THE ONE SHOW 1999 VOLUME 21

Advertising's Best Print, Radio, TV

BOB BARRIE
President

MARY WARLICK
Executive Director

MARY WARLICK
Editor

KRISTIN OVERSON
Editorial Consultant

DAVID CHANG, STEVE O'CONNELL
Editorial Assistants

ANNELOUISE BURNS & MARIA RUOTOLO
Designers

Cover Concept & Divider Pages

DOUG PEDERSEN
Art Director

CURTIS SMITH
Copywriter

JIMMY WILLIAMS
Photographer

STEPHANIE WALKER
Retouching

CD-ROM

KEVIN SWANEPOEL
Programming and Production
One Club Interactive

TODD GAFFNEY
Production
One Club Interactive

ROGER HORROCKS
ALAN ALSTON
Programming
Ogilvy Interactive, South Africa

Published and Distributed by

ROTOVISION S.A.
Sales Office: Sheridan House
112-116a Western Road
Hove, East Sussex, BN3 1DD
United Kingdom
Tel: +44 (0) 1273-72-7268
Fax: +44 (0) 1273-72-7269

In Association with

THE ONE CLUB FOR ART & COPY
32 East 21 Street
New York, NY 10010
Tel: 212-979-1900
Fax: 212-979-5006
e-mail: oneclub@inch.com
web site: www.oneclub.com

First Printing
ISBN 2-88046-475-7

Production and Separation by ProVision/Singapore
Tel: 65-334-7720
Fax: 65-334-7721

I

This year, we're going to be brave and forgo the usual "Message from the President" platitudes. Instead, we'll use an impressive 100% of this column to direct your attention to a great new feature of the One Show annual.

We call it "The Judges' Choice for Best of Show" and it appears on pages 98 to 101.

In addition to the fine overall "Best of Show" winner selected by highest collaborative point score, we asked each of the nineteen judges to select a personal favorite ad or campaign from the 13,674 entries. And we also asked each of them to elaborate on why this piece was so damn special to them.

You'll find this new feature intriguing in its range, educational in its commentary and controversial in its choices.

So, as you explore this latest installment of the most scrutinized showbook in advertising, please remember that you now have yet another reason to do so.

Enjoy.

Bob Barrie

BOB BARRIE

August, 1999

DOUG ADKINS
Hunt Adkins

DAVID ANGELO

DAVID BALDWIN
McKinney & Silver

ARTHUR BIJUR
Cliff Freeman and Partners

ALEX BOGUSKY
Crispin Porter & Bogusky

DEAN BUCKHORN
Fallon McElligott

JOHN BUTLER
Butler Shine & Stern

JANET CHAMP

GRAHAM CLIFFORD
Graham Clifford Design

DAVE COOK
Mad Dogs & Englishmen

TOM CORDNER
Team One Advertising

KERRY FEUERMAN
The Martin Agency

JERRY GENTILE
TBWA/Chiat/Day

KARA GOODRICH
Fallon McElligott

JOHN HEGARTY
Bartle Bogle Hegarty

STEVE LUKER

STEFFAN POSTAER
Leo Burnett

JEAN ROBAIRE
Robaire & Hogshead

SUSAN WESTRE
Ogilvy & Mather

This year, we're going to be brave and forgo the usual "Message from the President" platitudes. Instead, we'll use an impressive 100% of this column to direct your attention to a great new feature of the One Show annual.

We call it "The Judges' Choice for Best of Show" and it appears on pages 98 to 101.

In addition to the fine overall "Best of Show" winner selected by highest collaborative point score, we asked each of the nineteen judges to select a personal favorite ad or campaign from the 13,674 entries. And we also asked each of them to elaborate on why this piece was so damn special to them.

You'll find this new feature intriguing in its range, educational in its commentary and controversial in its choices.

So, as you explore this latest installment of the most scrutinized showbook in advertising, please remember that you now have yet another reason to do so.

Enjoy.

Bob Barrie

BOB BARRIE

August, 1999

DOUG ADKINS
Hunt Adkins

DAVID ANGELO

DAVID BALDWIN
McKinney & Silver

ARTHUR BIJUR
Cliff Freeman and Partners

ALEX BOGUSKY
Crispin Porter & Bogusky

DEAN BUCKHORN
Fallon McElligott

JOHN BUTLER
Butler Shine & Stern

JANET CHAMP

GRAHAM CLIFFORD
Graham Clifford Design

DAVE COOK
Mad Dogs & Englishmen

TOM CORDNER
Team One Advertising

KERRY FEUERMAN
The Martin Agency

JERRY GENTILE
TBWA/Chiat/Day

KARA GOODRICH
Fallon McElligott

JOHN HEGARTY
Bartle Bogle Hegarty

STEVE LUKER

STEFFAN POSTAER
Leo Burnett

JEAN ROBAIRE
Robaire & Hogshead

SUSAN WESTRE
Ogilvy & Mather

Mike Abadi
David Abbott
Jeffrey Abbott
Geoffrey W. Abraham
Will Adam
Yasmin Ahmad
Daniel Akesson
Darius Edward Alaie
Noel Albizo
Joe Alexander
Mike Alfonseca
Saadi Alkoualti
Blythe Alpern
David Altschiller
Olivia Altschuler
Patricia Alvey
Sharon Amato
Gideon Amichay
Matthew Ammirati
Ralph Ammirati
John Amodeo
Audrey Anderson
Matthew Anderson
Ron Anderson
Stephanie Anderson
Trudy Anderson
David Angelo
Anthony Angotti
Frank Anselmo
Frank Anton, Jr.
Chaco Aoki
J.P. Appelbaum
Jill Applebaum
Marcelo Aragao
David Arnold
Ron Arnold
Stephanie Arnold
Lorraine Arroll
Sam Ash
Larry Asher
Michael Ashley
Craig Astler
Enrique Astuy
Jayson Atienza
Brian Avenius
Chinnawut Awakul
Ruth Ayres
∎
Kristina Backlund
Ronald Bacsa
Tom Bagot
Chris Baier
Adam Bailine
Robert Baird
Larry Baisden
Chris Bakay
Albrecht Bake
Sandra Balboa
Mark Barber
Shannon-Megan Barreca
Bob Barrie
Daniel Barry
Gary Bassell
Jon Baucom
Steve Bautista
Esengul Baykal
Tim Bayless
Jennifer Bayne
Toygar Bazarkaya
Clifford Beach
Allan Beaver
Wendy Beck
Kris Becker
Wendy Becker
Brian Bellanca
Jarett Bellucci
Gordon Bennett
Ken Bennett
T.J. Bennett
Roger Bentley

Amanda K. Berger
Danielle Berger
Warren Berger
Joe Berkeley
Paul Bernasconi
David Bernstein
Grant Bernstein
Peter Berta
Fred Bertino
Eric Bertuccio
Dominique Biger Kahn
Arthur Bijur
Bruce Bildsten
Charles A. Black
Clay Black
Charles Blackwell
Brendon Blake
Laura Block
Steven Block
Warren Bloom
Steve Boase
Alex Bogusky
Mindy Bond
Javier Bonilla
John Boone
Brian Born
Peter Bossio
Kevin Botfeld
Nicole Botkier
Alix Botwin
Margaret Boyd
Rick Boyko
Mark Brady
Scott Brennan
Scott Brewer
Brad Brinegar
Jim Brodie
Bill Brokaw
Michael Bronowitz
Dara Brooks
Michael Brothers
George Brown
Mark Brown
Shameka M. Brown
Tim Brunelle
Sarah Bruns
Jane Bryson
Martin Buchanan
Rob Buck
Carol Buettner
Ron Burkhardt
Jon Burkhart
Pat Burnham
John Butler
∎
Larry Cadman
Andrew M. Cahill
Steve Callen
Luis Camano
Kelly Cammerota
Cathie Campbell
Paul Cappelli
Rob Carducci
Josephine Craig Carey
David Carlin
Gretchen Carswell
Jason Carter
Mark Catalina
Todd Cather
Marco Ceo
Anthony Cerniglia
Chad Chadwick
Mike Chadwick
Susanne Champ
Jennifer Chan
Ann Ting Chang
Joseph Chang
Maria Chang
Soo Mean Chang
Erin Cheeseman

Claire Chen
Kenny Chen
Chung-Mau Cheng
Jay Chiat
Vincent Chieco
Jeremy Chin
Niti Chitabra
Rebecca Chitty
Jennie Cho
Chin Chul Choi
Louie Chow
Marvin Chow
Tom Christmann
Tom Chung
Chris Churchill
Kirk Citron
Mark Clark
Tim Clarke
Bart Cleveland
Joel Cleveland
Cindy Clevenger
Wendy Clore
Henry Cochran
David Cohen
Josh Cohen
Michael Cohen
Joe Coldebella
Wynn Cole
Alicia Coles
Michael Comstock
Steve Connelly
Doug Cook
Diane Cook-Tench
August Cosentino
Colin Costello
Sharla Costello
Mark Henry Cousin
Michael Cox
Robert Cox
Rob Cramer
Court Crandall
Steve Crane
Juan Cravero
Richard Crean
Griffin Creech
Lourdes Crespo
Peter Crosby
Greg Crossley
Joseph Crowley
Kevin Cruickshank
Phyliss Cunningham
George Curi
Stephen Curry
Steven Cursou
∎
Bill D'Ambrosio
Joanna D'Avanzo
Marguerite D'Esposito
Chris D'Rozario
Alessandra Melo Da Silva
Kyle Daley
Sharon Dang
Keith Darby
Patricia Darcey
Adam David
Simon Davies
Bill Davis
Jeannine Marie Davis
Izzy DeBellis
Anthony Decarolis
Victor DeCastro
James Deckinger
Jay Deegan
Tony DeGregorio
Phil Delbourgo
Denise Dell'Olio
Jerry Della Femina
Charles DeMarco
Sharad Derarajan
John DeVito

Sal DeVito
Nicole DiIorio
Steve Dildarian
Greg DiNoto
Patrick Distasio
Angela Dominguez
Marty Donohue
Steve Doppelt
Tom Doud
Sean Dougherty
Rob Dow
James B. Downer
Michael Draper
Daniel J. Drexler
Joe Duffy
Dave Dumanis
Rosalyn Dunham
Laurence Dunst
Jim Durfee
Michael Dweck
Susan Dwyer
David Dyer
Andrew Dzija
∎
Yoshiko Ebihara
Jennifer Edson
Shannon Edwards
Barbara Eibel
Einar Gunnar Einarsson
Arthur Einstein
Gail Eisenberg
Prisca Ekkens
Stuart Elliott
Kevin Endres
Gary Ennis
Patricia Lynn Epstein
Marcelo Ernelindo
Elke Erschfeld
Eric Essig
Darryl Estrine
∎
Erik Fahrenkopf
Sarah Feldman
Steven Feldman
Mark R. Fenske
Scott Ferguson
Michael Fetsko
Kerry Feuerman
Michael Fine
Benjamin Finkel
Annie Finnegan
Matt Fischvogt
Tim Fisher
Betty Fitterman
Bob Fitzgerald
Mike Flegle
Ellen Fleischer
Katherine Flynn
Tim Foley
Nicole Forte
Jim Fortune
Grant Fraggalofch
Sela Francis
Cliff Freeman
Robert Fremgen
David M. Frieberg
Jerry Fury
∎
Tom Gabriel
Bryan Gaffin
Bob Gage
Allen Gallehugh
Sarah Galluzzo
Nicholas Gamma
Mark Ganton
Bertrand Garbassi
Gery Garcia
Salvador Garcia
David Gardiner
Beth Gardner

Tom Gardner
Lee Garfinkel
Amil Gargano
Rachel Garraffa
Lisa Garrone
Gianina Gauci
Dean Gemmell
John Gentile
Richard Gerdes
Greg Gerstrer
Marc Getter
Steven Giamarino
Kirk Gibbons
George Gier
Carla Gigante
C. Hayden Gilbert
John Gavin Gilbert
Brad Gilmore
David A. Gilmour
Frank Ginsberg
Jason Glassman
Kenneth Gleason
Marcus Glover
Max Godsil
George Goetz
Rhodessa Goings
Dan Goldgeier
David Goldoff
Chris Goldschmidt
Mark Goldstein
Ian Goldy
Mark A. Gonzalez
Andy Goodman
Melissa Gordon
Mitch Gordon
Michael Gorelick
Lori Grabowski
Roy Grace
David Gray
Jeff Graybill
Allan Greenberg
Rosalind Greene
Stephanie Greene
Norm Grey
Dick Grider
Jeff Griffith
Sarah Griswald
Philip Growick
Jeffrey Grutkowski
Roland Grybauskas
Michael Guarini
Kurt Guenther
Sunnie Gugllielmo
Gina Guiffrida
Paul Gumbinner
∎
Lori Habas
Stephen Hacker
Erika Ann Hadjoglou
Monica Hafner
Deb Hagan
James Hainis
Matthew Hallock
Trace Hallowell
Ada Halofsky
Bill Hamilton
Angela Hampton
Kirsten Hampton
Robert Hannan
Thomas C. Hansen
Wayne Hanson
Keith Harjes
Cabell Harris
Jackie Hathiramani
Jim Hayman
Blaise Hayward
Juliet Heeg
Brent Heindl
Cheryl Heller
Bradley Hensen

Roy Herbert
Rony Herz
Kenneth Herzog
Lee Hester
Ralf Heuel
Dawn Hibbard
Andy Hill
Bill Hillsman
Woody Hinkle
Andrew Hirsch
Joel Hladecek
Justin Hluboky
Amy Hoffar
Sigal Hofshi
Sally Hogshead
Annie Holdsworth
Barry Holland
Bert Holland
Bill Hollister
Dave Holloway
Jenine Holmes
Charlie Hopper
Jim Hord
Laurence Horvitz
Ryan Hose
Hugh Hough
Brian Howlett
Mike Hughes
Patrick Hunt
Jason Hunter
Kathy Hunter
John Hynes
■
Joan Iaconetti
Mauricio Mori Ikezaki
Nicole Infante
Michelle Ishay
Dick Jackson
Adrianna Jacobs
Chris Jacobs
Harry M. Jacobs, Jr.
Per Robert Jacobson
John Jaeckel
Holly Jaffe
Jaydee Jana
Crockett Jeffers
Adrian Jeffery
Bob Jeffrey
Mickey Jenkins
David Jensen
Andrew Jeske
Margarita Oliva Jiminez
Anthony A. Johnson
Kelly Johnson
Marcus Johnson
Mark Johnson
Raymond Johnson
Ed Jones
G. Hatton Jordan
Prachi Junankar
■
Tal Kagan
Ric Kallaher
Charles Kane
Daniel Kane
Melinda Kanipe
Grace Kao
Peter Kaplan
Scott Kaplan
Linus Karlsson
Marshall Karp
Shane Karshan
Rustie Kaster
Natalie Kaufman
Richard Kaufman
Leslie Kay
Woody Kay
Kristin Kelly
Lee Kelly
Robert L. Kelly

Tom Kelly
Sharon Kendrick
Jeff Kidwell
Joanne Kim
Elizabeth King
Richard Kintanar
Jeff Kirschner
Richard Kirshenbaum
Irina Kish
Leon Kislowski
John Klein
Leslie Herman Kolk
Andrew Knipe
Cynthia Knox
Nicole Kobeli
Natalie Kocsis
Klarisa Konstantinovsky
Benier Koranache
Evelyn Korfias
Paula Korpalski
Renee Korus
Sonja Korver
Jeff Kosloski
Robyn Kosoff
Maria Kostyk-Petro
Phil Koutsis Jr.
Judy Kozuck
Barry Krause
Sean Krause
Herta Kriegner
Ken Krimstein
Stewart Krull
Dave Kuhl
Krista Kuhn
Pradeep Kumar
Kuang-Chun Kuo
■
Robert LaBarge
Ben Lagunas
Ming Lai
Gary Lakey
Thomas Lam
Stephen Land
Steven Landsberg
Andy Langer
Anthony LaPetri
Eduardo Larios
Carole Larson
Kevin Laskoff
Joe Leahy
Eun-Jung Lee
Neil Leinwohl
Elizabeth Lemer
Dany Lee Lennon
Chag-Chag Leon
Dick Leonard
Jodie Leopold
Mike Lescarbeau
Sharon Lesser
Christian Lester
Chik Wan Leung
Robert Levenson
Kate Levin
Carol Lewis
Warren Lewis
Tom Lichtenheld
Susan Lieber
Morissa Liffman
Adrian Lim
Lisa Lipkin-Balser
Pierre Lipton
Wallace Littman
Steven Liu
Marcus Livesay
David Loew
George Lois
Ana Carmen Rivaben Longobardi
Frank Lopresti
Carson Lord

Jewell Lowe
Peter Lubalin
David Lubars
Marc Lucas
Andrea Luebbert
Francesca Lum
Vi Luong
Lisa Lurie
John Lutter
Michael Lyons
Sarah Lyons
■
Alicia Ma
Susanne Macarelli
Mike Maccaronio
Tony Macchia
Marcelo Machado
Diane Magid
Elyse Maguire
Chris Maiorino
Cheesoon Mak
Madhu Malhan
Karen Mallia
Paul Malmstrom
Peter Maloney
Jamie Mambro
Ken Mandelbaum
Jonathan Mandell
Bradley Manier
Mark Manion
John Mannion
Yoni Margulies
Louis Marino
Pam Mariutto
Kenneth Markey
Lawrence Marks
Rhoda Marshall
Dave Martin
Reynaldo Martinez
Arnold Marzan
Marzena
Diane Masal
Michael Maurer
Richard May
James Mazzola
Scott McAfee
Cal McAllister
Ed McCabe
Clem McCarthy
Dawn McCarthy
Kerry McCarthy
Peter McCarty
Katherine McConnell
Frank McGovern
Don McKinney
Michael McLaurin
Cameron McNaughton
Gabriel Medina
Michael Medina
Lynne Meena
Robert Mellett
Mark Mendelis
James Menefee
Kieber Menezes
Frank Meo
Tom Merrick
Luis Miguel Messianu
Mario G. Messina
Lyle Metzdorf
Terri Meyer
Greg Meyers
Bethann Miale
Jeanine Michna
Mark Millar
Christopher Miller
Reid Miller
Renee Miller
Alexia Milner
Bill Mitchell
Steven Mitsch

Marise Mizrahi
Ronald Modica
Sakol Mongkolkasetarin
Ty Montague
Pablo Monzon
Adam Morgan
Melvin Morgan
Rachel Mori Foster
Dawn Morris
Jacob Morris
Trevor Morris
Deborah Morrison
Aaron Mosher
Paul Most
Jim Mountjoy
Tom Moyer
Zak Mroueh
William Munch, Jr.
Kyle C. Murphy
Lexie Murray
■
Tracy Nader
Aruna Naimji
Thomas Nathan
Tamara Nathan-Gonzales
David Nathanson
Shane Nearman
Ted Nelson
Arun K. Nemali
Laura Neustadt
Joseph Ney
Patrick Ng
Thu Nguyen
Raymond Nichols
Amy Nicholson
Jennifer Noble
Susan Nobles
Olle Nordell
Ronald P. Northrop
Chris Nott
■
David Oakley
Bill Oberlander
James O'Brien
Mick O'Brien
Meghan O'Connell
Rip Odell
Allison O'Keefe
Kelly O'Keefe
Vicky Oliver
Alex Olmsted
Carolyn Oppenheim
Peter Oravetz
Ron Ordansa
Paul Orefice
Jason Orr
Martin Orzio
Mikio Osaki
Kwasi Osei
Seymon Ostilly
Cele Otnes
Amy Owett
■
Alvaro Paez
John Painter
Jack Palancio
Sharyn Panagides
Dick Pantano
Jennifer Pappalardo
Michael Parent
Sam Park
Brad Parks
Michael Pavone
Michael Payer
Doug Pedersen
Stephen Pederson
Richard Pels
Judy Penny
Lisa Hurwitz Peretz
Ellen Perless

Kelsie Petersen
David Piatkowski
Donna Pilch
Paul Piszko
Pichai Piyapongdacha
Terry Player
Jonathan Plazonja
Tuesday Poliak
Debra Polkes
Chris Pollock
Chris Poulin
Stan Poulos
Dave Prager
Chris Preston
Tim Price
Erik Proulx
Belinda Pruyne
Tony Pucca
Kendra Leigh Pukatch
Kay Colmar Pullen
Amy Putman
■
Nazneen Qazi
Keith Quesenberry
Aldo Quevedo
■
Tatjana Racic
Lynda Raihofer
Ryan Raith
Faria Raji
Rene Ramirez
Anselmo Ramos
Jeffrey Ranbom
Alissa Randall
Michael Rappaport
Jaime Raudenbush
John Rea
Mikal Reich
Steve Reich
Ian Reichenthal
Melissa Reilly
Kim Reit
Dave Remer
Liana Riccardi
Joseph Ricci
Erica Rice
Nancy Rice
Rob Rich
Allen Richardson
Kimball Richmond
Todd Riddle
Hal Riney
David Rittenhouse
John Robertson
Mark Robertson
Michael Robertson
Ginger Robinson
Scott Rockwood
Jeff Rodriguez
Jason B. Rogers
Gad Romann
Ana Maria Romay
Joe Rose
Katherine Rose
Gary Rosen
Rob Rosenthal
Bernie Rosner
Tom Rost
Rosanne Rotenberg
Mark Rothenberg
Carolyn Amorosi Rothseid
Amy Roy
Cary Ruby
Jonathan Ruby
Brian Rugeri
Paco Ruiz-Nicoli
John Russo
Mel Rustom
Nancy Rybczynski
Nora Ryder

Ted Sabarese
Dana Sacchetti
Steve Sage
Vinny Sainato
Lee St. James
Gabriel St. John
Jeffrey Salgado
Rajiv Samvatsar
Earle Sandberg
Mike Sanford
Emmanuel Santos
Lynne Sarella
Cindy Sargent
Carl Sastram
Ariel Saulog
Melanie Sawyer
Robert Saxon
Joanne Scannello
Ernie Schenck
Sandra Scher
Glenn Scheuer
Dennis Scheyer
Lou Schiavone
Joshua Schildkraut
Chris Schlegel
Timothy Schleif
R. Scott Schmehl
Lee Schmidt
Mario Schmidt
Paul Schmidt
Gail Schoen Brunn
Jonathan Schoenberg
Michael Schreier
Jill Schroeder
Eric Schutte
Michael Schwabenland
Edwin Schwartz
Lara Schwartz
Heinz Schwegler
John Scully
Adrianne Segal
Lee Seidenberg
Tod Seisser
Ivette Serur
Bill Shea
Molly Sheahan
Mike Sheehan
Lyle Shemer
Zhong Shen Shen
Hillary Shenk
Matthew Shepko
Chris Sheppard
Lori Sheppard
Matthew Sherring
Brett Shevack
Derek Shevel
Edward Shieh
Paul Shields
Lori Sibal
Desi Sibih
Tim Siedell
Mark Silveira
Jennifer Simon
Tonia Simon
Mark Sivertsen
Deborah Skaler
Pat Sloan
Mike Slosberg
Robert Slosberg
David A. Smith, Jr.
Gary S. Smith
Nancy Smith
Pete Smith
Sarah Smith

Bill Snitzer
Adriana Soler
Pedro Soler
Mo Solomon
Richard Solomon
Hari Sonitis
Vanessa Soto
Cheri Soukup
Mark Spector
John Spiteri
Douglas Spitzer
Helayne Spivak
Amy Spizler
Amy Spizzo
Aaron Killian Spratt
Kash Sree
John Staffen
Joseph Staluppi
Todd Stanton
Steven Stark
Bill Starkey
Scott Stefan
Dean Stefanides
Nancy Steinman
Michael Stelzer
Eric Stephens
Roger Stephens
Ginni Stern
Jared Stern
Keith Stetson
Chris Stoltz
David Stone
Randy Stone
Terence Stone
Rob Strasberg
Denzil Strickland
Christian D. Struzan
Bob Sullivan
Michael Sullivan
Leslie Super
Jack Supple
Marc Surchin
Nick Sustana
Kimberly Swanson
David Swartz
Steve Swartz
Joe Sweet
Leslie Sweet
Rich Swietek
John Szalay
Dean Szostczuk
■
Norman Tanen
Willie Tang
Donna Tarigo
Matthew Tarulli
C. Dow Tate
Blake Taylor
Kevin Teevens
Judy Teller
Nick Terzis
Danielle Teshner
Kevin Thoem
Anne Thomas
Greg Thomas
Rob Thompson
Eric Tilford

Laura Toch
John P. Topacio
Lisa Topol
Theodore Topolewski
Sally Totten
Mark Townsley
Roy Trimble
William Troncone
Matthew Trumino
Staz Tsiavos
Mario Tsikis
Roman Tsukerman
Aiti Tu
David Tuckman
Karl Turkel
Miles Turpin
■
Tom Ungar
Udi Urman
■
Victor Valadez
Peter Van Bloem
Schuyler G. Vanden Bergh
German Silva Vazquez
Paul Venables
Jessica Venegas
Amy Vensel
Deanna Vergara
Stephen Versandi
Matthew Vescovo
Carol Vick
Danielle Vieth
Larry Vine
Michael Vitiello
John Vitro
Eric Voigt
Joseph Volpicelli
■
James Wachira
Elaine Wagner
William Ernest Waites
Judy Wald
Marvin Waldman
Jim Walker
Thomas Walker
Ya-Li Wang
Walter Wanger
Michael Ward
Bob Warren
Deb Warrenfeltz
Shane Watson
Peter Watt
Karen Weber
Karen Weech
Joy Weeng
Iwan Weidmann
James Weiner
Les Weiner
Eric Weisberg

Marty Weiss
Lawrence G. Werner
Robert Shaw West
Bill Westbrook
Annette Wexler
Neal White
Nat Whitten
Enbruce Whou
Karl Wiberg
Ron Wilcox
Scott Wild
Richard Wilde
Clay Williams
Jay Williams
Tim Williams
Thema Wilson
Stewart Winter
David Wojdyla
Stefen Wojnarowski
David Wolff
Alan Wolk
Charles Tze Ho Wong
David A. Wong
Judy Wong
Rena Wong
Vivian Fay Wong
Peter Wood
Brian Woodruff
Laura B. Woods
■
Ted Xistris
■
Seiji Yamasaki
Betsy Yamazaki
Juyoon Yi
■
Joe Zagorski
Lynette Zator
Rainer Zierer
Mark Zito
Mat Zucker
Mark Zukor

PRESIDENT'S MESSAGE

This is a true story.

About five years ago, The One Club for Art and Copy received an unusual question from an individual who shall remain nameless. "How do I go about entering the Creative Hall of Fame?" they asked. Well, if this query were to be taken seriously, and it really was a "competition," the One Show's new category might look something like this: "Category 12A: To enter the Creative Hall of Fame, one must merely provide a lifetime of inspiration by consistently producing landmark advertising that people actually look forward to, thereby lifting the creative standards significantly and irrevocably for the entire industry. It also doesn't hurt to be a nice person."

Thirty-eight years ago, Leo Burnett was the first to win this prestigious honor. And only thirty-one other names have followed. Names like Bernbach. Ogilvy. Wells. Krone. McCabe. Riney. And Clow.

Tonight, we all gather to honor two new inductees named Wieden and Kennedy.

Congratulations, Dan and Dave. You've more than earned it. Your nominations were unanimously approved by the Board of Directors of The One Club. And your enduring legacy is still being written.

Oh, and thanks for entering.

**BOB BARRIE
PRESIDENT
THE ONE CLUB**

ON FEBRUARY 1, 1999
DAVID KENNEDY AND DAN WIEDEN
WERE INDUCTED INTO THE
CREATIVE HALL OF FAME AS THE
THIRTY-THIRD AND THIRTY-FOURTH
MEMBERS TO BE ACKNOWLEDGED FOR
THEIR LIFETIME CONTRIBUTION TO
ADVERTISING.

A foreigner who has the great good fortune to spend quality time inside the Bedlam known as Wieden & Kennedy gradually comes to three conclusions regarding its eponymous founders: They are outsiders; they are teachers; and they are kids. From April Fools' Day, 1982, when David Kennedy and Dan Wieden fled the constraints of a tiny Portland, Oregon boutique to open their even tinier novelty shop in the GranTree Rental Furniture Building, that combination has proved momentous. For of the handful of men and women who have contributed to the punctuated equilibrium of advertising's evolution, all boast one, or a pair, of these qualities. But few if any can claim all three, and none, perhaps, will ever again possess the transfiguring force of these childlike pedagogues from somewhere west of Laramie.

Portland is not just far in miles. It is a galaxy away from the emotional center of an advertising industry that, by its nature, is steeped in the new and the now. Founded by taciturn New Englanders who thought northeastern Puritanism a tad too libertine, Oregon's LARGEST CITY developed with what one historian termed "a preference for isolation." Big ideas were as unwelcome as strangers; in the second half of the 19th century, Portland citizens voted to exclude blacks, and at one point drove Chinese residents away. To this day, says one longtime advertising executive, Portland remains "difficult to penetrate."

Dan Wieden and David Kennedy were aliens to this isolationist culture, just as they were to the culture of advertising, which both grew up despising — paradoxically, because both were, in their way, born into it. Dan's father, Duke Wieden, was the chairman of the Gerber agency, known as "the Grey Advertising of Portland." Enormously popular, an amateur volleyball player of some note, Duke was simply unable to instill in his eldest son any love for his profession. Driven by the spirit of beat rebelliousness that underlay Portland's dominant conservatism, Dan tried everything possible to flee the life, trying his hand at poetry, short stories, and screenplays. Unable to make a living, he finally landed at the age of 33 at McCann-Erickson's Portland office, where he survived, he once said, by treating copywriting as "science fiction."

At McCann, he was teamed with an art director five years his senior named David Kennedy, who shared his complete disdain for advertising, but had built a curiously traditional career inside of it. The son and grandson of itinerant oil drillers, he'd gone to college to study geology, only to gravitate, out of a love for drawing, into fine art. But his artistic predilection conflicted with early-onset marriage and children so, soon after graduating, he found himself in Chicago, working for Young & Rubicam, Leo Burnett, Needham and Benton & Bowles. He flirted with various countercultures — at one point, he even helped produce the TV show "Soul Train" — but REMAINED unhappily tied to advertising. "There was no way I could get out of the business, and I just hated it," he once told me. Finally, fearful of the corrupting influence on his children of affluent suburban life, he uprooted his family for the Pacific Northwest.

ESPN "Balls and Bats"

MSN "Audrey"

Mothers,

there's a mad man

running in the

streets,

And he's

humming a tune,

And he's

snarling at dogs,

And he still

has

four

more

miles

to go.

Just do it.

NIKE "Running"

That attribute has been the root and branch of Wieden and Kennedy's system of advertising. Fun lies at the heart of the way their agency has produced advertising and in the center of the product itself. As arduous and painful as it is joyous and memorable, fun is a trait these two pre–Baby Boomers have in no small measure taught to the hundreds of ironically more conservative Boomers and Xers who've passed through their Northwestern realm. And fun, whether accomplished through the violation of pitching protocols, or by the employment of an untested independent film-maker, or via the re-purposing of an outlaw graphic designer has kept Wieden & Kennedy confusing and incomprehensible, removed from an ad industry mainstream that values "brand-speak," military-like efficiency and tough marketing cojones.

But make no mistake: Dan Wieden and David Kennedy have molded that mainstream in their image. In their appropriation of cultural fragments from the edges of design, art and film and their winking invitation that the audience disbelieve their every claim, they forcefully pushed advertising into the postmodern period. They made advertising safe for entertainment — no small feat in a time when commoditization was rendering "reason-why," product difference-oriented marketing moot. They helped godfather the era of attitude, in which the brand itself spoke with a voice neither palatable nor intelligible to a mass market they knew no longer existed, anyway.

From the start, Wieden and Kennedy complemented each other. While they shared an abhorrence for the conventional, they differed in correspondent ways. Dan was voluble where David was contem-plative. Dan was wild, David disciplined. Dan was always seeking the untried and unknown; David would find the precedent that could anchor it in a comprehensible reality. Most importantly, David — a man who was known to rummage through his office for, and yelp in excitement at finding, the exact right typeface for a comp — taught Dan that advertising could be fun.

THE MEEK MAY INHERIT THE EARTH,
BUT THEY WON'T GET THE BALL.

Just ask Charles Barkley. That's
why he likes the Nike Air Force.
Especially the cushioning of full-length
Nike-Air.® The traction from the
Center-of-Pressure™ outsole. And

when the league's toughest rebounder
thinks the Nike Air Force is the best
shoe under the
hoop, who's
gonna argue?

NIKE "Inherit the Earth"

Along the way, of course, they grew and grew and grew – not by merging or moving or acquiring, but by persuading some of the largest corporations in the world that, in an era of fragmentation and disaffection and uniformity, it was worth trekking to Portland. To the outside. To the kids.

So it's quite fitting that The One Club close this second millennium (after Christ, or the destruction of the Second Temple, or whatever) by inducting David Kennedy and Dan Wieden into the Creative Hall of Fame. There, they will join the other grandees of this industry, whose lessons they've largely ignored. Which is only appropriate because, teachers though they be, Wieden and Kennedy know the only advertising dictum worth heeding is this one: Just walk in stupid every day.

Would that we could all be so stupid.

RANDALL ROTHENBERG

NIKE "Marilyn"

AMERICAN INDIAN
COLLEGE FUND
"Sunny Walker"

NIKE "Frozen Moment"

GOLD AWARD
Newspaper Over 600 Lines:
Single

ART DIRECTOR
Neil Dawson

WRITER
Clive Pickering

PHOTOGRAPHER
Paul Reas

CLIENT
Volkswagen Group UK

AGENCY
BMP DDB/London

Gold, Silver, Bronze

GOLD AWARD
Newspaper Over 600 Lines:
Single

ART DIRECTOR
Neil Dawson

WRITER
Clive Pickering

PHOTOGRAPHER
Paul Reas

CLIENT
Volkswagen Group UK

AGENCY
BMP DDB/London

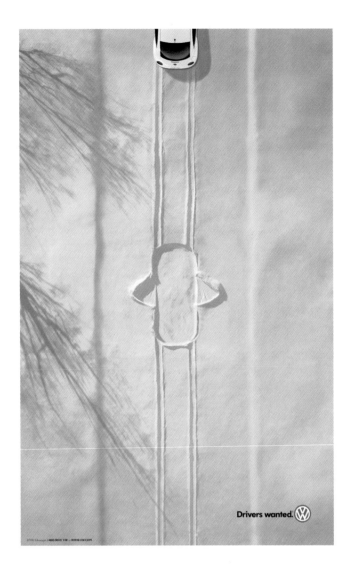

SILVER AWARD
Newspaper Over 600 Lines:
Single

ART DIRECTOR
Tim Vaccarino

WRITER
Shane Hutton

ILLUSTRATOR
Peter Levins

PHOTOGRAPHER
Steve Bronstein

CLIENT
Volkswagen

AGENCY
Arnold Communications/
Boston

BRONZE AWARD
Newspaper Over 600 Lines:
Single

ART DIRECTOR
Steve Sage

WRITER
Riley Kane

PHOTOGRAPHER
Michael Rausch

CLIENT
BMW of North America

AGENCY
Fallon McElligott/
Minneapolis

GOLD AWARD
Newspaper Over 600 Lines:
Campaign

ART DIRECTOR
Neil Dawson

WRITER
Clive Pickering

PHOTOGRAPHER
Paul Reas

CLIENT
Volkswagen Group UK

AGENCY
BMP DDB/London

TIME TO SWITCH TO TOSHIBA PROFESSIONAL LIGHTING.

AVAILABLE EXCLUSIVELY AT NOVENA LIGHTING, BLK 206, TOA PAYOH NORTH, #01-1215, S'PORE 310206, TEL: 255-7840, FAX: 253-2435.

TIME TO SWITCH TO TOSHIBA PROFESSIONAL LIGHTING.

AVAILABLE EXCLUSIVELY AT NOVENA LIGHTING, BLK 206, TOA PAYOH NORTH, #01-1215, S'PORE 310206, TEL: 255-7840, FAX: 253-2435.

SILVER AWARD
Newspaper Over 600 Lines:
Campaign

ART DIRECTOR
Gregory Yeo

WRITER
Justin Lim

ILLUSTRATORS
Yau Digital Imaging
Felix Wang

PHOTOGRAPHER
Eric Seow

CLIENT
Novena Lighting

AGENCY
TBWA/Singapore

TIME TO SWITCH TO TOSHIBA PROFESSIONAL LIGHTING.

AVAILABLE EXCLUSIVELY AT NOVENA LIGHTING, BLK 206, TOA PAYOH NORTH, #01-1215, S'PORE 310206, TEL: 255-7840, FAX: 253-2435.

BRONZE AWARD
Newspaper Over 600 Lines:
Campaign

ART DIRECTOR
Lance Paull

WRITERS
Lance Jensen
Josh Caplan
Robert Hamilton

PHOTOGRAPHER
Bill Cash

CLIENT
Volkswagen

AGENCY
Arnold Communications/
Boston

Is it possible to go backwards and
forwards at the same time?

Drivers wanted.

Hug it? Drive it? Hug it? Drive it?

Drivers wanted.

Comes with wonderful new features.
Like heat.

Drivers wanted.

Folha de S. Paulo Newspaper. Illustrating life with words for 77 years.

Folha de S. Paulo Newspaper. Illustrating life with words for 77 years.

Folha de S. Paulo Newspaper. Illustrating life with words for 77 years.

Folha de S. Paulo Newspaper. Illustrating life with words for 77 years.

BRONZE AWARD
Newspaper Over 600 Lines:
Campaign

ART DIRECTOR
Tomas Lorente

WRITER
Carlos Domingos

ILLUSTRATOR
Monica Kornfeld

PHOTOGRAPHER
Archive Image

CLIENT
Folha de São Paulo
Newspaper

AGENCY
DM9 DDB Publicidade/
São Paulo

GOLD AWARD
Newspaper 600 Lines
or Less: Single

ART DIRECTOR
Greg Bokor

WRITER
Jim Garaventi

PHOTOGRAPHER
Bruce Peterson

CLIENT
Swiss Army Brands

AGENCY
Mullen Advertising/
Wenham

JACK AND JILL went up the hill to fetch a pail of water. Jack fell down and Jill made an emergency tourniquet.——THE END.

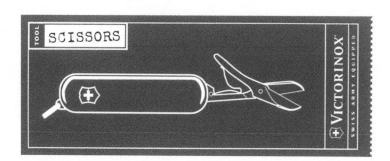

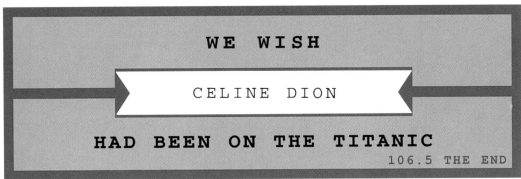

WE WISH

CELINE DION

HAD BEEN ON THE TITANIC

106.5 THE END

SILVER AWARD
Newspaper 600 Lines
or Less: Single

ART DIRECTOR
John Boone

WRITER
David Oakley

CLIENT
WEND 106.5

AGENCY
The Martin Agency/
Charlotte

BRONZE AWARD
Newspaper 600 Lines or
Less: Single

ART DIRECTOR
Ng Pei Pei

WRITER
Andy Greenaway

ILLUSTRATOR
Monica Kornfeld

PHOTOGRAPHER
John Clang

CLIENT
Mattel

AGENCY
Ogilvy & Mather/
Singapore

THE ONLY TIME YOU WILL BE DELIGHTED TO GET SYPHILIS

SCRABBLE

GOLD AWARD
Newspaper 600 Lines
or Less: Campaign

ART DIRECTOR
Ari Merkin

WRITER
Ari Merkin

CLIENT
5th Avenue Stamp Gallery

AGENCY
Hampel Stefanides/
New York

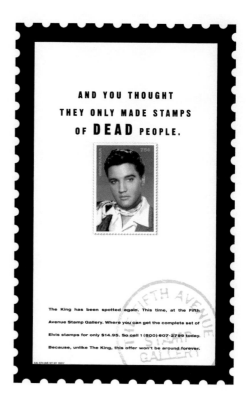

The Nanny
Weeknights 6 pm
TV12

Donny & Marie
Weekdays 2 pm
TV12

Deep Space 9
Wednesdays 9 pm
TV12

GOLD AWARD
Newspaper 600 Lines
or Less: Campaign

ART DIRECTOR
Ian Grais

WRITER
Alan Russell

PHOTOGRAPHER
Anthony Redpath

CLIENT
TV Twelve

AGENCY
Palmer Jarvis DDB/
Vancouver

SILVER AWARD
Newspaper 600 Lines
or Less: Campaign

ART DIRECTOR
Greg Bokor

WRITER
Jim Garaventi

PHOTOGRAPHER
Bruce Peterson

CLIENT
Swiss Army Brands

AGENCY
Mullen Advertising/
Wenham

JACK <u>AND</u> JILL went up the hill to fetch a pail of water. Jack fell down and Jill made an emergency tourniquet. —— THE END.

LONDON BRIDGE is falling down, falling down, falling down, London Bridge is falling down, my fair lady. Build it up with wood and clay, like that's gonna work. —THE END.

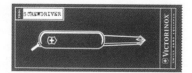

LITTLE MISS MUFFET sat on a tuffet, eating some curds and whey. Along came a spider, which she promptly burnt to a crisp. —— THE END.

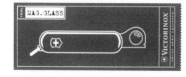

BRONZE AWARD
Newspaper 600 Lines
or Less: Campaign

ART DIRECTOR
John Boone

WRITER
David Oakley

CLIENT
WEND 106.5

AGENCY
The Martin Agency/
Charlotte

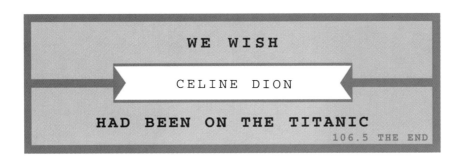

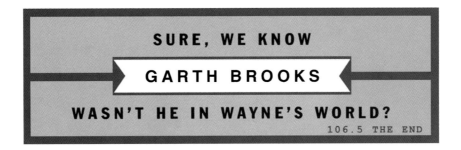

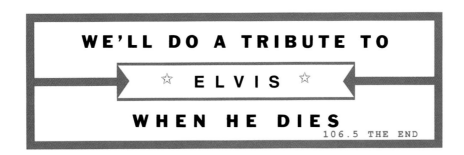

GOLD AWARD
Magazine B/W Full Page
or Spread: Single

ART DIRECTOR
Doug Pedersen

WRITER
Curtis Smith

PHOTOGRAPHER
Jim Arndt

CLIENT
Biltmore Estate

AGENCY
Loeffler Ketchum
Mountjoy/Charlotte

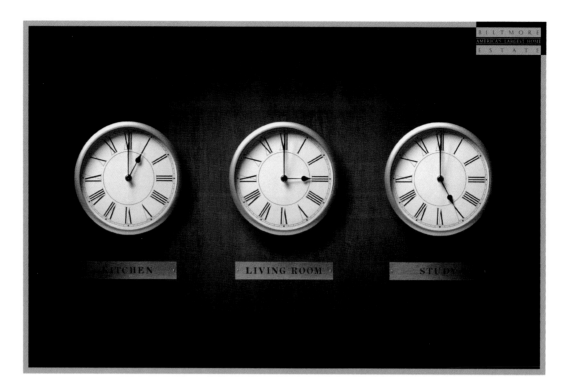

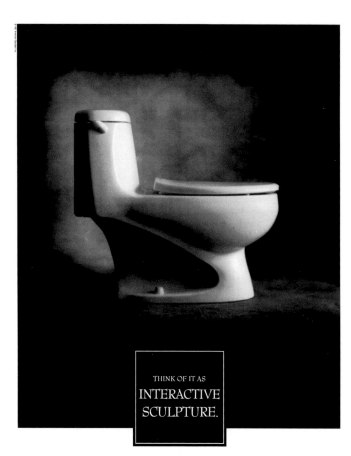

GOLD AWARD
Magazine Color Full Page
or Spread: Single

ART DIRECTORS
Erich Funke
Stuart Walsh

WRITERS
Stuart Walsh
Erich Funke

PHOTOGRAPHER
Michael Meyersfeld

CLIENT
Wonderbra

AGENCY
TBWA Hunt Lascaris/
Johannesburg

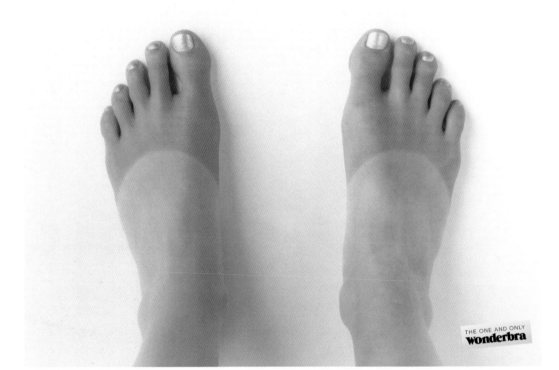

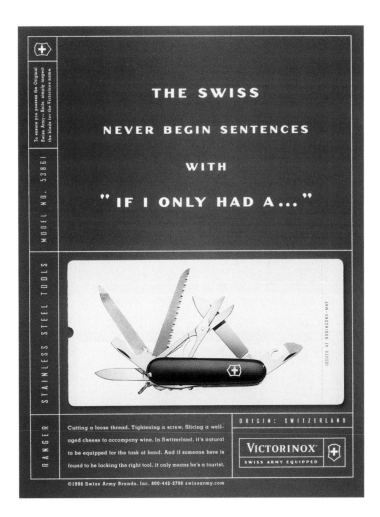

SILVER AWARD
Magazine Color Full Page
or Spread: Single

ART DIRECTOR
Monica Taylor

WRITER
Dylan Lee

PHOTOGRAPHERS
Geoff Stein

CLIENT
Swiss Army Brands

AGENCY
Mullen Advertising/
Wenham

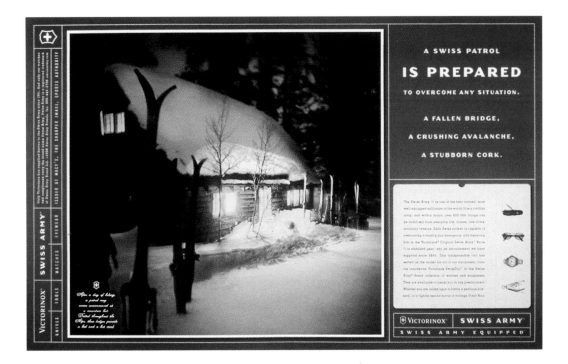

BRONZE AWARD
Magazine Color Full Page
or Spread: Single

ART DIRECTOR
Monica Taylor

WRITER
Dylan Lee

PHOTOGRAPHERS
Raymond Meeks
Geoff Stein

CLIENT
Swiss Army Brands

AGENCY
Mullen Advertising/
Wenham

GOLD AWARD
Magazine Color Full Page
or Spread: Campaign

ART DIRECTOR
Monica Taylor

WRITER
Dylan Lee

PHOTOGRAPHERS
Raymond Meeks
Geoff Stein
Stock

CLIENT
Swiss Army Brands

AGENCY
Mullen Advertising/
Wenham

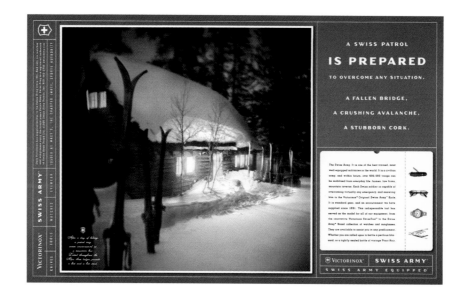

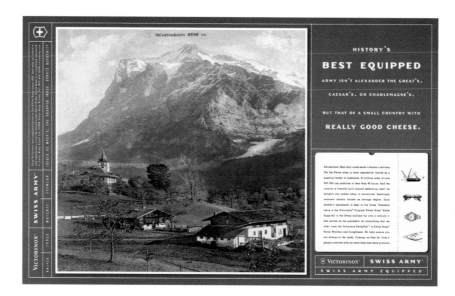

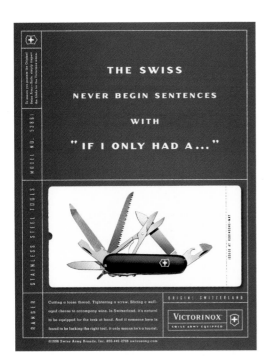

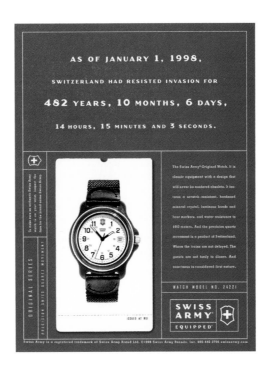

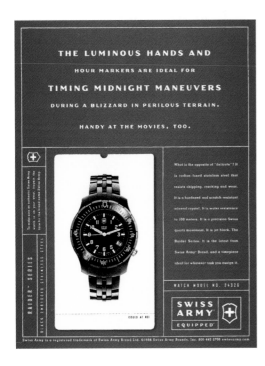

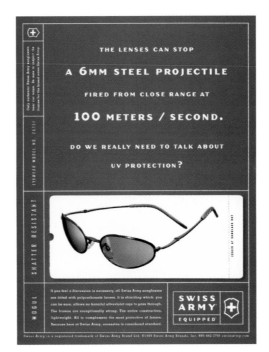

GOLD AWARD
Magazine Color Full Page
or Spread: Campaign

ART DIRECTOR
Monica Taylor

WRITER
Dylan Lee

PHOTOGRAPHER
Geoff Stein

CLIENT
Swiss Army Brands

AGENCY
Mullen Advertising/
Wenham

SILVER AWARD
Magazine Color Full Page
or Spread: Campaign

ART DIRECTOR
Bob Barrie

WRITER
Dean Buckhorn

PHOTOGRAPHERS
John Stanmeyer
Susan May Tell
Cynthia Johnson
Sygma
Joe Skipper

CLIENT
TIME

AGENCY
Fallon McElligott/
Minneapolis

If there's a story in there,
we'll find it.

The world's most interesting magazine.

Make sense of anything.
Almost.

The world's most interesting magazine.

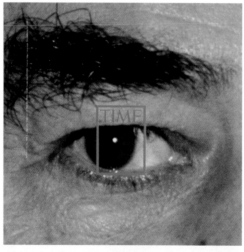

Iraq vs. the world.
Covered down to the last blink.

The world's most interesting magazine.

Always the truth.
Occasionally, the awful truth.

The world's most interesting magazine.

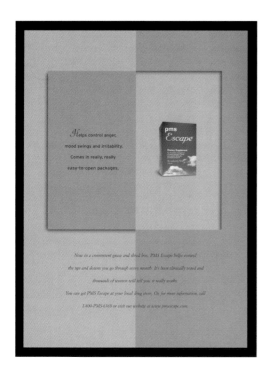

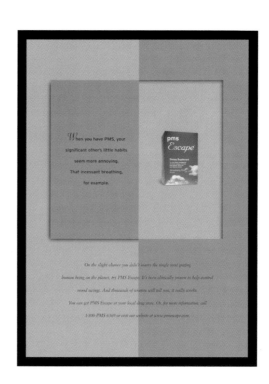

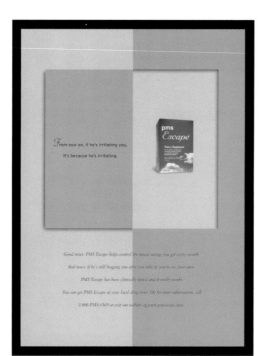

BRONZE AWARD
Magazine Color Full Page
or Spread: Campaign

ART DIRECTOR
Jim Amadeo

WRITER
Spencer Deadrick

PHOTOGRAPHER
Scott Goodwin

CLIENT
InterNutria

AGENCY
Clarke Goward
Advertising/Boston

SILVER AWARD
Magazine Less Than a Page
B/W or Color: Single

ART DIRECTOR
Andy Azula

WRITER
Dave Pullar

CLIENT
Nikon

AGENCY
Fallon McElligott/
Minneapolis

Tip #22:
Include people in
scenics to provide
a sense of scale.

The Nikon School

To get a firm grasp on landscape photography,
you'll need a little help. So we recommend taking
our 8-hour class, where our expert instructors will
teach you everything from basic composition to
advanced exposure techniques. You also get the
157-page Nikon School Handbook and a lunch,
all for $99. Call us at (516) 547-8666 for the date
and time a class will be offered in your city.

BRONZE AWARD
Magazine Less Than a Page
B/W or Color: Single

ART DIRECTOR
Koh Kuan Eng

WRITERS
Evelyn Tan
Amish Mehta

PHOTOGRAPHER
John Clang

CLIENT
Thomson Consumer
Electronics, Asia

AGENCY
Wunderman Cato Johnson/
Singapore

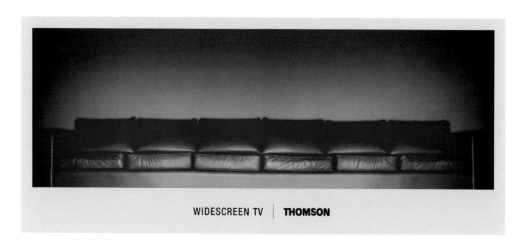

WIDESCREEN TV | THOMSON

AGENCY
Fallon McElligott/
Minneapolis

CLIENT
Nikon

WRITER
Dave Pullar

SILVER AWARD
Magazine Less Than a Page
B/W or Color: Campaign

ART DIRECTOR
Andy Azula

Tip #41:
Keep your
camera steady by
using a tripod.

The Nikon School

Tip #86:
In photojournalism,
shoot first.
Ask questions later.

The Nikon School

Tip #22:
Include people in
scenics to provide
a sense of scale.

The Nikon School

To get the best photos, you sometimes need a little help. Which is why we recommend taking our 8-hour class, where our expert instructors will teach you everything from basic composition to advanced exposure techniques. You also get the 157-page Nikon School Handbook and a lunch, all for $99. Call us at (516) 547-8666 for the date and time a class will be offered in your city.

Although everyone was okay, the photographer would've been really hurt if he didn't get this photo. So prepare for the unexpected by taking our 8-hour class, where you'll learn everything from basic composition to advanced exposure techniques. You also get the 157-page Nikon School Handbook and a lunch, all for $99. Call us at (516) 547-8666 to find out when a class will be offered in your city.

To get a firm grasp on landscape photography, you'll need a little help. So we recommend taking our 8-hour class, where our expert instructors will teach you everything from basic composition to advanced exposure techniques. You also get the 157-page Nikon School Handbook and a lunch, all for $99. Call us at (516) 547-8666 for the date and time a class will be offered in your city.

GOLD AWARD
Outdoor: Single

ART DIRECTOR
Ron Brown

WRITER
David Abbott

CLIENT
The Economist

AGENCY
Abbott Mead
Vickers.BBDO/London

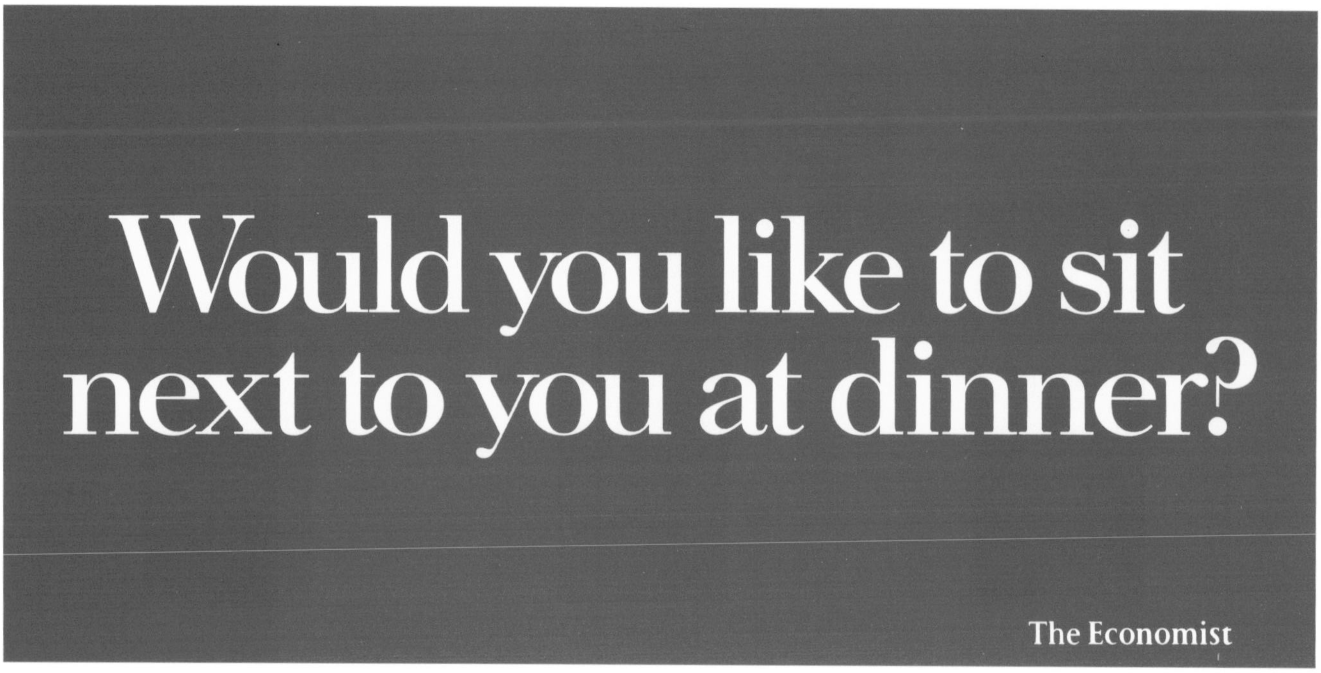

Would you like to sit next to you at dinner?

The Economist

0-60?

Yes.

Drivers wanted.® ⓋⓌ

©1998 Volkswagen 1-800-DRIVE-VW or WWW.VW.COM

SILVER AWARD
Outdoor: Single

ART DIRECTOR
Charles Pratt

WRITER
Lance Jensen

PHOTOGRAPHER
Bill Cash

CLIENT
Volkswagen

AGENCY
Arnold Communications/
Boston

BRONZE AWARD
Outdoor: Single

ART DIRECTOR
Mark Faulkner

WRITER
Steffan Postaer

PHOTOGRAPHER
Tony D'Orio

CLIENT
Callard & Bowser-Suchard

AGENCY
Leo Burnett/Chicago

GOLD AWARD
Outdoor: Campaign

ART DIRECTOR
Richard Flintham

WRITER
Andy McLeod

PHOTOGRAPHER
Neil Cummings

CLIENT
Volkswagen Group UK

AGENCY
BMP DDB/London

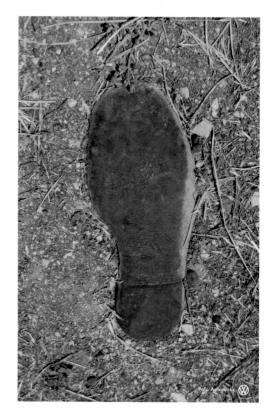

SILVER AWARD
Outdoor: Campaign

ART DIRECTORS
Greg Bokor
Gerard Caputo

WRITER
Jim Garaventi

PHOTOGRAPHERS
Susie Cushner
Shawn Michienzi
Nora Scarlet

CLIENT
Swiss Army Brands

AGENCY
Mullen Advertising/
Wenham

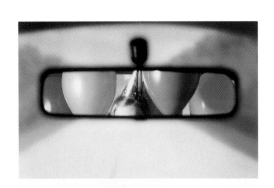

BRONZE AWARD
Outdoor: Campaign

WRITER
Alan Russell

CLIENT
TV Twelve

ART DIRECTOR
Ian Grais

PHOTOGRAPHER
Anthony Redpath

AGENCY
Palmer Jarvis DDB/
Vancouver

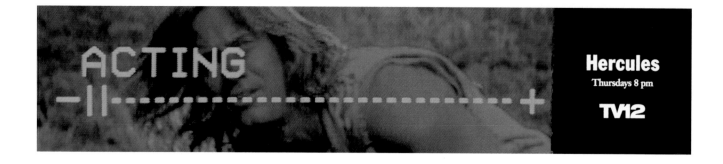

CLIENT	WRITER	SILVER AWARD
Wrangler	David Oakley	Guerilla Advertising
AGENCY	**PHOTOGRAPHER**	**ART DIRECTOR**
The Martin Agency/	Mike Carroll	John Boone
Charlotte		

SILVER AWARD
Guerilla Advertising

ART DIRECTOR
John Boone

WRITER
David Oakley

PHOTOGRAPHER
Mike Carroll

CLIENT
Wrangler

AGENCY
The Martin Agency/
Charlotte

BRONZE AWARD
Guerilla Advertising

ART DIRECTOR
Duncan Marshall

WRITER
Howard Willmott

PHOTOGRAPHER
John Vogel @ Vision

CLIENT
Virgin Clothing

AGENCY
Saatchi & Saatchi/
London

THE GREATEST DEADPAN
HUMORISTS EVER TO WALK THE EARTH

or

SECRETS OF THE AMISH.

Most reasonable people have, at one time or another, suspected that the Amish are really the penultimate madcap pranksters, relentless in their tomfoolery. To prove this once and for all, we spent months undercover, posing as Amish. We had our Mercedes pulled around by horses, wore only our black Armani suits and, at great personal sacrifice, refrained from bringing any hookers to barn raisings. When other Amish would come to our mansion and see our big-screen televisions, swimming pools and golden idols engraved in our own image, we simply told them, "Those aren't ours. They belong to our servants." Yes, the subterfuge was complete. And yet, somehow they never seemed to fully trust us. We tried everything – bribery, sexual favors, threats – yet nothing seemed to work with these people. So we went with our old standby method: we took them out to a bar and got them drunk off their asses.

The Amish call a spade a "undcini," illustrating their keen sense of humor

DEADPAN NIRVANA

To the Amish, even the most hilarious joke is ruined if someone laughs at it.

The Amish demonstrate their love of simple things by spending time with their families, studying the Bible and ripping up the countryside in their Mach-4 superbikes.

They've spent centuries perfecting the deadpan; they make the British look like Gallagher. In fact, we found that when the Amish are confronted and refuse to fight, they are really laughing to themselves, knowing that later they'll send out some goons to break your kneecaps.

To hide their humor from outsiders, the Amish have developed a secret language that allows them to openly tell jokes to each other. Fortunately, this code is but child's play for our brilliant team of Dublin cryptographers, who are deciphering this code at lightning speed. Already they have figured out that the phrase "Hello, neighbor" really means "Red afghan cow livers tepid marmalade clench." When we heard this, milk shot out of our noses, followed by a plate of spaghetti, garlic bread and three slices of cheesecake.

The Amish like to sneak into operating rooms and reenact their favorite episodes of "Quincy."

THE DEADPAN
COMMANDMENTS

Violation of deadpan law is a serious offense. Anyone so accused must pass several horrific tests, beginning with the 'Trial by Foot Tickling and escalating into the All-Out, Community-Wide Custard-Pie Fight. If the accused so much as smirks, he is stoned to death with anvils, cannonballs and engine blocks. Those who pass the test are stoned to death as well, but with smaller, less painful objects such as toasters, bricks and cell phones. If you're ever being stoned to death with cell phones, use one to call us at 213-960-3322 (Los Angeles) or 612-332-8864 (Minneapolis) so we can take you off our mailing list.

Rick and Jerry attempt the same Amish handshake, resulting in compound fractures to both men.

DUBLIN
PRODUCTIONS

IS IT HOT IN HERE OR IS IT JUST ME?

or

HUMOR IN HELL.

He is the most feared and loathed figure in all of history; he is called "Fallen Angel," "Lord of Darkness" and "Eater of Dung"; he is blamed for mankind's fall from the grace of God; and he is the comic genius responsible for such television hits as *Bosom Buddies* and *Alf.* "Clearly, He was jealous of me," Satan said when asked about the whole "God Fiasco," as he calls it. "He'd create these lame planets and then I'd have to go in and make them funny. Earth was just something He whipped up in a last, desperate attempt to one-up me. Now I'll be the first to admit that Earth is pretty hilarious, but what else has He done in the last few billion years? He's a one-hit wonder."

For proof of Satan's unmatched sense of humor one need look no further than his bulletin board, which is completely covered with *Family Circus* cartoons. Satan especially loves the ones in which dotted lines trace the path where little Billy has scampered all over the neighborhood. "Invariably little Billy assures his mother that he will come straight home," explains the

Jerry Pope attempts to "ride a balloon out of Hell."

Satan can be seen regularly during open-mike nights at many of Harlem's comedy clubs, where he tries out new jokes. To keep up with his demand for fresh material, Satan keeps thousands of writers locked up in small metal trailers in the Parking Lot of Misery. As incentive, the team that comes up with the best joke of the month gets to take the heat traps off their genitals and crack a window for ten minutes.

Lord of the Flies, "only to take a most circuitous route. How can one not delight in Billy's precociousness, and also in the knowledge that he is a liar and will burn in Hell."

MIND IF I SMOKE?

When he's not slashing people open and stuffing ravenous rats into their torsos, Satan loves nothing more than to spend an evening curled up with a big bowl of popcorn watching *America's Funniest Home Videos.* Beelzebub admits that his love of spontaneous, madcap humor may seem surprising. "While it's true that I am known for my vivisecting and gutting techniques, it's unfair to pigeonhole me as just another ruler of Hell. I am a complex, multifaceted

When constructing his new mansion, Satan saved a bundle by substituting humans for lumber.

individual with wide-ranging interests, including fine wine, French cuisine and ballroom dancing. Could you hand me that cranial saw?"

666-HA HA HA

Every Thursday night all the denizens of Hell gather to see Satan's ventriloquist act. The star of this show is not Satan so much as his little doll Woody. Dressed in their matching checkered sports jackets, Satan and Woody dazzle their rather captive audience for hours with skits that include: Satan drinking a cool glass of pink lemonade while Woody vomits boiling blood into the crowd, Satan dressing up in a frilly nightgown and bleating like a goat while being whipped by a leather-clad Woody, and Satan singing a medley from *The Sound of Music* while Woody causes screaming heads to rain from the sky. To receive an autographed 8" by 10" glossy of Woody and Satan playing Twister, call 612-332-8864 (Minneapolis) or 213-960-3322 (Los Angeles).

Satan's right-hand man, Rick Dublin, does nothing all day but drink souls.

DUBLIN
PRODUCTIONS

GOLD AWARD
Trade Color Full Page
or Spread: Single

ART DIRECTOR
Bob Barrie

WRITER
Dean Buckhorn

PHOTOGRAPHER
Francois Duhamel

CLIENT
TIME

AGENCY
Fallon McElligott/
Minneapolis

We cover art.

We cover life.

We cover art imitating life.

The world's most interesting magazine.

SILVER AWARD
Trade Color Full Page
or Spread: Single

ART DIRECTOR
Steve Mitchell

WRITER
Doug Adkins

PHOTOGRAPHER
Rick Dublin

CLIENT
Dublin Productions

AGENCY
Hunt Adkins/
Minneapolis

36 years after orbiting the earth,

this story is coming full circle.

The world's most interesting magazine.

BRONZE AWARD
Trade Color Full Page
or Spread: Single

ART DIRECTOR
Bob Barrie

WRITER
Dean Buckhorn

PHOTOGRAPHER
Ralph Morse

CLIENT
TIME

AGENCY
Fallon McElligott/
Minneapolis

SILVER AWARD
Trade Less Than a Page
B/W or Color: Single

ART DIRECTOR
Graham Clifford

WRITER
Neil Riley

CLIENT
The Economist

AGENCY
Mad Dogs & Englishmen/
New York

The Joneses.
Economist Subscribers

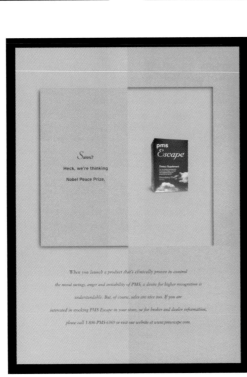

GOLD AWARD
Trade B/W or Color
Any Size: Campaign

ART DIRECTOR
Jim Amadeo

WRITER
Spencer Deadrick

PHOTOGRAPHER
Scott Goodwin

CLIENT
InterNutria

AGENCY
Clarke Goward
Advertising/Boston

SILVER AWARD
Trade B/W or Color
Any Size: Campaign

ART DIRECTOR
Bob Barrie

WRITER
Dean Buckhorn

PHOTOGRAPHERS
Francois Duhamel
Ralph Morse
Khalil Sensoi
NASA

CLIENT
TIME

AGENCY
Fallon McElligott/
Minneapolis

We cover art.
We cover life.
We cover art imitating life.

The world's most interesting magazine.

36 years after orbiting the earth,
this story is coming full circle.

The world's most interesting magazine.

A bomb explodes.
Ten thousand miles away,
you feel the impact.

The world's most interesting magazine.

From natural disasters to politics,
there is no better vantage point than
the eye of the storm.

The world's most interesting magazine.

BRONZE AWARD
Trade B/W or Color
Any Size: Campaign

ART DIRECTOR
Steve Mitchell

WRITER
Doug Adkins

PHOTOGRAPHER
Rick Dublin

CLIENT
Dublin Productions

AGENCY
Hunt Adkins/
Minneapolis

SILVER AWARD
Collateral: Brochures

ART DIRECTOR
Clif Wong

WRITER
Lance Jensen

CLIENT
Volkswagen

AGENCY
Arnold Communications/
Boston

BRONZE AWARD
Collateral: Brochures

ART DIRECTOR
Subashini Nadarajah

WRITERS
Sean O'Dell
Steve Wood

ILLUSTRATORS
Subashini Nadarajah
Sean O'Dell

CLIENT
Kansas City Ad Club

AGENCY
Bernstein Rein/
Kansas City

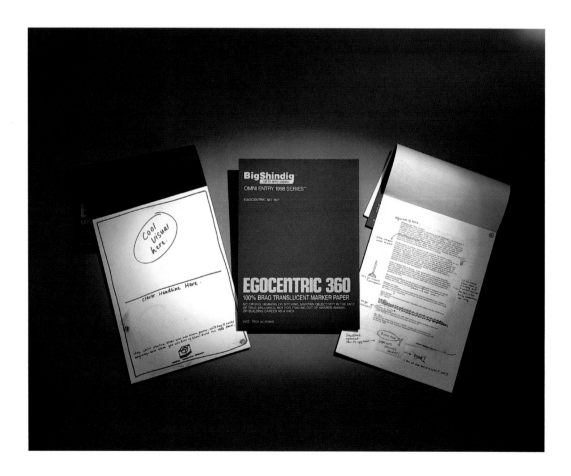

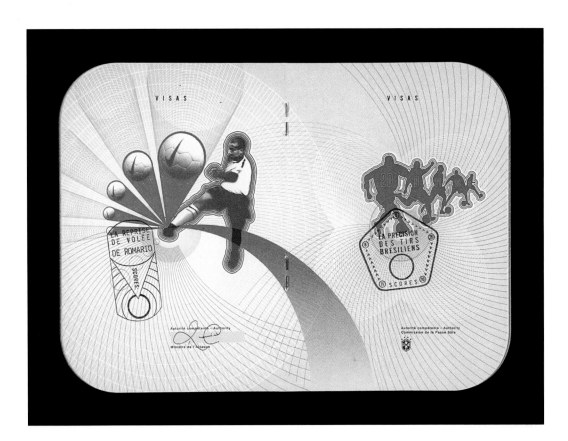

BRONZE AWARD
Collateral: Brochures

ART DIRECTOR
John Norman

WRITER
Tim Wolfe

ILLUSTRATOR
John Norman

CLIENT
Nike Europe

AGENCY
Wieden & Kennedy/
Amsterdam

SILVER AWARD
Collateral Direct Mail:
Single

ART DIRECTOR
Jac Coverdale

WRITER
Jerry Fury

ILLUSTRATORS
Bill Cook
Peter Siu
Kate Thomessen
Time Life Books

PHOTOGRAPHER
Raymond Meeks

CLIENT
Millennium Import
Company

AGENCY
Clarity Coverdale Fury/
Minneapolis

BRONZE AWARD
Collateral Direct Mail:
Single

ART DIRECTOR
Steve Sandstrom

WRITER
Peter Wegner

CLIENT
Graphic Arts Center

AGENCY
Sandstrom Design/
Portland

SILVER AWARD
Collateral Direct Mail:
Campaign

ART DIRECTOR
Rashid Salleh

WRITER
Peter Moyse

PHOTOGRAPHER
One-Twenty-One

CLIENT
Borneo Motors

AGENCY
Saatchi & Saatchi/
Singapore

GOLD AWARD
Collateral: Point of
Purchase and In-Store

ART DIRECTORS
Greg Bokor
Gerard Caputo

WRITER
Jim Garaventi

PHOTOGRAPHER
William Huber

CLIENT
Swiss Army Brands

AGENCY
Mullen Advertising/
Wenham

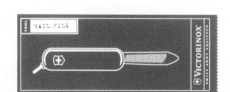

SILVER AWARD
Collateral: Point of
Purchase and In-Store

ART DIRECTORS
Greg Bokor
Gerard Caputo

WRITER
Jim Garaventi

PHOTOGRAPHER
William Huber

CLIENT
Swiss Army Brands

AGENCY
Mullen Advertising/
Wenham

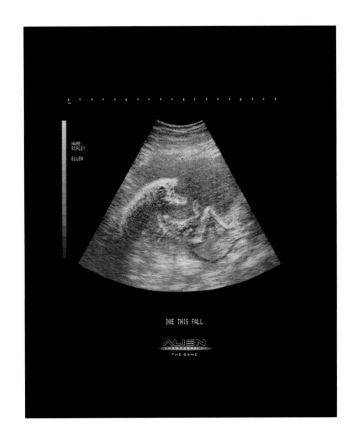

BRONZE AWARD
Collateral: Point of
Purchase and In-Store

ART DIRECTOR
Bradley Wood

WRITER
Alex Grossman

ILLUSTRATORS
I-Magic
Nick Dietrich

CLIENT
FOX Interactive

AGENCY
Butler Shine & Stern/
Sausalito

SILVER AWARD
Collateral: Self-Promotion

ART DIRECTORS
John Domas
Jean Robaire

WRITERS
Dave Holloway
Sally Hogshead

CLIENT
Robaire and Hogshead

AGENCY
Robaire and Hogshead/
Venice

CLIENT
Volvo España SA

AGENCY
Saatchi & Saatchi/
Madrid

GOLD AWARD
Collateral: Posters

ART DIRECTOR
Yuri Alemany

WRITER
Carlos Perrinó

SILVER AWARD
Collateral: Posters

ART DIRECTOR
Bradley Wood

WRITER
Ryan Ebner

CLIENT
Valor Tours

AGENCY
Butler Shine & Stern/
Sausalito

BRONZE AWARD
Collateral: Posters

ART DIRECTOR
Bradley Wood

WRITER
Ryan Ebner

CLIENT
Valor Tours

AGENCY
Butler Shine & Stern/
Sausalito

SILVER AWARD
Collateral: Posters

ART DIRECTOR
Rich Pryce-Jones

WRITER
David Chiavegato

PHOTOGRAPHER
Paul Weeks

CLIENT
Nearly Naked Lingerie

AGENCY
Palmer Jarvis DDB/
Toronto

GOLD AWARD
Public Service/Political
Newspaper or Magazine:
Single

ART DIRECTORS
Simon Langley
Richard Morgan

WRITERS
Richard Morgan
Simon Langley

CLIENT
Australian Red Cross

AGENCY
MOJO Partners/Sydney

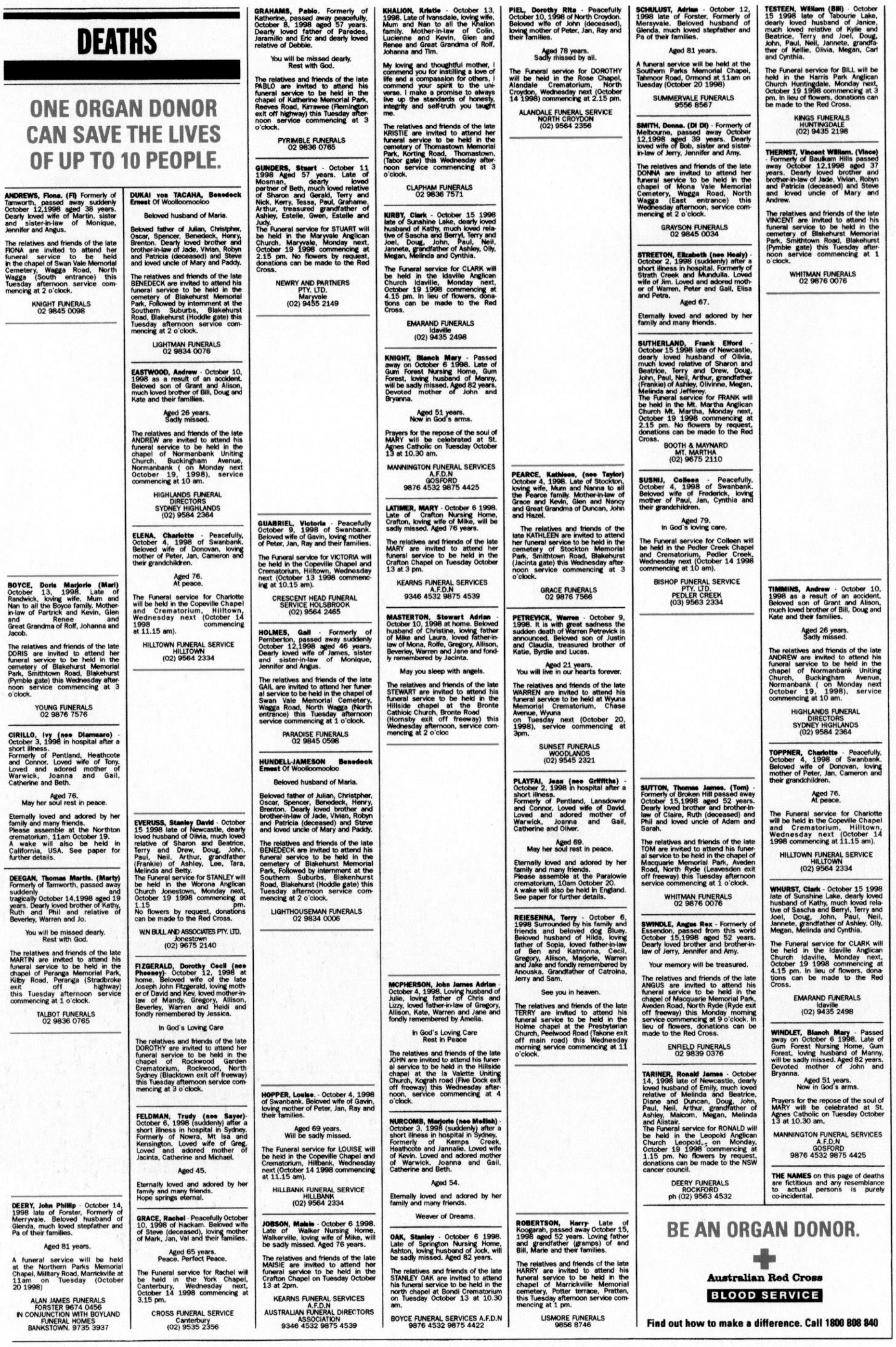

DEATHS

ONE ORGAN DONOR CAN SAVE THE LIVES OF UP TO 10 PEOPLE.

BE AN ORGAN DONOR.

Australian Red Cross
BLOOD SERVICE

Find out how to make a difference. Call 1800 808 840

THE NAMES on this page of deaths are fictitious and any resemblance to actual persons is purely co-incidental.

JOHN KENNEDY'S
FINGERPRINT.

Step back in time and
relive the space race.
The John F. Kennedy
Library & Museum
617-929-4523

SILVER AWARD
Public Service/Political
Newspaper or Magazine:
Single

ART DIRECTOR
Cliff Sorah

WRITER
Joe Alexander

PHOTOGRAPHER
NASA

CLIENT
John F. Kennedy
Library Foundation

AGENCY
The Martin Agency/
Richmond

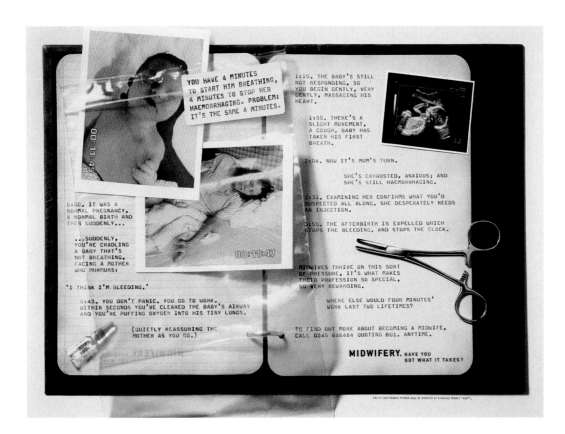

BRONZE AWARD
Public Service/Political
Newspaper or Magazine:
Single

ART DIRECTOR
Colin Jones

WRITER
Mike McKenna

PHOTOGRAPHER
Graham Cornthwaite

CLIENT
Department of Health/
COI

AGENCY
Saatchi & Saatchi/
London

GOLD AWARD
Public Service/Political
Newspaper or Magazine:
Campaign

ART DIRECTOR
Paul Belford

WRITER
Nigel Roberts

PHOTOGRAPHERS
Andreas Heumann
Michael Liam Cumiskey
Peter Knapp
Tessa Traeger
Bruno Munari

CLIENT
The Tate Gallery

AGENCY
TBWA Simons
Palmer/London

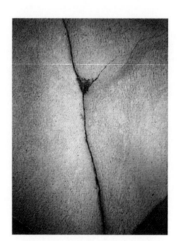

A rock, noticed after
a visit to the Tate.
Minds open from 10am.
TateGallery

A conker, noticed after
a visit to the Tate.
Minds open from 10am.
TateGallery

A vine, noticed after
a visit to the Tate.
Minds open from 10am.
TateGallery

Beansprouts, noticed after
a visit to the Tate.
Minds open from 10am.
TateGallery

A piece of wood, noticed
after a visit to the Tate.
Minds open from 10am.
TateGallery

SILVER AWARD
Public Service/Political
Newspaper or Magazine:
Campaign

ART DIRECTOR
Mark Mason

WRITERS
Mark Mason
Andrew Durkan
Mark Legward

ILLUSTRATOR
Wesley Lewis

CLIENT
Saatchi & Saatchi

AGENCY
Saatchi & Saatchi/
Cape Town

Blonde, Built & Beautiful

24 HRS

Full massage.

Hours of busty pleasure.

A lifetime of erotic memories.

★ ★ ★ ★ ★
Credit cards welcome

Call Pamela A.
480-9130

COME CHAT

Steamy telephone erotica.

24 hrs.

LIVE xxxx
First 3 mins FREE !
ADULTS ONLY
CALL: 480-9131

LIVE Gay Sex Chat

24 HRS

Hot telephone erotica.

Fully automated system.

First 3 mins FREE !
ADULTS ONLY
CALL: 480-9113

(Callers responding to this number received the following message.)

Hi, this is Pamela A. Unfortunately I can no longer offer my services, as I have just received the results of my most recent HIV test. So, if you want good, clean sex, I'm living proof that you should always wear a condom. Thank you.

(Callers responding to this number received the following message.)

Hi stranger, what's your name? You can call me Candy, but let's skip the foreplay cause I'm so wet I want you now. Take that big cock out and put it between my legs. Ooh yeah, now pump me big boy. Come on, stick it all in, ooh, harder, lover, yes make me come, ooh don't stop, just fuck me!

If this was more than just a phone call ask yourself if you'd have had the sense to wear a condom.

(Callers responding to this number received the following message.)

Hi, man... you ready for some hot cock... cause I got 12 inches of dick just waiting to shoot its load into your tight ass... You wanna come over here and spread that butt for me oh... yeah... that's good... you like my big dick in your ass... man.

If this was more than just a phone call buddy, ask yourself: would you have checked if I was wearing a condom.

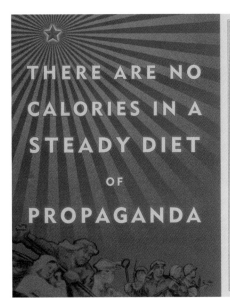

THERE ARE NO CALORIES IN A STEADY DIET OF PROPAGANDA

THE CHILDREN OF NORTH KOREA RECEIVE 110 CALORIES A DAY. THIS IS STARVATION LEVEL. CAUGHT BETWEEN A U.N. EMBARGO AND A POVERTY-STRICKEN GOVERNMENT, THE SURVIVAL OF AN ENTIRE GENERATION IS AT STAKE. BUT THERE ARE EFFORTS TO HELP.

THE CAMPAIGN FOR FAMINE RELIEF IN NORTH KOREA

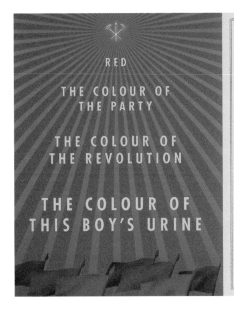

RED

THE COLOUR OF
THE PARTY

THE COLOUR OF
THE REVOLUTION

THE COLOUR OF
THIS BOY'S URINE

THE CHILDREN OF NORTH KOREA ARE DYING. DROUGHTS, FLOODS AND A RAVAGED GOVERNMENT HAVE LEFT A POPULATION HALF THE SIZE OF ETHIOPIA WITH A FAMINE THAT IS TWICE AS WORSE. BUT THERE IS HOPE.

THE CAMPAIGN FOR FAMINE RELIEF IN NORTH KOREA

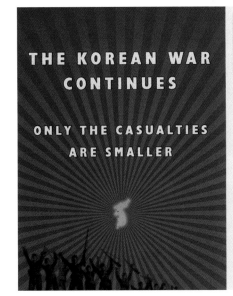

THE KOREAN WAR CONTINUES

ONLY THE CASUALTIES ARE SMALLER

HUNDREDS OF THOUSANDS OF NORTH KOREAN CHILDREN HAVE STARVED TO DEATH IN THE LAST THREE YEARS. NATURAL DISASTERS AND HARSH POLITICAL REALITIES THREATEN AN ENTIRE GENERATION. BUT THERE ARE EFFORTS TO HELP.

THE CAMPAIGN FOR FAMINE RELIEF IN NORTH KOREA

BRONZE AWARD
Public Service/Political
Newspaper or Magazine:
Campaign

ART DIRECTOR
Ted Royer

WRITER
Rowan Chanen

ILLUSTRATOR
Procolor

PHOTOGRAPHER
Tom Haskell

CLIENT
Campaign For Famine
Relief in North Korea

AGENCY
Saatchi & Saatchi/
Singapore

GOLD AWARD
Public Service/Political
Outdoor and Posters

ART DIRECTOR
Pedro Cappeletti

WRITER
Jader Rossetto

PHOTOGRAPHER
Alexandre Catan

CLIENT
Sao Paulo Museum of Art

AGENCY
DM9 DDB Publicidade/
São Paulo

Botero
at the São Paulo
Museum of Art.
From March 17 to May 17

SILVER AWARD
Public Service/Political:
Outdoor and Posters

ART DIRECTOR
Dave Sakamoto

WRITER
Brad Beerbohm

CLIENT
Lesbian & Gay Rights
Lobby of Texas

AGENCY
RIDE/Austin

BRONZE AWARD
Public Service/Political:
Outdoor and Posters

ART DIRECTOR
Nancy Steinman

WRITERS
Jeff Bossin
Bruce Dundore

PHOTOGRAPHER
Myron Beck

CLIENT
California Department
of Health Services

AGENCY
Asher & Partners/
Los Angeles

GOLD AWARD
Public Service/Political
Collateral: Brochures and
Direct Mail

ART DIRECTOR
Doug Pedersen

WRITER
Curtis Smith

ILLUSTRATOR
Floyd Coffey

PHOTOGRAPHER
Pat Staub

CLIENT
Outward Bound

AGENCY
Loeffler Ketchum
Mountjoy/Charlotte

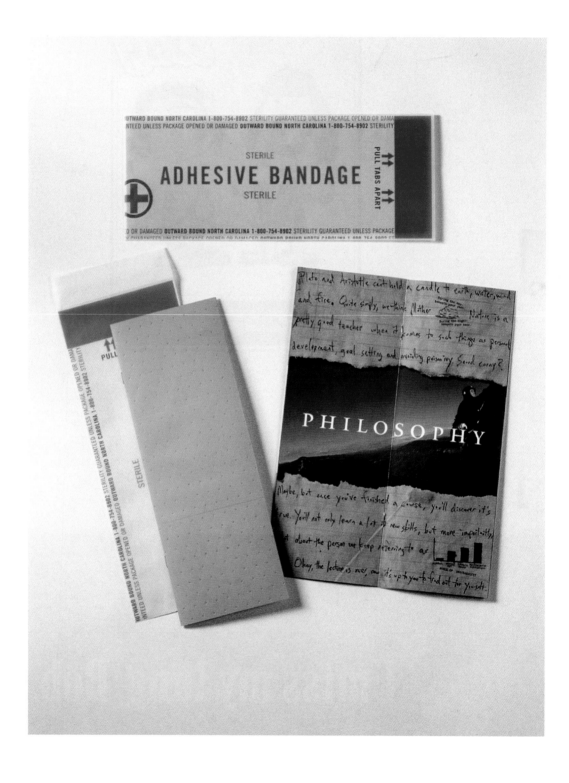

CLIENT
Middle Tennessee Council
Boy Scouts of America

AGENCY
Dye Van Mol &
Lawrence/Nashville

WRITER
Nelson Eddy

PHOTOGRAPHER
Michael Rutherford

BRONZE AWARD
Public Service/Political
Collateral: Brochures and
Direct Mail

ART DIRECTORS
Chuck Creasy
Kevin Hinson

GOLD AWARD
Public Service/
Political Television: Single

ART DIRECTORS
Greg Wells
Marne Brobeck

WRITER
Greg Collins

AGENCY PRODUCER
Julie Shannon

PRODUCTION COMPANY
November Films

DIRECTOR
Kyle Bergersen

CLIENT
Partnership for a
Drug-Free America

AGENCY
Team One Advertising/
El Segundo

HOST: *Once again, folks, item J-343 is—the surfing monkey coin bank! It's great for graduations, wedding gifts, and I believe we sold out on this one last time, so please, do not let this one pass you by. Now, let's go to caller… Scott in Nashville…*

SCOTT: *Hello.*

HOST: *Now Scott, I understand you just bought fifteen of our surfing monkey banks…is that true?*

SCOTT: *Yeah.*

SFX: *Pot-influenced laughter and coughing.*

SUPER: *Marijuana. A very expensive habit. Partnership for a Drug-Free America.*

SCOTT: *Chill, man… I'm on TV.*

SILVER AWARD
Public Service/
Political Television: Single

ART DIRECTORS
John Gorse
Paul Brazier

WRITER
Nick Worthington

AGENCY PRODUCER
Frank Lieberman

PRODUCTION COMPANY
Park Village

DIRECTOR
Roger Woodburn

CLIENT
DETR Seatbelts

AGENCY
Abbott Mead Vickers.
BBDO/London

ANNOUNCER: *Like most victims, Julie knew her killer.*

ANNOUNCER: *It was her son, who was sitting behind her without a seatbelt.*

ANNOUNCER: *After crushing her to death.*

ANNOUNCER: *He sat back down.*

SINGER (to "The Brady Bunch" theme music):

Here's the story

Of a chain-smoking lady.

Who smoked around her three lovely girls.

All of them had clothes that smelled.

Just like their mother's.

The youngest one–asthmatic.

Here's the story

Of a man who smoked daily.

Who was busy with three packs of his own.

His oldest son showed early signs of heart disease.

Because Dad smoked at home.

One day this lady bummed a smoke off this fellow.

The kids shared a risk of cancer with their folks.

Because this group would somehow form a family.

That's the way they became affected by Second-Hand Smoke.

Second-Hand Smoke.

Second-Hand Smoke.

That's the way they became affected by Second-Hand Smoke.

BRONZE AWARD
Public Service/
Political Television: Single

ART DIRECTORS
Paul Keister
Dave Clemans

WRITERS
Tim Roper
Tom Adams

AGENCY PRODUCER
Terry Stavoe

**PRODUCTION
COMPANY**
Voyeur Films

DIRECTOR
The Tozzis

CLIENT
Florida Tobacco Pilot
Program

AGENCY
Crispin Porter &
Bogusky/Miami

GOLD AWARD
Public Service/
Political Television:
Campaign

ART DIRECTOR
Rob Dow

WRITER
Nigel Dawson

AGENCY PRODUCER
Susie Cole

PRODUCTION COMPANY
Renegade Films

DIRECTOR
Aleksi Vellis

CLIENT
Transport Accident
Commission

AGENCY
Grey Advertising/
Melbourne

MUSIC: *"Twelve Days of Christmas."*

SUPER: *Monday.*

ALAN: *Whoooaa, hey big boy. Oh I've got you two!*

HANNAH: *Woooow!*

KAREN: *Ohhh...he's starting to swallow his own (laughs).*

ALAN: *Whack it on the tree.*

SUPER: *Wednesday.*

SFX: *Party noises; drinking, laughing, etc.*

ALAN: *A couple more weeks left, you should see her now, she's really big.*

WORKMATE: *Leave those girls alone, huh!*

LADY: *(Laughs)*

ALAN: *Come on.*

SFX: *Crash.*

DOCTOR: *I'm not sure how he's going to go.*

DOCTOR: *He's had a bad injury.*

DOCTOR: *Your husband does have a very serious head injury... we have to take him to our intensive care room.*

KAREN: *(Sobs)*

SUPER: *Should you be driving home tonight?*

SUPER: *If you drink, then drive, you're a bloody idiot. TAC.*

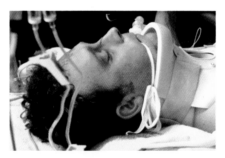

MUSIC: *"Twelve Days of Christmas."*

SUPER: *Thursday*

SFX: *Phone rings.*

HANNAH: *Where's Daddy, Daddy?*

DANIEL: *Hello... Daddy's not here, he's sick.*

GRANDPA: *It might take a few days but they come out of it.*

KAREN: *He'll be home, he'll be home.*

SUPER: *Sunday.*

DOCTOR: *The tests that we've done really confirm beyond... doubt that the... that Alan's brain has now stopped working and I can only tell you that we need to take him off the machine.*

GRANDMA: *Oh no.*

GRANDPA: *Oh no.*

GRANDPA: *See you later, Son.*

GRANDMA: *Don't take him away from me, Ohh don't take him, Ohhh God it's not fair, Ohh don't.*

SUPER: *Should you be driving home tonight?*

SUPER: *If you drink, then drive, you're a bloody idiot. TAC.*

Christmas Day

If you drink,
then drive,
you're a bloody idiot.

TAC

MUSIC: *"Twelve Days of Christmas."*

SUPER: *Christmas Eve.*

KAREN: *Mum! Stop fussing! You're fussing, you're fussing, shut up Mum! Just shut up!*

KAREN: *I'm fine, I'm fine, I'm alright.*

HANNAH: *Where are we going, Nana?*

GRANDMA: *We're going to the Church, darling.*

HANNAH: *Is Daddy going to be there?*

GRANDMA: *No, darling. Daddy won't be there.*

SUPER: *Christmas day.*

DANIEL: *Mummy, Mummy.*

HANNAH: *Wake up.*

KAREN: *Ohh, what time is it?*

DANIEL: *Do you like chocolate? Do you?*

KAREN: *Give me a kiss, careful, careful of Baby.*

HANNAH: *Can you open my thing?*

KAREN: *Yeah, hang on a minute, sweetheart, I'm just trying to get this.*

DANIEL: *Mummy, is Santa going to find Daddy?*

KAREN: *Um, no sweetheart he's not.*

DANIEL: *How do I open this?*

SUPER: *Should you be driving home tonight?*

SUPER: *If you drink, then drive, you're a bloody idiot. TAC.*

SILVER AWARD
Public Service/Political
Television: Campaign

ART DIRECTOR
Paul Keister

WRITER
Tim Roper

AGENCY PRODUCER
Terry Stavoe

**PRODUCTION
COMPANY**
JGF

DIRECTOR
Jeff Gorman

CLIENT
Florida Tobacco Pilot
Program

AGENCY
Crispin Porter & Bogusky/
Miami

EXECUTIVE 1: *You know, an operation like this does have a certain cost attached.*

ANNOUNCER: *What if there was a deadly, toxic substance? Harvested by man?*

NURSE: *42-year-old male, found down!*

DOCTOR: *NG to open barrel!*

ANNOUNCER: *Capable of killing thousands of people in a single day?*

PROTAGONIST: *In the last 24 hours about 8000 people just got six feet shorter.*

ANNOUNCER: *And what if someone manufactured this substance in massive quantities…?*

NURSE: *He's seizing!*

DOCTOR: *Let's tube him now!*

ANNOUNCER: *And a select group of people knew about it?*

PROTAGONIST: *A whole lot of people are dying. And a lot of other people are making money off of it.*

ANNOUNCER: *Then, what if the knowledge began to leak out…?*

EXECUTIVE 1: *Someone's gone public.*

EXECUTIVE 2: *Get creative with it.*

EXECUTIVE 1: *Mr. Senator, there's no conclusive evidence to suggest…*

SENATOR: *I have the death toll figures right here.*

ANNOUNCER: *Would anyone believe it?*

EXECUTIVE 1: *You don't just wipe out a population the size of Manhattan and wake up and play golf the next morning.*

EXECUTIVE 2: *Watch me.*

PROTAGONIST: *I'm not gonna wait around and become the spike on somebody's bar graph.*

SKEPTIC: *Dude, you watch way too many movies.*

PROTAGONIST: *This is not a movie.*

SUPER: *Tobacco. 3,000,000 deaths a year. And counting. Another TRUTH production.*

BRONZE AWARD
Public Service/Political
Television: Campaign

ART DIRECTOR
Lisa Francilia

WRITER
Dan Scherk

AGENCY PRODUCERS
Camielle Clark
Krista Brydges

**PRODUCTION
COMPANIES**
Coast Mountain Post
Production
Rainmaker Digital Pictures

DIRECTOR
Melanie Snagg

CLIENT
Vancouver International
Film Festival

AGENCY
Bryant Fulton & Shee/
Vancouver

MUSIC: *"Ma Vie En Rose" theme music.*

ANNOUNCER: *Growing up can be tough! Especially when you're the new kid in town! And a transvestite! But when little Ludo's caught trying to marry his father's boss' son, things really go to hell! But, with the help of an imaginary fairy princess, he realizes that when imagination is your passport to adventure, you can be a fairy princess too! At least until your candy-coated neighbors run you out of town on a rail! Critics have agreed, "Ma Vie En Rose is a foreign film!" Not that there's anything wrong with that…*

SUPER: *Same planet. Different worlds.*

SUPER: *Vancouver International Film Festival*

SUPER: *Vote for the Air Canada People's Choice Awards.*

AGENCY
Cliff Freeman and
Partners/New York

AGENCY PRODUCER
Arlene Adoremos

CLIENT
Hollywood Video

GOLD AWARD
Consumer Radio: Single

WRITERS
Adam Chasnow
Roger Camp
Ian Reichenthal

ANNOUNCER: *Hollywood Video presents..."Sixty Second Theater." Where we try (unsuccessfully) to pack all the action and suspense of a two-hour Hollywood production into 60 seconds. Today's presentation, "Scream 2."*

SFX: *Scary music chords.*

SIDNEY: *Well, it's just us seven incredibly attractive sorority girls here alone in our nightgowns...*

KILLER: *Must kill!*

DEBBIE: *Did you hear something?*

ALISON: *I'll go outside alone and investigate!*

SFX: *Door opening.*

KILLER: *Must kill!*

SFX: *Woman screaming; slashing sound; body falling.*

SIDNEY: *What was that?*

DEBBIE: *I'll go check!*

SFX: *Door opening.*

KILLER: *Must kill!*

SFX: *Woman screaming; slashing sound; body falling.*

HALLIE: *There's that noise again. I'm scared!*

CICI/HALLIE/LOIS: *Let's stick together!*

SFX: *Scary music.*

SIDNEY: *I've got a better plan! Lois, you hide in the utility shed with the gas-powered cutting and shearing equipment!*

LOIS: *Okay!*

SIDNEY: *Cici, you go up to the dark and slippery roof and hide right near the edge!*

CICI: *All right!*

SIDNEY: *Hallie, whatever you do, don't leave my side.*

HALLIE: *Good idea...I have to go the bathroom.*

SIDNEY: *Ooohh, there's an old outhouse near the swamp!*

HALLIE: *Perfect!*

CICI/HALLIE/LOIS: *Bye!*

SFX: *Door opening.*

KILLER: *Must kill! Must kill! Must kill!*

SFX: *Three women screaming; Three slashing sounds; Three bodies falling. Doorbell.*

SIDNEY: *Back already?*

SFX: *Door opening.*

KILLER: *Must kill!*

SIDNEY: *Oh my! Good thing I took that kickboxing class! Hi-ya!*

SFX: *Karate kicks; fighting sounds.*

Killer: *Ouch! No, not there!*

SFX: *Body falling.*

SIDNEY: *He sure looks dead.*

KILLER: *No, I'm not.*

SIDNEY: *I can't think of a better time to turn my back and put my guard down.*

KILLER: *Must...*

SFX: *Karate kick.*

KILLER: *...kill.*

SFX: *Hollywood Video theme music.*

ANNOUNCER: *If this doesn't satisfy your urge to see "Scream 2," and we can't say we blame you, then rent it today at Hollywood Video. Where "Scream 2" is guaranteed to be in-stock, or next time it's free. Welcome to Hollywood. Hollywood Video. Celebrity voices impersonated.*

SILVER AWARD
Consumer Radio: Single

WRITERS
Adam Chasnow
Ian Reichenthal

AGENCY PRODUCER
Arlene Adoremos

CLIENT
Hollywood Video

AGENCY
Cliff Freeman and
Partners/New York

ANNOUNCER: *Hollywood Video presents..."Sixty Second Theater." Where we try (unsuccessfully) to pack all the action and drama of a two-hour Hollywood production into 60 seconds. Today's presentation..."Good Will Hunting."*

SFX: *Chalk on chalkboard.*

PROFESSOR: *(Swedish accent) Class, it took me and my colleagues two years to solve this math problem.*

STUDENT: *It only took the janitor ten minutes.*

PROFESSOR: *Where is this genius-janitor?*

STUDENT: *In jail.*

PROFESSOR: *Why?*

Student: *He's an extremely violent genius-janitor.*

SFX: *Jail doors opening.*

PROFESSOR: *I'll get you out of jail, genius-janitor, if you teach me math and see a shrink.*

WILL: *(Matt Damon sound-alike; thick Boston accent) No, thanks.*

SFX: *Jail doors closing.*

CELLMATE: *(deep voice) Hi cutie, I'm your cellmate.*

WILL: *Whoaaa! Math and a shrink sounds good!*

SFX: *Door opening.*

MCGUIRE: *(Robin Williams sound-alike) Will, I'm Dr. McGuire.*

WILL: *You're a shrink? You're crazier than I am!*

MCGUIRE: *(Screaming) Don't you ever call me crazy! You got that chief! (Calmly) I'll see you next Thursday at 4:30?*

SFX: *Door closes. Car horn beeping.*

CHUCKIE: *(Ben Affleck sound alike; thick Boston*

accent) Hey Will, let's go to a Haavaahdd baahh and beat up some smaaahht kids.

WILL: *Or I could humiliate them with my vast knowledge of pre-revolutionary economic modalities.*

CHUCKIE: *Nah, let's just beat 'em up.*

SFX: *Car tires screeching to a stop.*

WILL: *Hey smaaahht kid, I'm smaahtaahh than you are.*

PREPPY: *You don't sound smart.*

WILL: *No one from Boston does.*

SKYLAR: *(Minnie Driver sound-alike; British accent) Hi, I'm Skylar.*

WILL: *Hi, Skylaaaah.*

SKYLAR: *No, Sky-LER. Wanna go back to my dorm room?*

SFX: *Key into door. Door opens.*

SFX: *Barry White-style music.*

SKYLAR: *I'm not going to shag you until I meet your friends.*

SFX: *Needle-scratch; music stops.*

WILL: *Chuckie, Billy, Maahgan this is Skylaahh. Skylaahh: Chuckie, Billy, Maahgan.*

SFX: *Barry White-style music again.*

SKYLAR: *I love you, Will.*

WILL: *I love you, Skylaaahh.*

SKYLAR: *It's Sky-LER! Skyler!!*

ANNOUNCER: *If this doesn't satisfy you urge to see "Good Will Hunting" (and we can't say we blame you) then rent it today at Hollywood Video. Where "Good Will Hunting" is guaranteed to be in-stock, or next time it's free. Welcome to Hollywood. Hollywood Video. Celebrity voices impersonated.*

AGENCY
TBWA Hunt Lascaris/
Johannesburg

AGENCY PRODUCER
Tracey Ashman

CLIENT
Nando's Chickenland

BRONZE AWARD
Consumer Radio: Single

WRITERS
Jonathan Davenport
Stuart Walsh
Rui Alves
Karl Dunn
Scott McClelland
Erich Funke

SFX: Soppy romantic music.

SFX: Woman sighing with ecstasy.

FEMALE: Stuart?

SFX: Sighing continues.

FEMALE: Stuart?

SFX: Sighing continues.

FEMALE: Stuart!

SFX: Muffled mumble.

FEMALE: That's enough foreplay, let's move on....

ANNOUNCER: And now for something else you've never heard before.
New from Nando's: three delicious flame-grilled chicken wings on a skewer
free with selected meals!

GOLD AWARD
Consumer Radio:
Campaign

WRITERS
Adam Chasnow
Ian Reichenthal
Wayne Best
Roger Camp

AGENCY PRODUCER
Arlene Adoremos

CLIENT
Hollywood Video

AGENCY
Cliff Freeman and
Partners/New York

ANNOUNCER: *Hollywood Video presents... "Sixty Second Theater." Where we try, unsuccessfully, to pack all the action and drama of a two-hour Hollywood production into 60 seconds. Today's presentation, "Tomorrow Never Dies."*

SFX: *Bond-style music sting.*

M: *007, a brilliant but evil madman is...*

BOND: *(Pierce Brosnan sound-alike)... threatening the security of the world, naturally. All right, where's "Q" with my gadgets?*

SFX: *Footsteps.*

Q: *Bond, here are your gadgets.*

BOND: *What does this pen do?*

Q: *Kills people.*

BOND: *This tie clip?*

Q: *Kills people.*

BOND: *What does this whoopee cushion do?*

SFX: *Whoopee cushion fart...*

Q: *Kills people.*

BOND: *Nasty. Then I'm off to an exotic destination.*

SFX: *Bond-style music sting.*

SFX: *Airplane landing...*

BOND: *Ah, here I am.*

SEXYPANTS: *(French accent) Hello, Mr. Bond. I'm Ms. Sexypants.*

BOND: *Splendid. Shall we get a room?*

SFX: *Kissing. Knocking on door.*

VILLAIN: *(Disguises his voice to sound like a maid) Housekeeping!*

SFX: *Door handle opening.*

VILLAIN: *(German accent) A-ha!*

SFX: *Bond music sting. Gun cocking.*

VILLAIN: *I have you now, James Bontt!*

BOND: *Bond. James Bond.*

VILLAIN: *What did I say?*

BOND: *Excuse me, would you like to sit on this whoopee cushion?*

VILLAIN: *(Laughs) Good!*

SFX: *Whoopee cushion fart then loud explosion.*

VILLAIN: *(Screams)*

SEXYPANTS: *The world is safe again. Oh, James.*

BOND: *Weren't you in on the plot to kill me?*

SEXYPANTS: *Yeah.*

BOND: *Oh, what the heck. You've got nice legs.*

SFX: *Hollywood Video theme music.*

ANNOUNCER: *If this doesn't satisfy your urge to see "Tomorrow Never Dies" (and we can't say we blame you) then rent it today at Hollywood Video. Where "Tomorrow Never Dies" is guaranteed to be in-stock, or next time it's free. Welcome to Hollywood. Hollywood Video. Celebrity voices impersonated.*

ANNOUNCER: *Hollywood Video presents... "Sixty Second Theater." Where we try (unsuccessfully) to pack all the action and suspense of a two-hour Hollywood production into 60 seconds. Today's presentation, "Scream 2."*

SFX: *Scary music chords.*

SIDNEY: *Well, it's just us seven incredibly attractive sorority girls here alone in our nightgowns...*

KILLER: *Must kill!*

DEBBIE: *Did you hear something?*

ALISON: *I'll go outside alone and investigate!*

SFX: *Door opening.*

KILLER: *Must kill!*

SFX: *Woman screaming; slashing sound; body falling.*

SIDNEY: *What was that?*

DEBBIE: *I'll go check!*

SFX: *Door opening.*

KILLER: *Must kill!*

SFX: *Woman screaming; slashing sound; body falling.*

HALLIE: *There's that noise again. I'm scared!*

CICI/HALLIE/LOIS: *Let's stick together!*

SFX: *Scary music.*

SIDNEY: *I've got a better plan! Lois, you hide in the utility shed with the gas-powered cutting and shearing equipment!*

LOIS: *Okay!*

SIDNEY: *Cici, you go up to the dark and slippery roof and hide right near the edge!*

CICI: *All right!*

SIDNEY: *Hallie, whatever you do, don't leave my side.*

HALLIE: *Good idea...I have to go the bathroom.*

SIDNEY: *Ooohh, there's an old outhouse near the swamp!*

HALLIE: *Perfect!*

CICI/HALLIE/LOIS: *Bye!*

SFX: *Door opening.*

KILLER: *Must kill! Must kill! Must kill!*

SFX: *Three women screaming; Three slashing sounds; Three bodies falling. Doorbell.*

SIDNEY: *Back already?*

SFX: *Door opening.*

KILLER: *Must kill!*

SIDNEY: *Oh my! Good thing I took that kickboxing class! Hi-ya!*

SFX: *Karate kicks; fighting sounds.*

KILLER: *Ouch! No, not there!*

SFX: *Body falling.*

SIDNEY: *He sure looks dead.*

KILLER: *No, I'm not.*

SIDNEY: *I can't think of a better time to turn my back and put my guard down.*

KILLER: *Must...*

SFX: *Karate kick.*

KILLER: *...kill.*

SFX: *Hollywood Video theme music.*

ANNOUNCER: *If this doesn't satisfy your urge to see "Scream 2," and we can't say we blame you, then rent it today at Hollywood Video. Where "Scream 2" is guaranteed to be in-stock, or next time it's free. Welcome to Hollywood. Hollywood Video. Celebrity voices impersonated.*

ANNOUNCER: *Hollywood Video presents... "Sixty Second Theater." Where we try (unsuccessfully) to pack all the action and drama of a two-hour Hollywood production into 60 seconds. Today's presentation, "As Good As It Gets."*

SFX: *Doorbell.*

MELVIN: *(Jack Nicholson sound-alike) All right. Who is it?*

SFX: *Many locks being unlocked quickly.*

SIMON: *(Greg Kinnear sound-alike) It's your artistic neighbor. Have you seen my little doggie?*

MELVIN: *Yeah. I stuffed the yapper down the trash chute.*

SIMON: *You are a cruel man!*

MELVIN: *I'm a hungry cruel man. I'm going to breakfast.*

SFX: *Door with bells swings open. Restaurant sounds.*

MELVIN: *You look bad today, even for a waitress.*

CAROL: *(Helen Hunt sound-alike) You are a cruel, obsessive, compulsive man.*

MELVIN: *You forgot rich.*

CAROL: *Get out!*

SFX: *Gets up from chair. Opens door.*

CAROL: *Did you say rich?*

SFX: *Door closes. Bells ring.*

MELVIN: *See ya.*

SFX: *Doorbell.*

MELVIN: *All right.*

SFX: *Many locks being unlocked quickly.*

MELVIN: *Well, if it isn't my "artistic" neighbor.*

SIMON: *You are a cruel man. Will you drive me to my parents' house?*

MELVIN: *Okay, can I bring the waitress?*

SIMON: *Does she like show tunes?*

SFX: *Tires screeching; Car driving. Show tunes play on car stereo. Tires screeching to a stop.*

MELVIN: *We're here.*

CAROL AND SIMON: *We don't like you. Let's go home.*

SFX: *Tires screeching; car driving. Show tunes on a car stereo. Tires screech to a stop.*

MELVIN: *We're home. Now can I be your boyfriend?*

SIMON: *Well, okay.*

MELVIN: *Not you. Her.*

SIMON: *What about me?*

MELVIN: *Well, you can be my roommate.*

SFX: *Hollywood Video theme music.*

ANNOUNCER: *If this doesn't satisfy your urge to see "As Good As It Gets" (and we can't say we blame you) then rent it today at Hollywood Video. Where "As Good As It Gets" is guaranteed to be in-stock, or next time it's free. Welcome to Hollywood. Hollywood Video. Celebrity voices impersonated.*

GOLD AWARD
Consumer Television
Over :30 Single

ART DIRECTOR
Thorbjorn Naug

WRITER
Aris Theophilakis

PRODUCTION COMPANY
Ferocious Films/London

DIRECTOR
Jorn Haagen

CLIENT
Audi of Norway

AGENCY
Bates Norway/Oslo

(An Audi TT Coupe is parked on a street. A passing car breaks frantically. The driver looks at the Audi and drives off, leaving skid marks on the street. The Audi TT Coupe starts and drives off. The parking space is immediately taken by a Mercedes SLK. Seconds later, a car passes the SLK without the driver noticing it.)

GOLD AWARD
Consumer Television
Over :30 Single

ART DIRECTOR
Tim Hanrahan

WRITER
Jerry Cronin

AGENCY PRODUCER
Ben Grylewicz

PRODUCTION COMPANY
Satellite

DIRECTOR
Jhoan Camitz

CLIENT
Nike

AGENCY
Wieden & Kennedy/
Portland

(A small boy runs with soccer ball towards his house. Inside house, the boy pulls a plate of meat out of the refrigerator and begins to ring it out, squeezing all the juice onto the ball. Then he picks up the piece of meat and rubs it all over the ball. The boy picks up ball and runs back outside. We see a shoe on top of the ball holding it in place. A large dog, chained up, growls; a chihuahua dog barks, a basset hound sneaks under fence. The boy screams as he notices all the dogs are starting to chase him.)

SUPER: *(What are you getting ready for?)*

SUPER: *Nike.*

(A man walks out front door of his house, starts his stop watch, starts running down the street. He is joined by a Kenyan runner, coming up behind him; the man looks nervously over his shoulder. Then Bob Kennedy runs up behind man; he looks over his shoulder at Kennedy and is puzzled. We see Uta Pippig carrying grocery bags to her house, dropping her groceries, stripping down to her running attire and joining the group. A group of University of Oregon runners joins the group. In an alley way children play ball; an elderly woman takes out the garbage. A cab comes screeching to a halt. Michael Johnson gets out of cab and joins the group. Someone from the group runs over a parked car, runners pass by a water table and push each other to get to it; water table collapses. Man runs towards his house, looking behind him at the runners; goes up the steps, into his house, and, closing the door behind him, checks his watch for his time.)

SUPER: *(What are you getting ready for?)*

SUPER: *Nike.*

SILVER AWARD
Consumer Television
Over :30 Single

ART DIRECTOR
Hal Curtis

WRITER
Chuck McBride

AGENCY PRODUCER
Donna Portaro

PRODUCTION COMPANY
Satellite

DIRECTOR
Jhoan Camitz

CLIENT
Nike

AGENCY
Wieden & Kennedy/
Portland

(A matador walks into an outdoor stadium with crowds of people cheering from the stands. A big crowd forms in the streets; some distance from the stadium people are banging on the door that holds back the bulls. The doors open; bulls start running through the city streets. Crowds on the sidelines of the street begin to cheer and yell. Football players in Panther uniforms climb over a railing and onto the crowded streets. The matador waits in the stadium for the bulls to arrive; runners come through the door and into the arena. The football players cut through crowd and stand in front of the stadium entrance, crouching into position, as the runners pass and jump over them. The bulls charge toward the football players, come head to head with them.)

SFX: *Grunting noises from bulls. (The crowd in the stadium rises out of their seats to see what happened. The matador is still waiting.)*

MATADOR *(in Spanish): Where are the bulls?*

SUPER: *(What are you getting ready for?)*

SUPER: *Nike.*

SILVER AWARD
Consumer Television
Over :30 Single

ART DIRECTOR
Rob Palmer

WRITER
Canice Neary

AGENCY PRODUCER
Jennifer Smieja

PRODUCTION COMPANY
@radical.media/London

DIRECTOR
Ralf Schmerberg

CLIENT
Nike

AGENCY
Wieden & Kennedy/
Portland

BRONZE AWARD
Consumer Television
Over :30 Single

ART DIRECTOR
Joanna Wenley

WRITER
Jeremy Craigen

AGENCY PRODUCER
Howard Spivey

PRODUCTION COMPANY
Gorgeous Enterprises

DIRECTOR
Frank Budgen

CLIENT
Sony

AGENCY
BMP DDB/London

(A man in his early 30s is standing in a city square filming his girlfriend eating a baguette with a camcorder. We see the camcorder's low battery sign flashing along with the man. The man lowers his camcorder, turns it off and unclips the battery.

Suddenly, a dog jumps up, takes a bite from the girlfriend's baguette and runs into the middle of the road. The dog running into the road causes a cyclist to swerve toward the path of an on-coming pick-up truck. The truck is carrying a load of milk churns. As the truck veers away from the bicycle, the milk churns begin to spill off. One of the churns hits the bottom of a scaffolding tower, knocking it sideways and unbalancing a man at the top. He's thrown off into a shop awning, from where he slides safely to the pavement. The neon sign he had been fixing falls off in a spectacular shower of electrical sparks.

Meanwhile, the truck causes a car to swerve out of its way. The car hits something at the edge of the road which launches it into the air. The car flies through the air and comes crashing down into the front of the shop.

Through the whole sequence camcorder man and girlfriend look on in frozen awe. His expression continues until his attention is caught by a final churn lid landing at his feet and clattering to a stop.

The camcorder man looks at his girlfriend, then down at his camcorder and across to the dead battery, and then back to his girlfriend–still with the same blank expression on his face.)

SUPER: *Don't change your battery, change your camcorder.*

SUPER: *The Sony Stamina Camcorder. Sony.*

(The outside of a Los Angeles hotel, then a hotel room. Ben is getting dressed to go to rehearsal as members of the Wu-Tang are splayed out on the bed, watching Goldie Hawn, Diane Keaton and Bette Midler singing the "You Don't Own Me" theme song from "The First Wives Club.")

BEN: *Okay, guys I've got to cut out to go to rehearsal.*

RZA: *Yo easy, B... this is the best part.*

METHOD MAN: *Yo, Ben, you should book one of them birds on the show.*

GHOSTFACE: *Yeah, Diane Keaton is bangin'.*

BEN: *Yeah, gee, I dunno. Diane Keaton? I mean, she's great, but, you know, it's the Video Music Awards... I don't see...*

RZA: *Oh, I get it. You an actor/director, she's an actor/director. Ain't no room for two. Man, that ain't right.*

METHOD MAN: *Straight up, G. You know, the show's bigger than you. It ain't the damn Ben Stiller Awards.*

BEN: *It's not an ego thing, Killah, it's just... I don't know what we'd get her to do.*

RZA: *Get her ass to co-host, yo. She won an Oscar, I'm pretty sure she can co-host the damn Video Music Awards...*

BEN: *Yeah, well, I'm pretty sure you can put some of the wet towels in the hamper, that's what I'm pretty sure of.*

ANNOUNCER: *It's the MTV Video Music Awards. Live from L.A. September 10th at 8:00 Hosted by Ben Stiller.*

Ben starts leaving the room.

RZA: *Yeah, later Ben Gay.*

METHOD MAN:... *Zipper.*

BEN: *Stop it with the zipper, already.*

GOLD AWARD
Consumer Television
Over :30 Single

ART DIRECTORS
Tom Kuntz
Mike Maguire
Tim Abshire

WRITERS
Tom Kuntz
Mike Maguire
Allan Broce

AGENCY PRODUCERS
Michael Engleman
Benita Husband
Marcy Lacanere

**PRODUCTION
COMPANY**
MTV

DIRECTORS
Mike Maguire
Tom Kuntz
Tim Abshire

CLIENT
MTV: Video Music
Awards

AGENCY
MTV/New York

(Ben is, in his hotel's gym, on a treadmill/stairmaster. Madonna walks up to him, appearing as though she has just finished working out.)

MADONNA: *Hey, Ben.*

BEN: *Oh, uh... hey Madonna... in town for the awards?*

MADONNA: *Yeah, you're hosting, right?... uh, anyway, I was gonna say, I have these reservations tonight at Spago and I figured, you might want to...*

BEN: *REALLY?!... I'd... well, I'd...*

MADONNA: *You would?*

BEN: *I'd love to.*

MADONNA: *Great.*

BEN: *Great. (Ben gets off the elevator with a handful of flowers, walks up to Madonna's room, adjusts his tie, etc. Before knocking.)*

MADONNA: *Hey, Ben...*

BEN: *Well...*

MADONNA: *Anyway, you're such a sweetheart for helping us out tonight... (Over Madonna's shoulder appears a handsome gentleman. Ben then looks in the room and sees some kids' show on the tv.)*

MADONNA: *We'll be back around 2:00. Don't let her eat too many sweets. And if she gets hungry, there's breast milk in the refrigerator.*

ANNOUNCER: *It's the MTV Video Music Awards. Live from L.A. September 10th at 8:00. Hosted by Ben Stiller.*

(Ben, now in the suite, is sprawled out on the floor, with baby bottle of milk in his hand. He gives a subtle look around, then takes a swig off the bottle.)

SILVER AWARD
Consumer Television
Over :30 Campaign

ART DIRECTORS
Hal Curtis
Tim Hanrahan
Rob Palmer

WRITERS
Chuck McBride
Jerry Cronin
Canice Neary

AGENCY PRODUCERS
Donna Portaro
Jennifer Smieja
Ben Grylewicz

**PRODUCTION
COMPANIES**
@radical.media/London
Satellite

DIRECTORS
Ralf Schmerberg
Jhoan Camitz

CLIENT
Nike

AGENCY
Wieden &
Kennedy/Portland

(A man walks out front door of his house, starts his stop watch, starts running down the street. He is joined by a Kenyan runner, coming up behind him; the man looks nervously over his shoulder. Then Bob Kennedy runs up behind man; he looks over his shoulder at Kennedy and is puzzled. We see Uta Pippig carrying grocery bags to her house, dropping her groceries, stripping down to her running attire and joining the group. A group of University of Oregon runners joins the group. In an alley way children play ball; an elderly woman takes out the garbage. A cab comes screeching to a halt. Michael Johnson gets out of cab and joins the group. Someone from the group runs over a parked car, runners pass by a water table and push each other to get to it; water table collapses. Man runs towards his house, looking behind him at the runners; goes up the steps, into his house, and, closing the door behind him, checks his watch for his time.)

SUPER: *(What are you getting ready for?)*

SUPER: *Nike*

BRONZE AWARD
Consumer Television
Over :30 Campaign

ART DIRECTOR
Lisa Rubisch

WRITERS
Tom Kuntz
Mike Maguire

AGENCY PRODUCER
Benita Husband

PRODUCTION COMPANY
MTV

DIRECTOR
Lisa Rubisch

CLIENT
MTV: Movie Awards

AGENCY
MTV/New York

SAMUEL: *Sure, Samuel L. Jackson's a big star now. Making the big bucks. Making feature films. Hosting the MTV Movie Awards. But hey, it wasn't always like that. I had to get my start just like everyone else.*

Clips of Samuel in pineapple outfit dancing at a children's show, in paper towel commercial.

SAMUEL: *A little job here... A lucky break there... Then finally, my big break...*

SUPER: *(from "famous" '70's porn film): Bad Cat... Big Bat!*

SAMUEL: *Hollywood... iz awl good.*

ANNOUNCER: *It's the 1998 MTV Movie Awards with your host Samuel L. Jackson.*

(Masterpiece Theatre style.)

NARRATOR: *In an effort to get people to remember our name, Outpost.com, we contacted the local high school marching band and asked them to help us out.*

High school kids in band outfits playing their instruments and spell out Outpost.com.

NARRATOR: *And to help make this memorable, next we decided to release a pack of ravenous wolves.*

Band members screaming, dropping instruments, running off.

NARRATOR: *That's good stuff.*

SUPER: *Send complaints to Outpost.com.*

SUPER: *Outpost. com. The place to buy computer stuff online.*

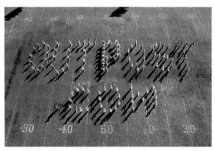

GOLD AWARD
Consumer Television
:30 Single

ART DIRECTOR
Roger Camp

WRITER
Eric Silver

AGENCY PRODUCER
Nick Felder

PRODUCTION
COMPANY
Hungry Man

DIRECTOR
John O'Hagan

CLIENT
Outpost.com

AGENCY
Cliff Freeman and
Partners/New York

(Masterpiece Theatre style.)

NARRATOR: *Hello. We want you to remember our name, Outpost.com. That's why we've decided to fire gerbils out of this cannon through the "O" in Outpost.*

NARRATOR: *Cute little guy. Fire!*

NARRATOR: *And again.*

NARRATOR: *So close.*

SFX: *Siren going off.*

SUPER: *Send complaints to Outpost.com.*

SUPER: *Outpost.com. The place to buy computer stuff online.*

SILVER AWARD
Consumer Television
Over :30 Single

ART DIRECTOR
Roger Camp

WRITER
Eric Silver

AGENCY PRODUCER
Nick Felder

PRODUCTION
COMPANY
Hungry Man

DIRECTOR
John O'Hagan

CLIENT
Outpost.com

AGENCY
Cliff Freeman and
Partners/New York

BRONZE AWARD
Consumer Television
:30 Single

ART DIRECTOR
Wayne Best

WRITER
Adam Chasnow

AGENCY PRODUCER
Liz Graves

**PRODUCTION
COMPANY**
JGF

DIRECTOR
Jeff Gorman

CLIENT
FOX Sports

AGENCY
Cliff Freeman and
Partners/New York

(Man reads 2:30am on clock radio)

MAN: *Wake up, honey. C'mon, honey. Wake up! Wake up!*

(Man enters his kids' room, turns on the light, hits the sides of their beds and pulls the covers off of them.)

MAN: *Okay...up, up, up, up,up! Let's go!*

SFX: *all singing "Happy Birthday" to the mother. Baby crying loudly.*

SUPER: *Get everything out of the way. There's a full day of Super Bowl pregame coverage.*

SFX: *Baby crying.*

MAN: *All right, everyone back to bed.*

SUPER: *FOX Super Bowl XXXIII. Pregame 11am ET/8am PT.*

GOLD AWARD
Consumer Television
:30 Campaign

ART DIRECTOR
Kilpatrick Anderson

WRITER
Kevin Roddy

AGENCY PRODUCER
Nick Felder

**PRODUCTION
COMPANY**
MJZ

DIRECTOR
Rocky Morton

CLIENT
FOX Sports

AGENCY
Cliff Freeman and
Partners/New York

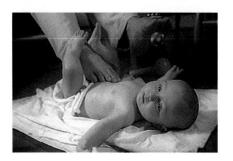

(A pair of men's feet adeptly change an infant's diaper with a diaper pin acting amazingly like hands.)

ANNOUNCER: *These feet belong to Roger Camp, an extraordinary man who overcame a tremendous challenge. Roger is determined to lead an ordinary life, to perform the everyday tasks that you and I take for granted... so he won't miss a second of Fox Sports.com.*

Whether it's daily insights from John Madden or real-time scores and stats, it's like having the NFL on FOX, online.

(Man shakes rattle with toes over baby on the floor on a blanket.)

SUPER: *foxsports.com. Making A Difference.*

(Inner city playground; teenagers hanging out; man walking up to them)

ANNOUNCER: *Meet Wayne Best. He saw the kids in his community without direction and did something about it...*

(Same teenagers are now working: painting, cleaning up trash and leaves, etc.)

ANNOUNCER: *He got them off the street and put them to work, teaching important lessons in community service, responsibility and helping others.*

(One of the youths vacuuming in Wayne Best's home.)

ANNOUNCER: *So he can spend all his time on FOX Sports.com. Where he enters his zip code to get the latest on his favorite home teams. It's like FOX Sports Net, online.*

(One of the kids continues vacuuming under the man's chair, accidentally knocking it, disturbing his concentration and irritating him. Outside home kids are preforming all kinds of chores.)

SUPER: *foxsports.com. Making A Difference.*

(An elderly man with a walker struggles to reach for a jar on shelf and can't get it.)

ANNOUNCER: *This man is 98 years old. Life's not so easy for him anymore. But every day he learns the importance of being independent...*

(Man finally gets jar but his frail hands drop it and the jar smashes.)

ANNOUNCER: *And self-reliant, thanks to this man...*

(A younger man is sitting at a table, with the elderly man behind him; he seems irritated at the disturbance.)

ANNOUNCER: *Meet Nick Felder. Nick ignores him and spends all day on FOX Sports.com. With breaking news and inside scoop from the pros, its like FOX Sports, online.*

(Elderly man stares down at mess of peaches, unable to clean them up.)

MAN: *Nick?*

SUPER: *foxsports.com. Making A Difference.*

SILVER AWARD
Consumer Television
:30 Campaign

ART DIRECTOR
Roger Camp

WRITER
Eric Silver

AGENCY PRODUCER
Nick Felder

PRODUCTION COMPANY
Hungry Man

DIRECTOR
John O'Hagan

CLIENT
Outpost.com

AGENCY
Cliff Freeman and
Partners/New York

(Masterpiece Theatre style.)

NARRATOR: *Hello. We want you to remember our name, Outpost.com. That's why we've decided to fire gerbils out of this cannon through the "O" in Outpost.*

NARRATOR: *Cute little guy. Fire!*

NARRATOR: *And again.*

NARRATOR: *So close.*

SFX: *Siren going off.*

SUPER: *Send complaints to Outpost.com.*

SUPER: *Outpost.com. The place to buy computer stuff.*

SILVER AWARD
Consumer Television
:30 Campaign

ART DIRECTORS
Leslie Ali
Tim Hanrahan
Hal Curtis

WRITERS
Derek Barnes
Canice Neary
Chuck McBride

AGENCY PRODUCERS
Beth Barrett
Donna Portaro
Amy Davenport

PRODUCTION COMPANIES
M-80 Films
Satellite
The Director's Bureau

DIRECTORS
Jhoan Camitz
Mike Mills
Tenney Fairchild

CLIENT
Nike

AGENCY
Wieden & Kennedy/
Portland

MUSIC: *Soft piano jazz.*

(A guy proceeds to climb out on the ledge of a building and looks as if he is about to jump. Barrett Christy appears carrying a snowboard.)

BARRETT: *Hey. This looks pretty steep.* (She straps into the board, looks at the guy. He looks scared and confused. People inside the building are watching to see what will happen. Barrett jumps off, lands on the blow up pad and gets up.)

BARRETT: *Ow.* (She looks at the paramedic coming over to help her.)

BARRETT: *What?*

SUPER: *(What are you getting ready for?)*

SUPER: *Nike.*

ANNOUNCER: *That last egg's looking real good. You've had quite a few, though. Maybe you shouldn't. But... if you make a light choice here, maybe you will have room for just one more. See there? When you live the High Life, you can live it both ways.*

BRONZE AWARD
Consumer Television
:30 Campaign

ART DIRECTOR
Jeff Williams

WRITER
Jeff Kling

AGENCY PRODUCER
Jeff Selis

PRODUCTION COMPANY
@radical.media

DIRECTOR
Errol Morris

CLIENT
Miller Brewing
Company

AGENCY
Wieden & Kennedy/
Portland

ANNOUNCER: *It's hard to respect the French when you have to bail 'em out of two big ones in one century. But we have to hand it to 'em on mayonnaise. Nice job, Pierre.*

GOLD AWARD
Consumer Television
:20 and Under: Single

ART DIRECTOR
Jeff Williams

WRITER
Jeff Kling

AGENCY PRODUCER
Jeff Selis

PRODUCTION COMPANY
@radical.media

DIRECTOR
Errol Morris

CLIENT
Miller Brewing Company

AGENCY
Wieden & Kennedy/
Portland

SILVER AWARD
Consumer Television
:20 and Under: Single

ART DIRECTOR
Jeff Williams

WRITER
Jeff Kling

AGENCY PRODUCER
Jeff Selis

PRODUCTION COMPANY
@radical.media

DIRECTOR
Errol Morris

CLIENT
Miller Brewing Company

AGENCY
Wieden & Kennedy/
Portland

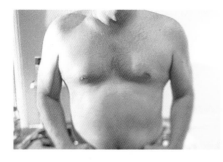

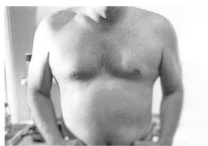

ANNOUNCER: *Is your name Sally? Sally the salad eater? No, you're a High Life man, and you don't care who knows it. You're not scared to enjoy Miller Time.*

GOLD AWARD
Consumer Television
:20 and Under: Campaign

ART DIRECTORS
Taras Wayner
Roger Camp

WRITER
Kevin Roddy

AGENCY PRODUCER
Liz Graves

PRODUCTION COMPANY
HKM

DIRECTOR
Noam Murro

CLIENT
FOX Sports

AGENCY
Cliff Freeman and
Partners/New York

(A guy fills a shopping cart with concrete blocks, bags of cement; begins pushing cart fast across parking lot. Cart smashed into another guy crouching in parking lot wearing catcher's gear.)

GUY 1: *Did that look like Bernie Williams? (Actual Catcher cam game footage of Bernie Williams charging home plate.)*

Game Announcer: *Here comes Williams… he's out at the plate. A major collision but Wilson was able to hang on…*

SUPER: *FOX Catcher Cam. Don't Try it at Home.*

SUPER: *Major League Baseball. FOX Saturday Game of the Week.*

GUY 1: *Ready?*

GUY 2: *Uh-umm.*

(The guy swings a huge sledge hammer and hits a flag pole as hard as he can, directly opposite the other guy's ear.)

SFX: *Loud metal thud.*

(Actual game footage of a Ken Griffey, Jr. home run hitting the foul pole.)

Game Announcer: *Junior cracks it down the right field line... he hit the foul pole. A little music for his trot.*

SUPER: *FOX Sounds of the Game. Don't Try it at Home.*

SUPER: *Major League Baseball. FOX Saturday game of the week.*

(A guy lies with his head on the ground of empty dirt field.)

SFX: *Footsteps running, getting closer.*

(Another guy runs, does a stand-up slide, feet first, into the head of guy laying down.)

SFX: *Sliding through dirt.*

GUY 1: *That sounded like Larkin.*

(Guy on the ground spits out a mouthful of dirt)

Game Announcer: *And Larkin is safe at second. That's his third stolen base of the game. He's really hot today...*

SUPER: *FOX Sounds of the Game. Don't Try it at Home.*

SUPER: *Major League Baseball. FOX Saturday game of the week.*

GOLD AWARD
Consumer Television
Varying Lengths Campaign

ART DIRECTOR
Jeff Williams

WRITER
Jeff Kling

AGENCY PRODUCER
Jeff Selis

PRODUCTION COMPANY
@radical.media

DIRECTOR
Errol Morris

CLIENT
Miller Brewing Company

AGENCY
Wieden & Kennedy/
Portland

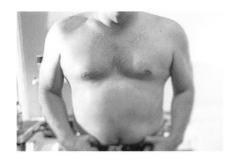

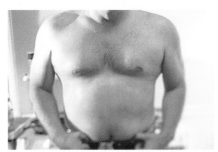

ANNOUNCER: *Is your name Sally? Sally the salad eater? No, you're a High Life man, and you don't care who knows it. You're not scared to enjoy Miller Time.*

ANNOUNCER: *Sometimes a man gets too hungry to clean his hands properly. The powdered sugar on this donut puts a semi-protective barrier between your fingerprint and your nutrition. But even if some grease does get on that donut, that's just flavor to a High Life man.*

SFX: *Refrigerator motor sound.*

ANNOUNCER: *Hear that? That's music to a man's ears. That's the sound of one friend keeping another friend cold. Thank you, refrigerator.*

ANNOUNCER: *This is enough to put a High Life man off his lunch. Time was, a man knew how to command his own vehicle. Just how far are we willing to fall? Better re-acquaint yourself with the High Life, soldier, before someone tries to take away your Miller Time.*

SILVER AWARD
Consumer Television
Varying Lengths Campaign

ART DIRECTOR
Jeff Williams

WRITER
Jeff Kling

AGENCY PRODUCER
Jeff Selis

PRODUCTION COMPANY
@radical.media

DIRECTOR
Errol Morris

CLIENT
Miller Brewing Company

AGENCY
Wieden & Kennedy/
Portland

BRONZE AWARD
Consumer Television
Varying Lengths
Campaign

ART DIRECTOR
Rob Palmer

WRITERS
Jamie Barrett
Jim LeMaitre

AGENCY PRODUCER
Jennifer Smieja

**PRODUCTION
COMPANY**
@radical.media

DIRECTOR
Frank Todaro

CLIENT
Nike

AGENCY
Wieden & Kennedy/
Portland

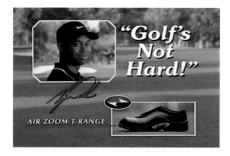

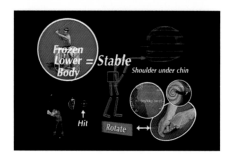

MUSIC: *Upbeat.*

ANNOUNCER: *"Golf's not hard" with Tiger Woods and the Air Zoom T-Range.*

TIGER: *Too many people over-complicate the golf swing. Today, we're gonna make it simple*

First, place the ball off the inside of your left heel. Second, bend your knees slightly And finally, keep the left arm straight. Voila, you're on the way to a better golf swing.

(Tiger swings.)

TIGER: *Of course, you'll also want to maintain the triangle, too. And lead with your hips. And other than taking the club back low and slow, that's all there is to it!*

(A computerized diagram of golfer with each teaching point made comes up on screen.)

TIGER: *As long as you shift your weight to the inside of your right foot and keep the club face square and your left heel planted and the "v" between your thumb and fore finger pointed to your right shoulder and the club gripped gently like a wounded bird and your left shoulder under your chin allowing your hands to rotate through the impact area and maintaining a stable lower body position and finishing with your belt buckle facing the target with your rear elbow hinged... That should help take the mystery out of the golf swing. This is Tiger Woods, reminding you that we can all be better.*

GOLD AWARD
Consumer Television
Under $50,000 Budget:
Single

ART DIRECTOR
Matt Mowat

WRITER
Chuck Meehan

AGENCY PRODUCER
James Horner

**PRODUCTION
COMPANY**
Five Union Square

DIRECTOR
Tom Schiller

CLIENT
Ameristar Casinos

AGENCY
Goldberg Moser O'Neill/
San Francisco

(Slightly overweight boy climbs ladder to diving board, stops to prepare for dive.)

ANNOUNCER: *Stevie Moyer will be attempting a forward three-and-one-half somersault with two-and-one-half twists.*

SUPER: *No Chance.*

SFX: *Coins hitting metal tray.*

SUPER: *Ameristar Casinos.*

SUPER: *Chance.*

LARRY: *Hi, I'm Larry Shanet, President of Comedy Central. I'd like to remind you that Comedy Central has quality comedy programming while other networks don't. CNN, not funny, VH1, not funny, C-Span, not funny. The Discovery Channel, well, those baboons with the red asses, they're kind of funny. But how often do you see those things? Comedy Central, that's your best bet.*

SILVER AWARD
Consumer Television
Under $50,000 Budget:
Single

ART DIRECTORS
Lori Campbell
Stephen Pearson
Scott Vitrone

WRITERS
Lori Campbell
Stephen Pearson
Scott Vitrone

PRODUCTION COMPANY
Hungry Man

DIRECTORS
Hank Perlman
Mark Foster

CLIENT
Comedy Central

AGENCY
Dweck and Campell/
New York

SFX: *Doorbell.*

(Man dressed as Arctic Ground Squirrel answers door.)

DELIVERY MEN: *Dial-A-Mattress*

SQUIRREL: *Hey, I'm glad you're here. We're gonna put this around back... What? What are you looking at?*

WIFE: *(Angrily from inside the house) Can you shut the door?*

SQUIRREL: *Can you shut your pie hole! Thank you!*

(Delivery men head with mattress to the basement)

SQUIRREL: *Anyone with a brain knows that an Arctic Ground Squirrel should be down by now. But I gotta clean the gutters, I gotta clean the roof... But you know, that's my life. Sorry you had to see that thing with the wife there... little... tiff. Listen. How about it, you guys coming with me or you going to stand there. Come on. Move. Move. Move.*

(The delivery men set up the mattress, the squirrel feels it)

SQUIRREL: *Ahh... This is good. Let me just tell you something, you would hibernate, too, for eight months if you had to live with what I live with upstairs. Nut? Some walnuts? Almonds? Got anything you want. Beautiful.*

Wife: *Honey, what's going on down there?*

SQUIRREL: *(screams) I'm talking to the mattress guys! Thank you!... I'm sorry I'm taking this out on you. You know what it is... lack of sleep. So, I appreciate it... thank you for all your hard work.*

(Delivery men hand him a form)

SQUIRREL: *Love to, but... three fingers. My wife signs for everything. Let that woman let you out... thank you, boys. Ahh. Eight months of peace and quiet. That's good, that's just nice right there.*

SUPER: *Dial-A-Mattress. Always out there.*

BRONZE AWARD
Consumer Television
Under $50,000 Budget:
Single

ART DIRECTORS
Lori Campbell
Stephen Pearson
Scott Vitrone

WRITERS
Lori Campbell
Stephen Pearson
Scott Vitrone

AGENCY PRODUCER
Larry Shanet

PRODUCTION COMPANY
Hungry Man

DIRECTOR
John O'Hagan

CLIENT
Dial-A-Mattress

AGENCY
Dweck and Campbell/
New York

GOLD AWARD
Non-Broadcast
Cinema: Single

ART DIRECTOR
Richard Flintham

WRITER
Andy McLeod

AGENCY PRODUCER
Howard Spivey

**PRODUCTION
COMPANY**
Academy Commercials

DIRECTOR
Peter Cattaneo

CLIENT
Volkswagen Group UK

AGENCY
BMP DDB/London

MUSIC: *German version of "Pump Up The Jam."*

(Woman sitting at bar notices man walk in and order a drink; leans toward him)

Woman (in German with Subtitles): Is that a ruler in your pocket or are you just pleased to see me?

(The man considers the question, then takes a ruler out of his pocket and puts it on the bar.)

SUPER: *The Passat. A car born out of obsession.*

SILVER AWARD
Non-Broadcast Cinema:
Single

ART DIRECTOR
Theo Ferreira

WRITER
Alistair Morgan

AGENCY PRODUCER
Yolandi Mes

**PRODUCTION
COMPANY**
Fresh Water Films

DIRECTOR
Lourens Van Rensburg

CLIENT
Virgin Atlantic

AGENCY
Net#Work/Johannesburg

ANNOUNCER: *Wonderworld is proud to present a new motion picture by debut director Carlos Martinez.*

SUPER: *"The most disturbing movie of the decade."*
– The New York Reviewer

ANNOUNCER: *A movie that's taken America by storm with its vivid portrayals of violence and explicit sex. A feast for the eyes. Six Miles to Skellerin. How far can you go in six miles?*

SUPER: *Now you see why we offer personal TV screens for all passengers. Virgin Atlantic*

**Now you see why we offer
personal TV screens for every passenger.**

virgin atlantic

(This film was shown in the commercial break of the SHOTS advertising VHS magazine. The message from Germany's biggest film production company was only visible in fastforward-mode: A big hello to all fastforward-users from Markenfilm, Germany.)

GOLD AWARD
Non-Broadcast
Out-of-Home: Single

ART DIRECTOR
Arndt Dallmann

WRITER
Guido Heffels

AGENCY PRODUCERS
Arndt Dallmann
Guido Heffels

**PRODUCTION
COMPANIES**
Markenfilm
Wedel

DIRECTOR
Oliver Bock

CLIENT
Markenfilm

AGENCY
Springer & Jacoby
Werbung GmbH/
Hamburg

(A man about 30 years old is driving his Renault Clio. On the opposite side of the road a truck is overtaking another car and they both start coming towards the man's car. Before the lorry knocks into it, the scene "freezes" and the only thing that continues happening in real time is what happens inside the car. In the back seat an elegantly dressed man who constantly plays with a baton which has a skull at the end.)

DEVIL: *It's time to put a price on your soul.*

DRIVER: *But it was him.*

DEVIL: *Don't ask me to be fair, you only ask (looks and points upward)... for justice. And I am the Devil – your soul – and I will save you.*

DRIVER: *No.*

DEVIL: *And women. The most beautiful women in the world.*

(Three beautiful women appear inside the car, looking at driver, trying to tempt him. The driver thinks it over but denies again and the women disappear.)

DEVIL: *Money. Money.*

(A whirlpool of dollars surrounds the car in slow motion but the driver denies himself again.)

DEVIL: *And power.*

DRIVER: *(shouts): No, no. I don't want your power.*

DEVIL: *Obviously you know nothing about life.*

DRIVER: *No, it's you who knows nothing – about cars.*

(The outside scene unfreezes and the Clio pulls out at high speed and with a spectacular maneuver is able to evade the truck that was coming towards it. The devil is consumed in flames until he disappears completely.)

ANNOUNCER: *Renault Clio. Big inside.*

SILVER AWARD
Foreign Language
Commercial Television:
Single

ART DIRECTOR
Pablo Stricker

WRITER
Leandro Raposo

AGENCY PRODUCER
Alejandro Di Michele

**PRODUCTION
COMPANY**
2001

DIRECTOR
Pucho Mentasti

CLIENT
Renault Argentina

AGENCY
Agulla & Baccetti/
Buenos Aires

GOLD AWARD
Multi-Media Campaign

ART DIRECTORS (PRINT)
Neil Dawson
Andrew Fraser

WRITERS (PRINT)
Clive Pickering
Andrew Fraser

PHOTOGRAPHERS
Paul Reas
Simon Condlyffe

ART DIRECTORS (TV)
Andrew Fraser
Ewan Paterson
Paul Angus

WRITERS (TV)
Andrew Fraser
Ewan Paterson
Ted Heath

AGENCY PRODUCER
Howard Spivey

PRODUCTION COMPANIES
Stark Films
Framstore

DIRECTORS
Steve Reeves
Paul Angus
Ted Heath

CLIENT
Volkswagen Group U.K.

AGENCY
BMP DDB/London

(Two men are at the top of a long, steep staircase, slowly making their way down carrying a heavy piano.)

GARY: *Can you just bring your end round?... don't go 'til I'm ready.*

GEOFF: *These stairs are a nightmare.*

GARY: *I tell you, I just hope this goes in your van.*

GEOFF: *Easy... how's that motor of yours?*

GARY: *I got rid of that one...*

GEOFF: *Yeah, how much did that set you back?*

(Gary looks up at Geoff, who is finding it difficult to keep hold of the piano.)

GARY: *I'll tell you later.*

SUPER: Volkswagen. *Surprisingly ordinary prices.*

(In an ordinary suburban home, a mother is sitting in a comfortable chair holding her newborn baby. The father is also in the room, and so is the mother's young brother.)

SFX: *Light pop music on the radio.*

(The mother offers the baby to her brother and he is initially reluctant to take it. However, after some encouragement he takes the baby and holds it awkwardly in his arms.)

SFX: *DJ saying, "We'll be right back after the break..."*

SFX: *Ad announcer saying, "Come and visit your local Volkswagen dealer, where you can now pick up a brand new Volkswagen Golf..."*

(The mother looks at the radio, and a worried look comes over her face. She looks back at her brother who seems to be even less comfortable with the baby.)

SFX: *"... complete with twin air bags and ABS for..."*

(The mother looks anxiously at the father and the father looks back at her. They both look at the baby.)

SFX: *"... an on the road price of..."*

(The father leans over and switches the radio off.)

SUPER: *Volkswagen. Surprisingly ordinary prices.*

(A man is working at his desk late at night. The office is empty, and he is on his own. The man keeps shaking himself; he is desperately trying not to fall asleep. Finally he gets up, flicks a kettle on and picks up a jar of instant coffee from the shelf. He scoops up a teaspoon of coffee and is about to put it into a mug when something catches his attention: an illuminated poster. It reads, "Polo, only 8,290." He pauses for a moment, looking at the teaspoon of coffee. He puts the coffee back in the jar, and the jar back on the shelf. He walks back to his desk and starts work again.)

SUPER: *Volkswagen. Surprisingly ordinary prices.*

ATTENTION

THE FOLLOWING PIECE OF FILM
CONTAINS SCENES THAT SOME
PEOPLE MAY FIND SHOCKING
AND WHICH MIGHT CAUSE
DISTRESS TO THOSE VIEWERS
OF A NERVOUS DISPOSITION

Polo L £8,290

Surprisingly ordinary prices.

www.volkswagen.co.uk

SUPER: *Warning. The following piece of film contains scenes that some people may find shocking and which may cause distress to those viewers of a nervous disposition.*

SUPER: *POLO £8.290.*

SUPER: *Volkswagen. Surprisingly ordinary prices.*

GOLD AWARD
Multi-Media Campaign

**ART DIRECTORS
(PRINT)**
Neil Dawson
Andrew Fraser

WRITERS (PRINT)
Clive Pickering
Andrew Fraser

PHOTOGRAPHERS
Paul Reas
Simon Condlyffe

ART DIRECTORS (TV)
Andrew Frader
Ewan Paterson
Paul Angus

WRITERS (TV)
Andrew Frader
Ewan Paterson
Ted Heath

AGENCY PRODUCER
Howard Spivey

**PRODUCTION
COMPANIES**
Stark Films
Framstore

DIRECTORS
Steve Reeves
Paul Angus
Ted Heath

CLIENT
Volkswagen Group UK

AGENCY
BMP DDB/London

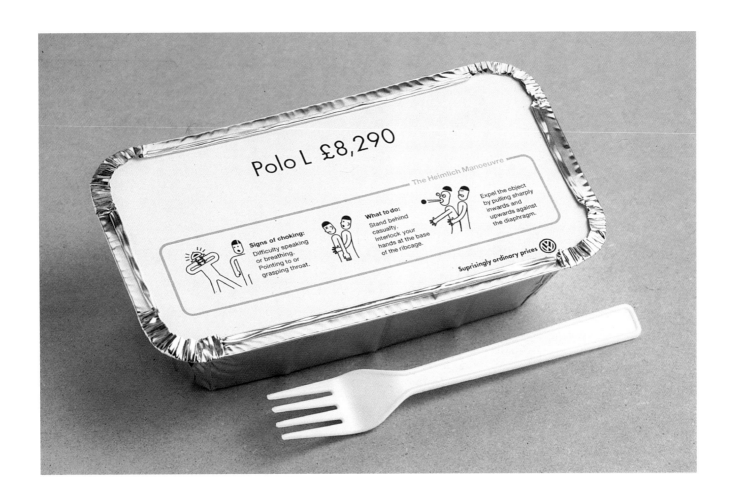

SILVER AWARD
Multi-Media Campaign

ART DIRECTOR
Paul Angus

WRITER
Ted Heath

ILLUSTRATOR
Grundy Northedge

CLIENT
Volkswagen Group UK

AGENCY
BMP DDB/London

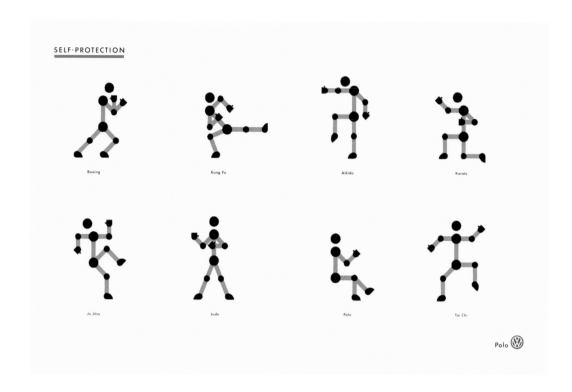

SELF-PROTECTION

Boxing   Kung Fu   Aikido   Karate

Ju Jitsu   Judo   Polo   Tai Chi

Polo

(Open on a big gymnasium. Ten or more people of various ages are gathered wearing tracksuits, loose clothing or martial arts type clothes. They are led through a series self-defense moves by an instructor. The group executes the moves precisely, fluidly, and more or less in time together. The last move the group performs is raising their left hands, extending their thumbs and forefingers, and moving their hands slowly from left to right – as if adjusting rear view mirror. We then see the outside of the building at street level, and the Polo sitting outside the entrance. The instructor emerges from the door of the building and opens the car door.)

SUPER: *Self defence by Polo.*

SUPER: *VW Polo.*

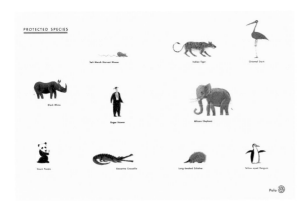

GOLD AWARD
College Competition

ART DIRECTOR
Chris Carraway

WRITER
Jacob Baas

SCHOOL
VCU Adcenter/
Richmond

ASSIGNMENT
Promote *one. a magazine*
the quarterly publication
about creative advertising

SILVER AWARD
College Competition

ART DIRECTOR
Amanda Berger

WRITER
Steve McElligott

SCHOOL
VCU Adcenter/
Richmond

Time for a new look?

Ready for some new ideas?

Need some inspiration?

93

BRONZE AWARD
College Competition

ART DIRECTOR
Nic Fantl

WRITER
Tom Randall

SCHOOL
VCU Adcenter/
Richmond

Because God isn't that kind. one. a magazine.

Until it's this easy. one. a magazine.

Luck has nothing to do with it. one. a magazine.

ART DIRECTOR
Kilpatrick Anderson

WRITER
Kevin Roddy

AGENCY PRODUCER
Nick Felder

**PRODUCTION
COMPANY**
MJZ

DIRECTOR
Rocky Morton

CLIENT
FOX Sports.com

AGENCY
Cliff Freeman and
Partners/New York

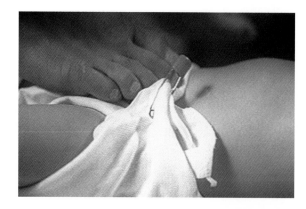

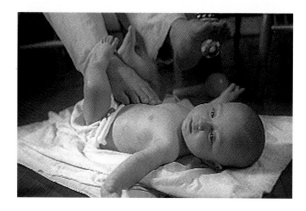

(A pair of men's feet adeptly change an infant's diaper with a diaper pin acting amazingly like hands.)

ANNOUNCER: *These feet belong to Roger Camp, an extraordinary man who overcame a tremendous challenge. Roger is determined to lead an ordinary life, to perform the everyday tasks that you and I take for granted... so he won't miss a second of Fox Sports.com.*

Whether it's daily insights from John Madden or real-time scores and stats, it's like having the NFL on FOX, online.

(Man shakes rattle with toes over baby on the floor on a blanket.)

SUPER: *foxsports.com. Making A Difference.*

(Inner city playground; teenagers hanging out; man walking up to them)

ANNOUNCER: *Meet Wayne Best. He saw the kids in his community without direction and did something about it...*

(Same teenagers are now working: painting, cleaning up trash and leaves, etc.)

ANNOUNCER: *He got them off the street and put them to work, teaching important lessons in community service, responsibility and helping others.*

(One of the youths vacuuming in Wayne Best's home.)

ANNOUNCER: *So he can spend all his time on FOX Sports.com. Where he enters his zip code to get the latest on his favorite home teams. It's like FOX Sports Net, online.*

(One of the kids continues vacuuming under the man's chair, accidentally knocking it, disturbing his concentration and irritating him. Outside home kids are preforming all kinds of chores.)

SUPER: *foxsports.com. Making A Difference.*

(An elderly man with a walker struggles to reach for a jar on shelf and can't get it.)

ANNOUNCER: *This man is 98 years old. Life's not so easy for him anymore. But every day he learns the importance of being independent...*

(Man finally gets jar but his frail hands drop it and the jar smashes.)

ANNOUNCER: *And self-reliant, thanks to this man...*

(A younger man is sitting at a table, with the elderly man behind him; he seems irritated at the disturbance.)

ANNOUNCER: *Meet Nick Felder. Nick ignores him and spends all day on FOX Sports.com. With breaking news and inside scoop from the pros, its like FOX Sports, online.*

(Elderly man stares down at mess of peaches, unable to clean them up.)

MAN: *Nick?*

SUPER: *foxsports.com. Making A Difference.*

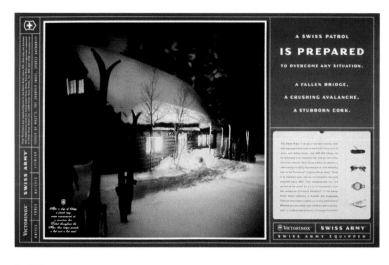

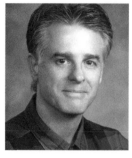

How do you reinvent a brand that everyone understands, appreciates, owns or has owned, and recommends for its usefulness and authenticity. Check out the campaign for Swiss Army knives, not the watch. They make you want to find your old one, open it up and relive the moment you bought it. More importantly, it's introducing a whole new target to a timeless brand with values that have never changed, only been re-examined in a fresh new way. I wish I was the art director or writer who created this campaign.

TOM CORDNER, TEAM ONE ADVERTISING

CLIENT
Swiss Army Brands

AGENCY
Mullen

CATEGORY
Multi-Media
Campaign

CLIENT
Volkswagen Group
UK

AGENCY
BMP DDB/London

Genius is not about doing the simple things well but the complex things simply.

**GRAHAM CLIFFORD,
GRAHAM CLIFFORD DESIGN**

Every time I see this campaign I'm more and more amazed at how intelligent it is. If you were to explain these ads to someone, most people would say, "That's nice." The executions bring the ads to a whole new level. There's a subtlety that very few clients would comprehend, let alone ad agencies.

JERRY GENTILE, TBWA/CHIAT/DAY

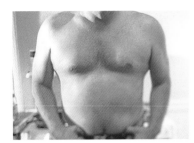
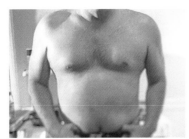

CLIENT
Miller Brewing
Company

AGENCY
Wieden & Kennedy/
Portland

The creators of this campaign took a worn-out old macho beer strategy and did the difficult. They made it fresh, transforming it into a tongue-in-cheek tribute to manliness. It poked fun at the simple-minded caveman in all of us and reminded us how much we like him.

The executions are perfect. The funky retro style harkens back to the days before the homogenization of the sexes. The writing brilliantly toyed with banal truths in a suitably no muss, no fuss style. And oh yeah, it was really funny. Sometimes hilarious. I just wish I didn't have to talk about this campaign in the past tense. The fact that it missed in the marketplace just underscores the vagaries of beer advertising. It certainly worked for me.

ARTHUR BIJUR, CLIFF FREEMAN AND PARTNERS

Everyone wanted to find some overlooked gem to reveal as their Personal Best of Show. In all honesty, I think it's more of a challenge to force myself to commit to one of the at least four incredible TV campaigns that I saw. Depending on a mood swing any one could easily be judged the best. However, my favorite is the Miller High Life campaign. It's pretty damn perfect. The voiceover, the personality of the work, the writing, the strategy, the casting, the look of the film, the way the deviled eggs were styled, and, I can only imagine, the way the light shone in the window the day the creative team came up with the idea. The highest praise I can give, it invoked in me sincere and profound feelings of jealous rage.

KARA GOODRICH, FALLON MCELLIGOTT

Picking a Best of Show this year was somewhat like trying to pick your favorite Beatles song. Among the television entries alone, there were so many great things: Outpost.com, the Fox Sports stuff (all of it), the Nike "What are you getting ready for?" campaigns, a great series of spots featuring Ben Stiller for MTV, and let us never forget "Evil Beaver" for Miller Lite. They're all brilliant.

But I think Best of Show for me has to go to the Miller High Life campaign. All the cliché's apply, yet none of them were used. It's simple, subtle, funny and wonderfully executed. I wish I had done them. But I didn't. And now life must go on."

DAVID BALDWIN, MCKINNEY & SILVER

My vote for Best of Show is the Miller High Life campaign. The ideas are simple and unencumbered by, well, crap. I'm guessing James Cameron didn't direct the spots. Oh yes — and the writing is brilliant. Change one word in any of the scripts and they'd be diminished. Nice job, Pierre.

DOUG ADKINS, HUNT ADKINS

CLIENT
Miller Brewing
Company

AGENCY
Fallon McElligott/
Minneapolis

It's got beer, a motor bike and an evil beaver. The ad I'd watch over and over again. Four thumbs up! Eeeeevil beeeeaver! Eeeeevil beeeeaver!

DAVE COOK, MAD DOGS & ENGLISHMEN

CLIENT
Volkswagen

AGENCY
Ogilvy & Mather/
Cape Town

Most advertising tries to say too much and in doing so ends up doing less. Writing less and saying more also requires confidence and confidence requires courage. If you display those characteristics your consumers will reward you. Which is why this ad for the Golf is an object lesson in great advertising.

JOHN HEGARTY, BARTLE BOGLE HEGARTY

CLIENT
Nike

AGENCY
Wieden & Kennedy/
Portland

I admit, I loved nearly every spot in Nike's "What are you getting ready for?" campaign. But the Heimlich spot just killed me. I loved the political incorrectness. I loved how effortlessly it sucks the viewer into the story. I loved how quiet the end line is. But mostly, I just loved it because it makes every spot I've ever done seem like a chewed-up, slobbery hunk of meat bouncing across a restaurant floor.

No, wait, I hated that part.

DEAN BUCKHORN, FALLON MCELLIGOTT

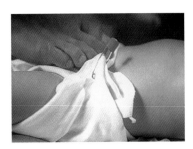

CLIENT
FOX Sports

AGENCY
Cliff Freeman and
Partners/New York

This is the most cunning and brilliant "misdirect"
I have ever seen. Funny as hell and dead-on in terms
of insight into the fanatical nature of sports fans. The
whole campaign is great but this spot is brilliant.

STEFFAN POSTAER, LEO BURNETT

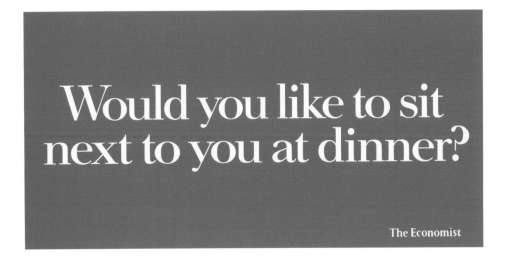

Would you like to sit next to you at dinner?

The Economist

CLIENT
The Economist

AGENCY
Abbott Mead
Vickers.BBDO

I can't tell you how many spots and ads made me laugh
out loud while judging this year's One Show. Let's just say
a lot. On the other hand, I can tell you how many made me
think. One.

For years The Economist campaign has repeatedly demon-
strated how powerful intelligence, wit and the color red
can be. As a writer I've envied it. As a consumer I've been
persuaded by it. But even without all that history, this ad
would have stopped me. With just twelve words it made me reflect on what kind of person I am. Am I interesting? Or boring. Am I worldly and informed? Or, like the souffle served at dinner, a bit empty.

This ad is my personal Best of Show because it is just that: personal. It involved me. And I'm a little wiser
for it. Still, I'm not sure I'd want to sit next to me quite yet.

KERRY FEURMAN, THE MARTIN AGENCY

GOLD AWARD
Newspaper Over
600 Lines: Single

CLIENT
Volkswagen Group
UK

AGENCY
BMP DDB/London

Surprisingly ordinary prices

What a marvelous feeling it is to be here in front of so many old friends, some from far afield, to see the years of struggling to bring up our baby finally come to fruition. And how proud we, the parents, feel at this moment. I'd like to thank you all for joining us here today, but some people deserve particular mention for their part in bringing about this happy event.

First of all there are, of course, the Best Man, Dave Dye, and the Matron of Honour, Jeremy Craigen, who helped to bring the happy couple together in the first place. A big thank you also to the Right Reverend Tony Cox/Larry Barker, who presided over the wedding, and our usher, Adrian Reilly, as well as Dave Buchanan and his organ.

Then there are Kerry Harvey, Sarah Hannam and Katie Ward who organized the invitations, and the boys from FGDS who have done such a magnificent job with the decorations. Thanks also to Mary O'Tea, for the food and drink — a wonderful spread — and to Uncle Sean Doyle for the entertainment.

Last but not least there is our photographer Paul Reas. He just wanted me to say he's available for Bar Mitzvahs and Christenings, as well as weddings. His number is 171-931-3633.

Finally, a toast from us, the parents. Ladies and gentlemen, we give you the happy couple.

CLIVE PICKERING
NEIL DAWSON

GOLD AWARD
Newspaper Over
600 Lines: Campaign

CLIENT
Volkswagen Group
UK

AGENCY
BMP DDB/London

We'd like to say there was some blinding moment of inspiration that led us to come up with these ads, but there wasn't. We'd give you some amusing anecdote about how they originated, but we can't. Actually they were the product of a long, hard, surprisingly ordinary slog, in the course of which many ideas were (quite rightly) rejected. In fact, we found it so hard that we had to rely on Andrew Fraser to come up with the third execution (good to see him graduate from mere television). Anyway at least the ads are more interesting than this. Sorry.

**NEIL DAWSON
CLIVE PICKERING**

GOLD AWARD
Newspaper 600 Lines
or Less: Single

CLIENT
Swiss Army Brands

AGENCY
Mullen Advertising/
Wenham

JACK AND JILL went up the hill to fetch a pail of water. Jack fell down and Jill made an emergency tourniquet. —— THE END.

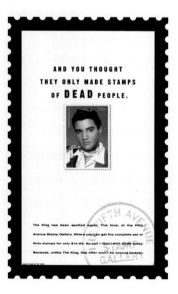

Michael Jordan turned us down.

Charles Barkley turned us down.

Mia Hamm turned us down.

Dennis Hopper turned us down.

A small dog with a Spanish accent turned us down.

Mark McGwire turned us down.

Tiger Woods turned us down.

Picabo Street turned us down.

We got Jill.

GREG BOKOR
JIM GARAVENTI

GOLD AWARD
Newspaper 600 Lines
or Less: Campaign

CLIENT
5th Avenue Stamp
Gallery

AGENCY
Hampel Stefanides/
New York

THE BACK.
YOU'RE SUPPOSED TO LICK
THE BACK.

THE JERRY GARCIA STAMP.
LICK AT YOUR OWN RISK.

AND YOU THOUGHT
THEY ONLY MADE STAMPS
OF **DEAD** PEOPLE.

I owe it all to the art director.

ARI MERKIN

The Nanny TV12
Weeknights 6 pm

Donny & Marie TV12
Weekdays 2 pm

GOLD AWARD
Newspaper 600
Lines or Less:
Campaign

CLIENT
TV Twelve

AGENCY
Palmer Jarvis DDB/
Vancouver

Deep Space 9 TV12
Wednesdays 9 pm

TV12 has programming that pretty much appeals to the average couch potato. All the shows are light, fun, and entertaining, and we felt that the brand personality of the station should reflect this sentiment. We decided "Truth In Advertising" was the way to go, by poking fun at our own product. After all, when was the last time anyone watched Pamela Anderson for the riveting dialogue and profound subtext?

At first, the idea of using the volume control bar as a device for the station seemed a little too simple. However, the more we started applying it against individual shows, with words that were funny truisms, the more the concept came to life. Once the campaign was running, people became really involved in it. Even DJs on local radio started inventing their own words for various shows.

IAN GRAIS
ALAN RUSSELL

GOLD AWARD
Magazine B/W
Full Page or Spread:
Single

CLIENT
Biltmore Estate

AGENCY
Loeffler Ketchum
Mountjoy/Charlotte

Get assignment.

Go into office.

Close door.

Look at clock.

Talk about movies.

Look at clock.

Tell jokes.

Look at clock.

Look at clock again.

Jot down idea.

Look at clock.

Hey, time to go home.

**DOUG PEDERSEN
CURTIS SMITH**

GOLD AWARD
Magazine Color
Full Page or Spread:
Single

CLIENT
Wonderbra

AGENCY
TBWA Hunt
Lascaris/
Johannesburg

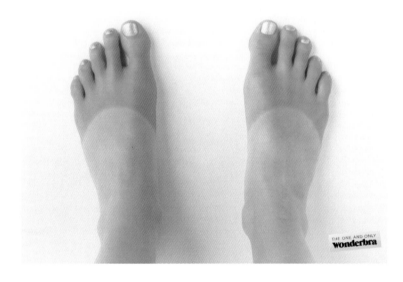

"Okay we've got a Wonderbra brief."

"Yes, please!"

"Yeah, but let's do it differently."

"What do you mean?"

"None of the usual imagery. No pouting
supermodels, no barely clothed Evas
or Caprices, no seductive poses, no
lingering "come hither" looks and
definitely no breasts. It'll be completely
unlike any other bra ad."

"Er...sounds great, but how?"

"Well... we could show the tan-lines
on her feet caused by her enhanced
breasts."

"Hey! That's a brilliant idea."

So we cast around South Africa for
fifty-two of the top models in the country,
all of them with drop-dead gorgeous,
full-breasted bodies. And called them
in... to look at their feet.

What a stupid idea.

**ERIC FUNKE
STUART WALSH**

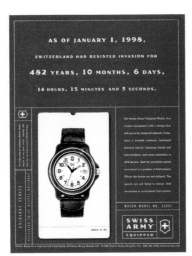

GOLD AWARD
Magazine Color
Full Page or Spread:
Campaign

CLIENT
Swiss Army Brands

AGENCY
Mullen Advertising/
Wenham

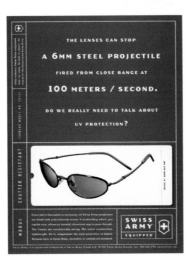

So as we sat on the deck of our chalet at the foot of the Alps, we turned to each other and began discussing the assignment.

"Hand me a slice of cheese, Dylan."

"Oh, Monica, this doesn't even feel like advertising, does it?"

"Mmmphhhh…"

"Silly girl. No more Gruyère for you."

The two weeks of "research" were almost at an end. Monica had learned to ski. Dylan had brushed up on his French.

"So, what do you think we should do for these ads, Dylan?"

"Monica, où-est le WC?"

**MONICA TAYLOR
DYLAN LEE**

GOLD AWARD
Magazine Color
Full Page or Spread:
Campaign

CLIENT
Swiss Army Brands

AGENCY
Mullen Advertising/
Wenham

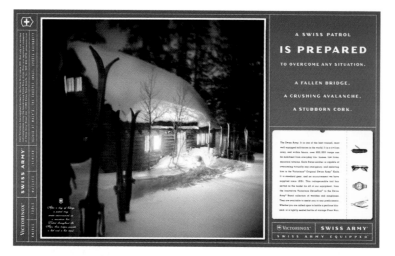

So as we sat in the car on the three-hour drive back from Shelton, Connecticut, we turned to each other and began discussing the assignment.

"It's f—— hot in here, Dylan."

"Bite me."

"So, I'm going to Idaho next week for the shoot."

"Yeah, for one ad. What the hell are we going to do for the other two? The client can only afford one stock shot."

"I've got this antique postcard I found at a flea market."

The two weeks of driving back and forth and back and forth and presenting campaign after campaign after campaign were almost at an end. Monica had learned to drive stick. Dylan had caught up on his books on tape: The Hobbit Anthology.

"So, what do you think we should do for these ads, Dylan?"

"I need to pull over to this rest stop."

"Again?"

MONICA TAYLOR
DYLAN LEE

Years ago a journalist on one of London's evening newspapers retired from writing a weekly column on advertising to concentrate on writing fiction. (Not much of a change you might think.) Her last column was a personal recollection of all that she had found interesting or not in the advertising industry. I was nominated as one of the two most boring people she had met. Ever since then I've been a social wreck.

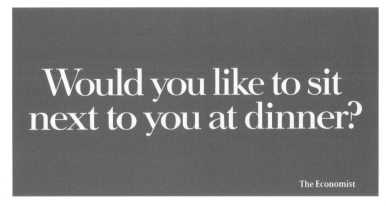

Would you like to sit next to you at dinner?

The Economist

GOLD AWARD
Outdoor: Single

CLIENT
The Economist

AGENCY
Abbott Mead
Vickers.BBDO/
London

At cocktail parties I'm alert for the moment when the person I'm talking to darts a quick look over my shoulder to summon help. In fact, the only people I now see socially are my children and grandchildren who are genetically programmed to find me vaguely amusing.

I have always plundered my own life to create advertising, so the genesis of this poster is clear. When I tried the line out on Ron Brown, he smiled politely as his eyes flicked over my shoulder to see if anyone interesting was coming into the office with me.

DAVID ABBOTT

This campaign was a labor of love really. We spent over a year walking around with disposable cameras in our pockets, snapping discarded left shoes wherever we saw them. After that it was simply a case of giving the client our best hurt-puppy looks until he agreed to run it.

RICHARD FLINTHAM
ANDY MCLEOD

GOLD AWARD
Outdoor: Campaign

CLIENT
Volkswagen Group
UK

AGENCY
BMP DDB/London

GOLD AWARD
Trade Color Full
Page or Spread:
Single

CLIENT
TIME

AGENCY
Fallon McElligott/
Minneapolis

Perhaps the most ironic thing about this ad for TIME was that it was based on a movie that was based on a book that was based on reality as interpreted by an anonymous author who turned out to work for *Newsweek*.

BOB BARRIE
DEAN BUCKHORN

GOLD AWARD
Trade B/W or Color
Any Size: Campaign

CLIENT
InterNutria

AGENCY
Clarke Goward
Advertising/Boston

When we first sat down to discuss the campaign, our client, Wendy Kramer, brought up a very sobering issue: "How can two men possibly think they're qualified to advertise a product for PMS?" After careful consideration, Jim explained, "I grew up with five sisters. Believe me, I know what PMS is all about."

She bought it.

However we still had one more challenge: how do you advertise a product for women to an audience that is predominantly male? Four campaigns later we figured it out. We had a product category that's not over-crowded, a product name that's incredibly illustrative, a client who trusted us and the crushing realization that we couldn't afford Kim Alexis.

Thanks to Wendy Kramer, Julie Rosso, Carolina Cotman, Anne Saleh, Karen Dinsmore, Terry Clarke, Mike Norton.

JIM AMADEO
SPENCER DEADRICK

The gate to your shuttle closes in four minutes. You're three minutes away — at the metal detector. Several small, missile-like objects have just been detected in your bag. They're inscribed with the words "Swiss Army."

You make your flight. You wonder if you'll ever be this lucky again.

GREG BOKOR
GERARD CAPUTO
JIM GARAVENTI

GOLD AWARD
Collateral: Point of Purchase and In-Store

CLIENT
Swiss Army Brands

AGENCY
Mullen Advertising/ Wenham

We hadn't got pictures. We didn't feel like writing. We only had a few pages bought. So, we found a bubble plastic (bubble wrap). We stuck it on and the client approved it.

CARLOS PERRINÓ
YURI ALEMANY

GOLD AWARD
Collateral: Posters

CLIENT
Volvo Espana SA

AGENCY
Saatchi & Saatchi/ Madrid

This was one of those rare ads on which people's lives literally depend. An opportunity that makes boosting the sales figures of some new washing powder or chocolate bar pale into insignificance. To be able to contribute to the cause and also be personally rewarded for it like this is quite a privilege.

It was a classic case of getting the brief, then 'digging' a little deeper for a fresh angle from which to work. Upon discovering that one organ donor can save the lives of up to ten people, the challenge then became finding an unexpected way to demonstrate it. Eventually, whilst staring at the blank page, we drew a complete blank. Ten of them, actually.

Thanks again to a brave client and for all the people who supported us. And remember, if this ad touches your heart, maybe, one day, someone else could use it.

RICHARD MORGAN
SIMON LANGLEY

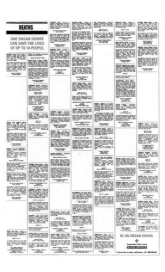

GOLD AWARD
Public Service/ Political Newspaper or Magazine: Single

CLIENT
Australian Red Cross

AGENCY
MOJO Partners/ Sydney

GOLD AWARD
Public Service/
Political Newspaper
or Magazine:
Campaign

CLIENT
The Tate Gallery

AGENCY
TBWA Simons
Palmer/London

A rock, noticed after
a visit to the Tate.
Minds open from 10am.
TateGallery

A vine, noticed after
a visit to the Tate.
Minds open from 10am.
TateGallery

A conker, noticed after
a visit to the Tate.
Minds open from 10am.
TateGallery

Beansprouts, noticed after
a visit to the Tate.
Minds open from 10am.
TateGallery

A piece of wood, noticed
after a visit to the Tate.
Minds open from 10am.
TateGallery

Some people appreciate art. Some people think, for appearances sake, that they should appreciate art. And the remaining majority think that spending an afternoon gazing at the inspiration for a set of table mats ranks pretty low on their list of preferred leisure activities. "Bugger," thought the Tate, "we need some kind of a brand campaign." "This kind?" we asked. And they said, "Hmmm, might work." Did work.

**NIGEL ROBERTS
PAUL BEDFORD**

GOLD AWARD
Public Service/
Political Outdoor
and Posters

CLIENT
São Paulo
Museum of Art

AGENCY
DM9 DDB
Publicidade/
São Paulo

In 1990 a man was sentenced to six and a half years in prison for having thrown some paint on Rembrandt's "The Nightwatch."

The Dutchman that stabbed Picasso's "Woman Nude Before Garden" was arrested and sent to a clinic for mentally ill people.

We threw a Botero on the floor and got a big prize for it.

**PEDRO CAPPELETTI
JADER ROSSETTO**

Botero
at the São Paulo
Museum of Art.
from March 3? to May 1?

112

By the fourth day of the Outward Bound trip the client was nice enough to send us on, we had the idea for the catalog. The only problem was, we still had four days left.

**DOUG PEDERSEN
CURTIS SMITH**

GOLD AWARD
Public Service/
Political Collateral:
Brochures and
Direct Mail

CLIENT
Outward Bound

AGENCY
Loeffler Ketchum
Mountjoy/Charlotte

GOLD AWARD
Public Service/
Political Television:
Single

CLIENT
Partnership for a
Drug-Free America

AGENCY
Team One
Advertising/
El Segundo

"Caller Scott" is actually a really good friend of ours. And, truth be told, he and his lovely wife Teresa bought a Chi-Wash-Wa home car-washing system, a Star Trek Collectors' Plate and a Michael Jordan "In Flight" pewter statuette off of QVC. All in one night.

Must've been some bubonic chronic.

Hilarious story, but still, all that stuff was a little too much to cram into a 30-second spot. Somehow, Greg Wells remembered a goofy surfing monkey coin bank he had as a kid. Luckily for us, they're still in plentiful supply down in Tijuana. $300 later, we had a finished spot that seems to touch people in a funny and resonant way.

**GREG COLLINS
GREG WELLS**

GOLD AWARD
Public Service/
Political Television:
Campaign

CLIENT
Transport Accident
Commission

AGENCY
Grey Advertising/
Melbourne

It is likely that a shiver will crawl up your spine and the hint of a tear will well in an eye as you watch these commercials.

You are not alone.

Chris Reed, our big, strong DOP had to walk to one side and collect himself after shooting the scene in which the devastated family prepares to leave for the father's funeral on Christmas Eve and the little daughter asks, "Is Daddy going to be there?" When the father died as he was disconnected from life support, he actually broke down and wept while in the crushingly sad atmosphere of Intensive Care the family said goodbye.

In this campaign we wanted to confront drunk drivers with the ripple effect of their tragic stupidity upon their loved ones. Can you imagine your wife waking up alone in bed on Christmas morning, having buried you the day before, with your three-year-old asking if Santa's going to find Daddy?

In ten years of TAC advertising we have never shirked from showing the public the absolute emotional reality of road trauma, leading them to the inescapable conclusion that "That could so easily be me."

It is working. Today the state of Victoria has one of the lowest road tolls in the world, and the December toll was the second lowest since 1952. But don't congratulate us.

Today I read in the newspaper of the court case concerning a young mother who, on December 23rd last year, drank heavily and drove into a tree, killing her two-year-old son. Her barrister described her as "The most destroyed human being I have ever seen."

We have a long way to go.

NIGEL DAWSON
ROB DOW

After this spot ran, people called Hollywood Video to complain that we were giving away the ending to the movie. One person even called Cliff directly. Well, it's true. At the end of Scream 2, like the end of Scream 1, and the end of every other horror movie ever made, pretty much everyone dies.

Sorry to give that away.

IAN REICHENTHAL
ADAM CHASNOW
ROGER CAMP

GOLD AWARD
Consumer Radio:
Single

CLIENT
Hollywood Video

AGENCY
Cliff Freeman and
Partners/New York

We could never have produced these spots without help from Roy Kamen and everyone at Kamen Audio, the kind of guys that will spend hours researching, recording and digitally manipulating the sound of a fart until it sounds wet enough.

IAN REICHENTHAL
ADAM CHASNOW
WAYNE BEST
ROGER CAMP

GOLD AWARD
Consumer Radio:
Campaign

CLIENT
Hollywood Video

AGENCY
Cliff Freeman and
Partners/New York

GOLD AWARD
Consumer Television
Over :30 Single

CLIENT
Audi of Norway

AGENCY
Bates Norway/Oslo

When working on this brief we could remember at least five or six recent commercials that depicted the car as something every-body turned to look at. "Ooh, look a new Toyota!! How fantastic." No matter how good or funny these commercials were though, the car always seemed to be a let-down. These were average cars with average styling and looks, and what moron would really drop his baby just because a new Corolla rolled by? But when finally a different car came along like the Audi TT Coupe, it was hard to be yet another who shouted "Wolf, wolf!" — unless of course you could poke fun at those other cars. So we took the best ad we could find on this proposition, and thought "Why are those skid marks really there?"

We usually never refer to other ads in our ads, and Audi never picks fights with its competitors, but here it seemed like the right thing to do. The "story behind the story" approach could not have been used if it wasn't for the spectacular product itself. But Audi got what it deserved, a spectacular ad.

THORBJØRN NAUG
ARIS THEOPHILAKIS

GOLD AWARD
Consumer Television
Over :30 Single

CLIENT
Nike

AGENCY
Wieden & Kennedy/
Portland

We thought it was a nice idea, and presented it for a Superbowl commercial. The client said it was too dull. Six months later, they needed a spot for the World Cup at the last minute, and they reluctantly agreed to resurrect it. We showed them the cut, and they still thought it was dull. Now they like it and always have.

JERRY CRONIN
TIM HANRAHAN

GOLD AWARD
Consumer Television
Over :30 Single

CLIENT
MTV: Video Music
Awards

AGENCY
MTV/New York

We'd like to thank everyone who worked on this year's One Show. It's a privilege to be among the other winners on these pages.

TOM KUNTZ
MIKE MAGUIRE

GOLD AWARD
Consumer Television
:30 Single

CLIENT
Outpost.com

AGENCY
Cliff Freeman and
Partners/New York

The One Show does not list credits for the editor or the editorial company for commercials. That has always proved baffling. Perhaps no one there has ever worked with a truly great editor. We would like to thank Gavin Cutler of MacKenzie Cutler (along with his partner Ian MacKenzie) who cut these spots, as well as Hollywood Video and the vast majority of FOX. Put simply, the spots would not have worked without your vision.

ERIC SILVER
ROGER CAMP

GOLD AWARD
Consumer Television
:30 Campaign

CLIENT
FOX Sports

AGENCY
Cliff Freeman and
Partners/New York

In the year 2018, some kid from art school will find this annual on a dusty shelf in a used book store and start rifling through it looking for an idea he thinks no one will remember. I won't use this opportunity to preach ethics to him, but I would like to ask that kid in the future a few questions from here in 1999.

Question #1: Have apes taken over the planet in the future? Do they speak English, wear clothing and perform experimental brain surgery? Have humans been defeated and become nothing more than a primitive slave culture tolerated but completely dominated by these apes? If so, look for a monkey named Cornelius, he'll be sympathetic and can help you escape to a place called the Forbidden Zone. Feel free to look me up when you get there.

Question #2: Is food made from people who've been squished into a little square wafer in the future? I saw that in a movie once and think it'd be cool. I hope I still have teeth and can eat Michelle-Pfeiffer-in-a-wafer in the future.

Question # 3: Does Eric Silver still have the nicest ass in advertising in the future? I mean, do you just want to bite it or what? Is Eric Silver even in advertising any more? Did that thing about him and the little boys ever go public? I guess all that doesn't really matter. All that matters is that he's got a nice ass right now. In 1999. Sure it's a little on the flat side, but when he wears the right pants you don't even notice. It'd sure be a loss for all humanity if he didn't still have a nice ass in the future.

Good luck in your advertising career. Give Eric a call, I'm sure he'd love to show you his incredibly nice ass.

KEVIN RODDY

FOX CATCHER CAM
DON'T TRY IT AT HOME

GOLD AWARD
Consumer Television
:20 and Under:
Campaign

CLIENT
FOX Sports

AGENCY
Cliff Freeman and
Partners/New York

Ladies and gentlemen, we'd like to introduce you to our country's newest hero, your children's greatest role model, and television's brightest young superstar. This is a man among men. He sweats courage, bleeds daring and oozes machismo. Ladies, you should have sex with this man and let him father your children. And men, you should step aside and let him. His name is Chris "Critter" Antonucci... and he's a stuntman. This is his story:

"Shopping Cart": The cart was fastened to a safety cable that was supposed to stop it inches before it actually hit "Critter." Unfortunately, on the last take the cable snapped and the cart really did ram him...at full speed, with full force, head on.

We cheered.

"Head": The runner was supposed to keep his foot a few inches above "Critter's" head so we could fake the impact with camera angles and post-production tricks. Unfortunately, he missed and planted his foot square into "Critter's" face.

We cheered again.

"Pole": On this one, we were a little disappointed with "Critter" because after only a dozen or so takes, he had to stop because his head was ringing and his ear started to bleed. But after we called him a "wussie" and a "cry baby"— being the pro that he is — he got right back up there for a few more whacks at his head.

Now maybe you can understand why we idolize this man. If it weren't for his pain and suffering, his cuts, contusions, and permanent scarring and if he hadn't sacrificed his left front tooth to make these commercials, we wouldn't have won a Gold Pencil. Which is obviously the most important thing.

Thank you "Critter." We're all naming our first boys after you.

**KEVIN RODDY
TARAS WAYNER
ROGER CAMP**

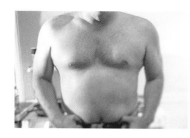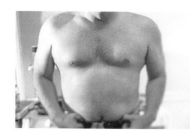

GOLD AWARD
Consumer Television
Varying Lengths
Campaign

CLIENT
Miller Brewing
Company

AGENCY
Wieden & Kennedy/
Portland

Gracious thanks for this kind recognition.

We also owe great thanks to a nice, thoughtful client.

We are most grateful, however, for the opportunity to have introduced Herbal Mind Essence into the ingestion habits of pentagenarian director Errol Morris. Until mind essence, Errol's wife would catch him standing for hours in the middle of the bedroom. What's wrong? she'd ask, and he'd say, socks. Someone should invent a knitted, tube-like structure, closed at one end, that slips over the foot. A pair of them could be called socks. They did, she'd say, and you have several mismatched pairs in your top dresser drawer. And he'd say, dressers? They make those now?

Now, with Mind Essence, Errol enjoys the mental strength of ten Japanese schoolchildren on a diet rich in fish. Just try to stump him! During the shoot (after enough time had passed to allow significant absorption of the Herbal Mind Essence product), one PA reported successfully lifting Errol's wallet, only to find that Errol had cleverly removed any money from it!

Long division, sans pencil, can't be far off.

Thanks also to @.radical media for the enormous kickback and steady influx of lavish gifts.

Do we deserve any of it? No! But thanks just the same. Love, Jeffs.

JEFF WILLIAMS
JEFF KLING

GOLD AWARD
Consumer
Television Under
$50,000 Budget:
Single

CLIENT
Ameristar Casinos

AGENCY
Goldberg Moser
O'Neill/ San
Francisco

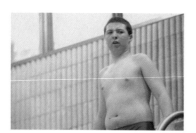

We were looking for a slightly overweight thirteen-year-old who could be believable. As the kids shuffled in (some were overweight, others obese) the director asked them how old they were, and then asked each kid to take his shirt off. The casting session quickly degenerated into a Calvin Klein spot. It was getting ugly, and it was looking like we weren't going to have a spot at all — and then our kid, little Stevie Moyer, walked in. If he hadn't, we definitely wouldn't be writing this.

We'd like to thank our account guy, Weinstein, for hitting Raczka on the "cell" enough times to make the project happen. And of course, "Slash" Noble and our producer James Horner, who did a yeoman's job.

MATT MOWAT
CHUCK MEEHAN

GOLD AWARD
Non-Broadcast
Cinema: Single

CLIENT
Volkswagen Group
UK

AGENCY
BMP DDB/London

The hardest bit of this commercial was choosing which music should be playing in the bar. It was going to be Nena's 1984 classic "99 Luftballons," but then we found the German version of "Pump Up the Jam" by Frank Meyer-Thurn. No contest, obviously.

RICHARD FLINTHAM
ANDY MCLEOD

GOLD AWARD
Non-Broadcast
Out-of-Home: Single

CLIENT
Markenfilm

AGENCY
Springer & Jacoby
Werbung GmbH/
Hamburg

After winning a Gold Pencil for our last piece of work for Springer & Jacoby, there is only one thing we could have done better: we could have run it as the first piece of work for HEIMAT, our own agency instead. Would you give us a call for a job in Berlin, anyway?: +49-171-2269593.

ARNDT DALLMANN
GUIDO HEFFELS

GOLD AWARD
Multi-Media
Campaign

CLIENT
Volkswagen Group
UK

AGENCY
BMP DDB/London

"Well done on that Price campaign you did for Volkswagen, and for winning all those awards," the account men all say. "Now you've proved you can crack a difficult brief — here's another one."

A big thank you to the One Show jury. You've made our lives a misery.

ANDREW FRASER
CLIVE PICKERING
NEIL DAWSON
EWAN PATERSON
TED HEATH
PAUL ANGUS

When we began to concept our campaign for one. a magazine, the first thing we tried to do was to eliminate all the clichéd rules of advertising. After all, we were trying to communicate with some of the sharpest minds in the industry — the last thing we wanted to do was put out advertising that was dull and unoriginal.

So, with this in mind, we set out to create some truly original stuff. We worked day and night, trying to come up with something that would set our creative director on fire. We walked into the first day of Concept class, armed with a multitude of great thumbnails. Hours later we emerged, bruised and broken. Nothing had survived, even the best concepts. Where had we gone wrong?

After several more failed attempts, we realized that what we had been trying to avoid was exactly the message we needed to get across. Everyone wants to avoid the clichéd idea, that which has been done to death.

One way to stay ahead is one. a magazine, which is consistently full of new ideas and original work. That night we went to work finding the most ridiculous rules of advertising, and put them to work for us. In just a little while, we had our campaign.

CHRIS CARRAWAY
JACOB BAAS

GOLD AWARD
College Competition

ART DIRECTOR
Chris Carraway

WRITER
Jacob Baas

SCHOOL
VCU Adcenter/
Richmond

MERIT AWARD
Newspaper Over 600
Lines: Single

ART DIRECTOR
Paul Renner

WRITER
David Abend

ILLUSTRATOR
Lilly Lee

PHOTOGRAPHER
Daniel Proctor

CLIENT
American HealthCare

AGENCY
Arnold Communications/
Boston

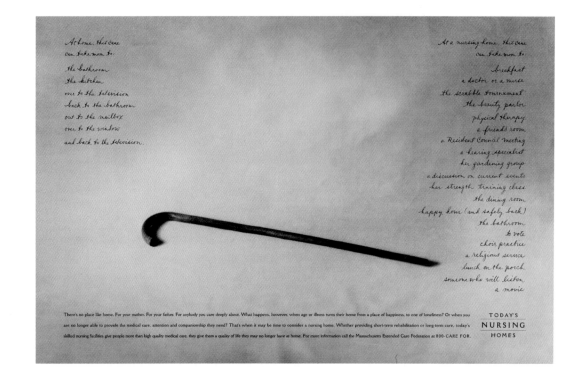

MERIT AWARD
Newspaper Over 600
Lines: Single

ART DIRECTOR
Lance Paull

WRITER
Stuart D'Rozario

PHOTOGRAPHER
Bill Cash

CLIENT
Volkswagen

AGENCY
Arnold Communications/
Boston

Comes with wonderful new features.
Like heat.

MERIT AWARD
Newspaper Over 600
Lines: Single

ART DIRECTOR
Lance Paull

WRITER
Lance Jensen

PHOTOGRAPHER
Bill Cash

CLIENT
Volkswagen

AGENCY
Arnold Communications/
Boston

Lime.

Also comes in red, black, silver, white, dark blue, and bright blue. And of course, a lemon yellow. **Drivers wanted.**

MERIT AWARD
Newspaper Over 600
Lines: Single

ART DIRECTOR
Lance Paull

WRITER
Lance Jensen

PHOTOGRAPHER
Bill Cash

CLIENT
Volkswagen

AGENCY
Arnold Communications/
Boston

Is it possible to go backwards and
forwards at the same time?

Drivers wanted.

MERIT AWARD
Newspaper Over 600
Lines: Single

ART DIRECTOR
Neil Dawson

WRITER
Clive Pickering

ILLUSTRATOR
Typo Fads

TYPOGRAPHER
Kevin Clarke

CLIENT
Volkswagen Group UK

AGENCY
BMP DDB/London

We have chosen not to disturb your Sunday morning with a
'Surprisingly ordinary prices' advertisement.

MERIT AWARD
Newspaper Over 600
Lines: Single

ART DIRECTOR
Andrew Fraser

WRITER
Andrew Fraser

PHOTOGRAPHER
Paul Reas

CLIENT
Volkswagen Group UK

AGENCY
BMP DDB/London

MERIT AWARD
Newspaper Over 600
Lines: Single

ART DIRECTOR
Neil Dawson

WRITER
Clive Pickering

PHOTOGRAPHER
Paul Reas

CLIENT
Volkswagen Group UK

AGENCY
BMP DDB/London

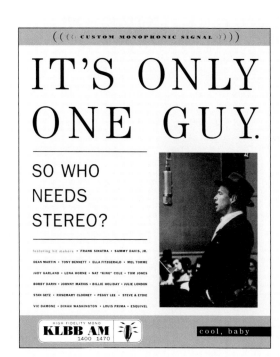

MERIT AWARD
Newspaper Over 600
Lines: Single

ART DIRECTOR
Randy Tatum

WRITER
Phil Calvit

PHOTOGRAPHER
KLBB Archives

CLIENT
KLBB AM Radio

AGENCY
Carmichael Lynch/
Minneapolis

MERIT AWARD
Newspaper Over 600
Lines: Single

ART DIRECTOR
B. Ramnathkar

WRITER
Agnello Dias

PHOTOGRAPHER
Sanjeev Angne

CLIENT
Heinz India

AGENCY
Chaitra Leo Burnett/
Mumbai

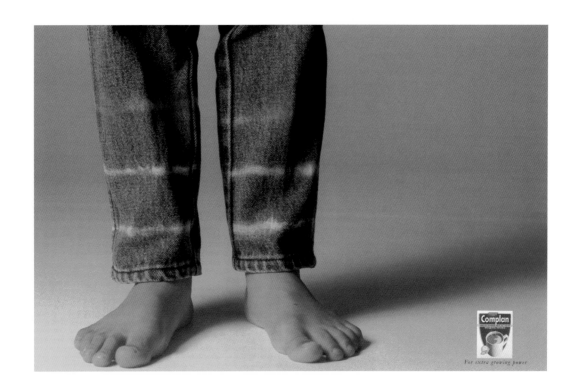

MERIT AWARD
Newspaper Over 600
Lines: Single

ART DIRECTOR
David Swartz

WRITER
Tim Roper

PHOTOGRAPHER
Bruce DeBoer

CLIENT
Giro Sport Design

AGENCY
Crispin Porter & Bogusky/
Miami

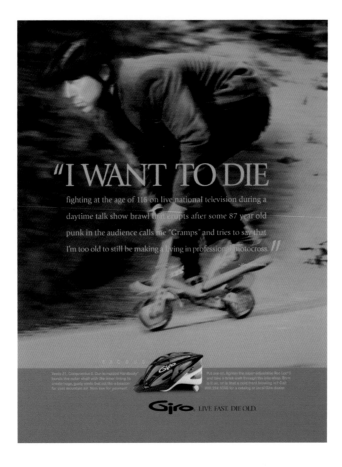

Wool is so scratchy.

They may well inspire you to have your shirts tailored with the sleeves a bit too short.

Leaving champagne and caviar out for Santa Claus was sheer genius.

MERIT AWARD
Newspaper Over 600
Lines: Single

ART DIRECTOR
Steve Sage

WRITER
Riley Kane

PHOTOGRAPHER
Michael Rausch

CLIENT
BMW of North America

AGENCY
Fallon McElligott/
Minneapolis

Now with more room for little white arrows.

The Ultimate Driving Machine

MERIT AWARD
Newspaper Over 600
Lines: Single

ART DIRECTOR
Rick Yamakoshi

WRITER
Greg Hahn

CLIENT
United Airlines

AGENCY
Fallon McElligott/
Minneapolis

*United: The world leader
in curvy red lines.*

You've seen the maps a thousand times. But what do these lines really represent? Well, when it comes to your travel plans they mean flexibility. With 35 international destinations from Chicago and an additional 339 with Star Alliance, United is bound to have a flight that fits within your schedule. Plus, of all U.S. based airlines, we have the largest fleet of 747s and the only fleet of 777s. So next time you need to travel, call United. We're sure to be the easiest way to get there. Wherever "there" may be.

UNITED
RISING

MERIT AWARD
Newspaper Over 600
Lines: Single

ART DIRECTOR
Vanessa Pearson

WRITER
Lawrence Seftel

CLIENT
Nike/South Africa

AGENCY
The Jupiter Drawing
Room/Johannesburg

MERIT AWARD
Newspaper Over 600
Lines: Single

ART DIRECTOR
Peter Nicholson

WRITER
Scott Wild

PHOTOGRAPHER
Lars Topelmann

CLIENT
Adidas

AGENCY
Leagas Delaney/
San Francisco

MERIT AWARD
Newspaper Over 600
Lines: Single

ART DIRECTOR
Jason Ross

WRITER
Paul Ruta

PHOTOGRAPHER
John Clang

CLIENT
British Airways

AGENCY
M+C Saatchi/
Singapore

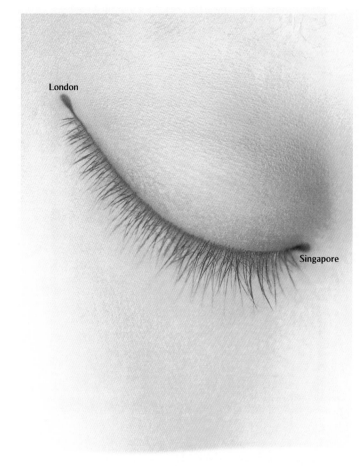

MERIT AWARD
Newspaper Over 600 Lines:
Single

ART DIRECTOR
John Boone

WRITER
David Oakley

PHOTOGRAPHER
Gilles Mingasson

CLIENT
Wrangler

AGENCY
The Martin Agency/
Charlotte

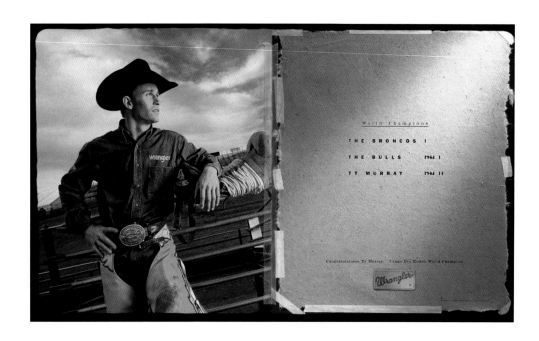

GOT TO BE GUINNESS

MERIT AWARD
Newspaper Over
600 Lines: Single

ART DIRECTOR
Eugene Cheong

WRITER
Andy Greenaway

ILLUSTRATOR
The Lounge

PHOTOGRAPHER
Shaun Pettigrew

CLIENT
Guinness Asia Pacific

AGENCY
Ogilvy & Mather/
Singapore

GOT TO BE GUINNESS

MERIT AWARD
Newspaper Over 600
Lines: Single

ART DIRECTOR
Eugene Cheong

WRITER
Andy Greenaway

ILLUSTRATOR
The Lounge

PHOTOGRAPHER
Shaun Pettigrew

CLIENT
Guinness Asia Pacific

AGENCY
Ogilvy & Mather/
Singapore

MERIT AWARD
Newspaper Over
600 Lines: Single

ART DIRECTOR
Eric Yeo

WRITER
Lim Soon Huat

ILLUSTRATORS
Bold
Procolour

PHOTOGRAPHER
Bold

CLIENT
Tung Lok Group

AGENCY
Ogilvy & Mather/
Singapore

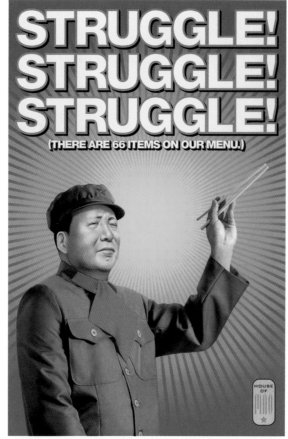

MERIT AWARD
Newspaper Over 600
Lines: Single

ART DIRECTOR
Eric Yeo

WRITER
Lim Soon Huat

ILLUSTRATORS
Bold
Procolour

PHOTOGRAPHER
Bold

CLIENT
Tung Lok Group

AGENCY
Ogilvy & Mather/
Singapore

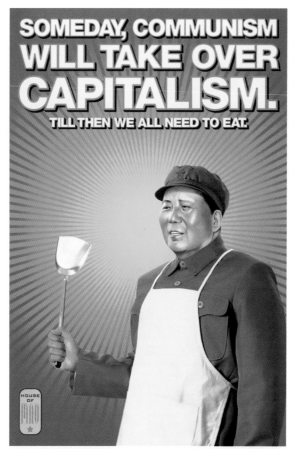

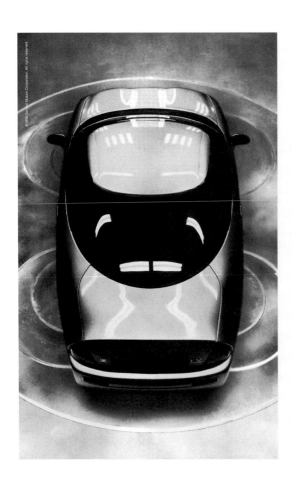

IT HARDLY MAKES A NOISE. REVOLUTIONS ALWAYS BEGIN THAT WAY.

THE ELECTRIC CAR IS HERE.

1.800.25ELECTRIC or www.gmev.com

MERIT AWARD
Newspaper Over 600
Lines: Single

ART DIRECTOR
Mike Mazza

WRITER
Jack Harding

PHOTOGRAPHER
R.J. Muna

CLIENT
EV1/General Motors

AGENCY
Publicis & Hal Riney/
San Francisco

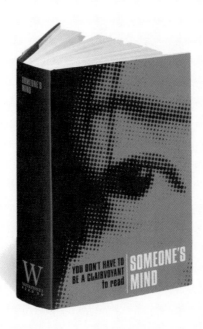

MERIT AWARD
Newspaper Over 600
Lines: Single

ART DIRECTOR
Paul Belford

WRITER
Nigel Roberts

ILLUSTRATOR
Paul Belford

PHOTOGRAPHER
Laurie Haskell

CLIENT
Waterstone's Booksellers

AGENCY
TBWA GGT Simons
Palmer/London

MERIT AWARD
Newspaper Over 600
Lines: Single

ART DIRECTOR
Paul Belford

WRITER
Nigel Roberts

ILLUSTRATOR
J.P.

PHOTOGRAPHER
Laurie Haskell

CLIENT
Waterstone's Booksellers

AGENCY
TBWA GGT Simons
Palmer/London

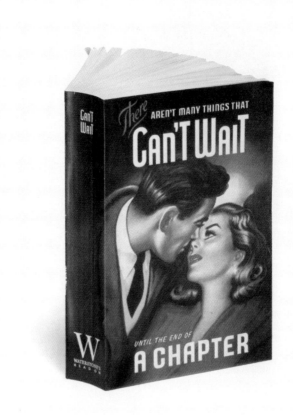

MERIT AWARD
Newspaper Over 600
Lines: Single

ART DIRECTORS
Erich Funke
Stuart Walsh

WRITERS
Stuart Walsh
Erich Funke

PHOTOGRAPHER
Michael Meyersfeld

CLIENT
Wonderbra

AGENCY
TBWA Hunt Lascaris/
Johannesburg

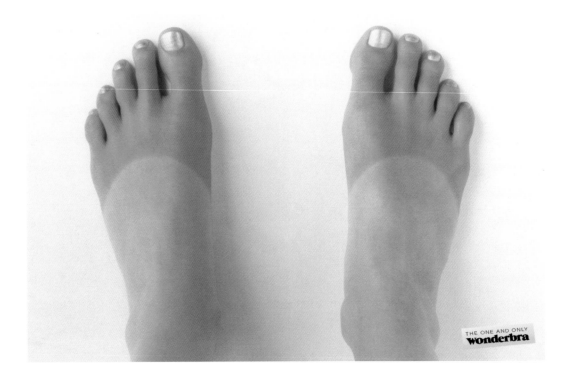

HOT CHILI FLAVOR
Set your mouth on fire.

MERIT AWARD
Newspaper Over 600
Lines: Single

ART DIRECTOR
Jordi Comas

WRITER
Siscu Molina

PHOTOGRAPHER
Leandre Escorsell

CLIENT
Ruffles/Frito Lay

AGENCY
Tiempo/BBDO/Barcelona

MERIT AWARD
Newspaper Over 600
Lines: Single

ART DIRECTOR
Pablo Cappelletti

WRITER
Gustavo Bussot

CLIENT
Disco

AGENCY
Young & Rubicam/
Buenos Aires

MERIT AWARD
Newspaper Over 600
Lines: Single

ART DIRECTOR
Cassio Moron

WRITERS
Anselmo Ramos
Jose Maria Pujol

ILLUSTRATOR
Cassio Moron

CLIENT
Iruna Rugby Club

AGENCY
Young & Rubicam/
Madrid

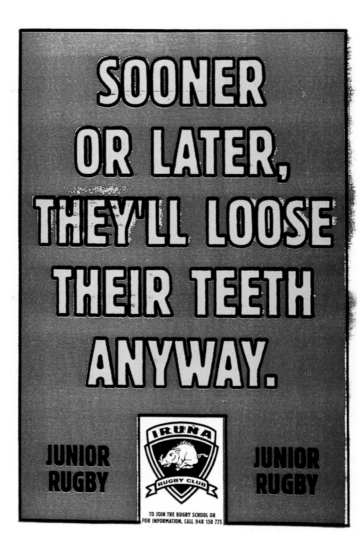

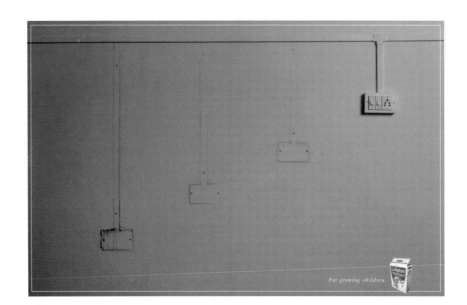

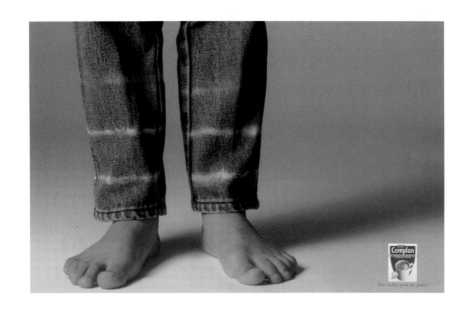

MERIT AWARD
Newspaper Over 600
Lines: Campaign

ART DIRECTORS
B. Ramnathkar
Yayati Godbole

WRITERS
Agnello Dias
Gokul Krishnan

PHOTOGRAPHER
Sanjeev Angne

CLIENT
Heinz India

AGENCY
Chaitra Leo Burnett/
Mumbai

MERIT AWARD
Newspaper Over 600
Lines: Campaign

ART DIRECTOR
Barrett Whitfield

WRITER
Ed Crayton

CLIENT
Duke's Barber Shop

AGENCY
DGWB Advertising/Irvine

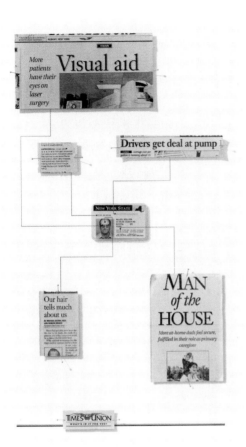

MERIT AWARD
Newspaper Over 600
Lines: Campaign

ART DIRECTOR
Wade Devers

WRITER
John Simpson

PHOTOGRAPHER
Jack Richmond

CLIENT
Times Union

AGENCY
Ingalls Advertising/Boston

MERIT AWARD
Newspaper Over 600
Lines: Campaign

ART DIRECTORS
Ed Evangelista
Phil Kelly

WRITERS
Steve Salinaro
Chris D'Rozario
Jon Koffler
Leslie Stern

PHOTOGRAPHER
Steve Hellerstein

CLIENT
Debeers

AGENCY
J. Walter Thompson/
New York

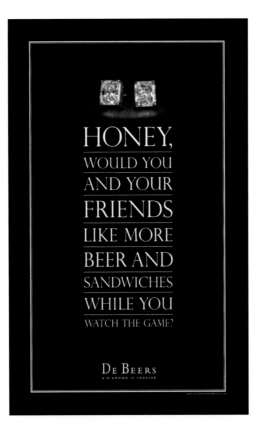

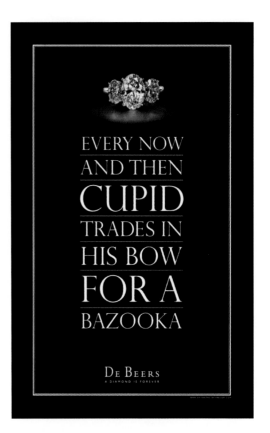

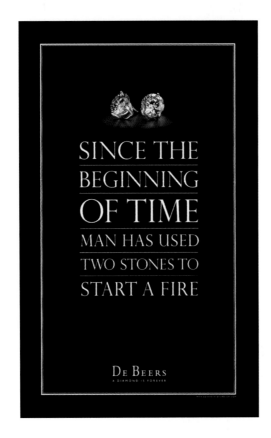

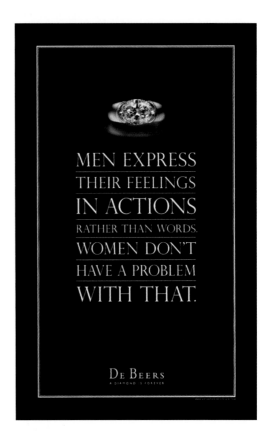

Are you ready for a store like this? ⊙ **TARGET.** Now in Commack and Westbury, L.I.

Are you ready for a store like this? ⊙ **TARGET.** Now in Commack and Westbury, L.I.

Are you ready for a store like this? ⊙ **TARGET.** Now in Commack and Westbury, L.I.

MERIT AWARD
Newspaper Over 600
Lines: Campaign

ART DIRECTOR
Julian Pugsley

WRITER
Andrew Bruck

PHOTOGRAPHER
Guzman

CLIENT
Target

AGENCY
Kirshenbaum Bond &
Partners/New York

MERIT AWARD
Newspaper Over 600
Lines: Campaign

ART DIRECTOR
Mark Fairbanks

WRITERS
Dave Hanneken
Rob Franks

ILLUSTRATOR
Jim McDonald

PHOTOGRAPHER
Dave Altman

CLIENT
Milwaukee Brewers
Baseball Club

AGENCY
Kohnke Hanneken/
Milwaukee

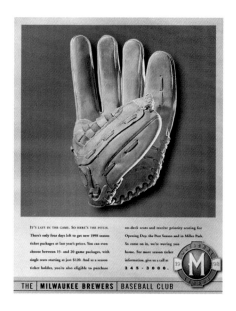

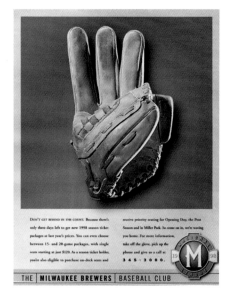

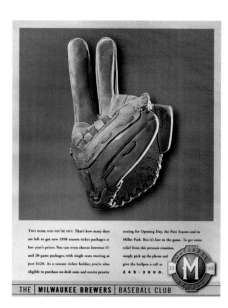

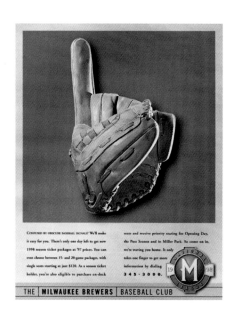

MERIT AWARD
Newspaper Over 600
Lines: Campaign

ART DIRECTOR
Eugene Cheong

WRITER
Andy Greenaway

ILLUSTRATOR
The Lounge

PHOTOGRAPHER
Shaun Pettigrew

CLIENT
Guinness Asia Pacific

AGENCY
Ogilvy & Mather/
Singapore

MERIT AWARD
Newspaper Over 600
Lines: Campaign

ART DIRECTOR
Eric Yeo

WRITER
Eugene Cheong

ILLUSTRATOR
Procolour

PHOTOGRAPHER
Joyce Choo

CLIENT
Mattel

AGENCY
Ogilvy & Mather/
Singapore

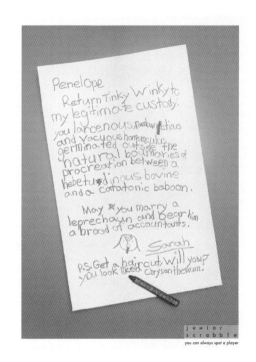

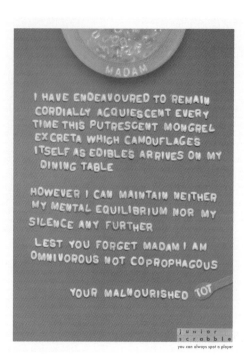

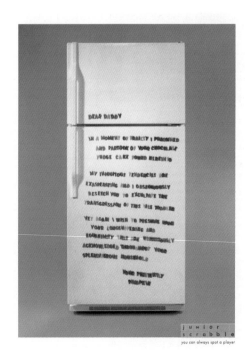

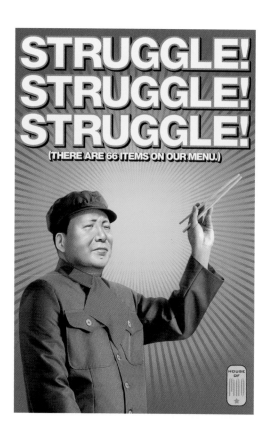

MERIT AWARD
Newspaper Over 600
Lines: Campaign

ART DIRECTOR
Eric Yeo

WRITER
Lim Soon Huat

ILLUSTRATORS
Bold
Procolour

PHOTOGRAPHER
Bold

CLIENT
Tung Lok Group

AGENCY
Ogilvy & Mather/
Singapore

MERIT AWARD
Newspaper Over 600
Lines: Campaign

ART DIRECTORS
Francis Wee
Tay Guan Hin

WRITER
Calvin Soh

ILLUSTRATORS
Anthony Wong
Procolor

PHOTOGRAPHERS
Simon Taplin
Shooting Gallery

CLIENT
Pidemco Land

AGENCY
Saatchi & Saatchi/
Singapore

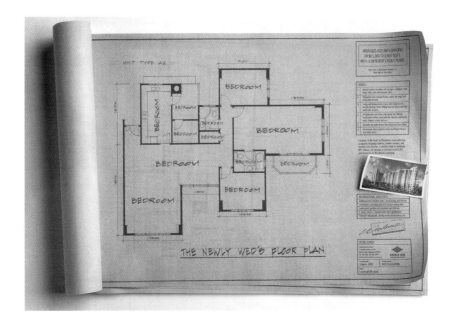

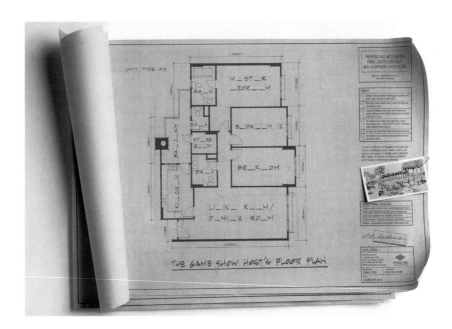

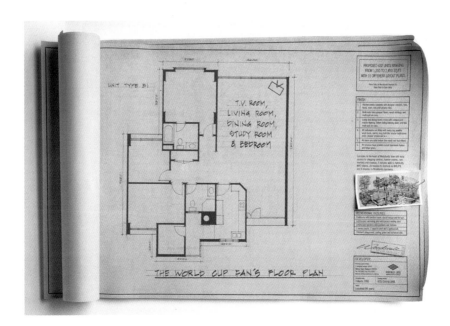

Here's the deal.
We'll take a few thousand off,
but we keep the change
we found in the seats.

'97 Jetta GLX

After all it will go to good use. You see, every pre-owned vehicle we get in must

first pass our initial inspection. Basically to determine if it's a car we would buy

ourselves. If it is, we back it with a Volkswagen of America warranty, set a fair

price and give it a good old fashioned spit shine. That way you can be confident

you're getting a great car with a whole company standing behind it.

Drivers wanted. Ⓥ

©1998 Volkswagen

MERIT AWARD
Newspaper 600 Lines or
Less: Single

ART DIRECTOR
Tim Vaccarino

WRITER
Shane Hutton

CLIENT
Volkswagen

AGENCY
Arnold Communications/
Boston

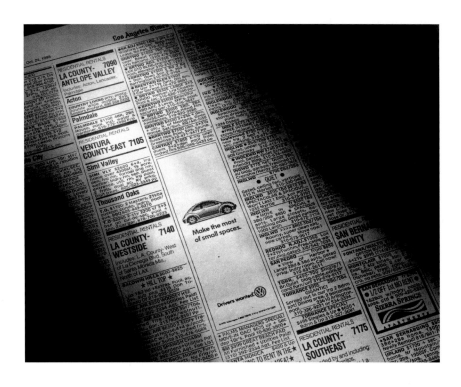

MERIT AWARD
Newspaper 600 Lines
or Less: Single

ART DIRECTOR
Will Uronis

WRITER
David Weist

CLIENT
Volkswagen

AGENCY
Arnold Communications/
Boston

MERIT AWARD
Newspaper 600 Lines
or Less: Single

ART DIRECTOR
James Clunie

WRITER
Susan Ebling

CLIENT
Deckers Outdoor
Corporation

AGENCY
Cohn Godley Norwood/
Boston

Slide foot in. Don't walk backwards.

Simple.

©1998 Deckers Outdoor Corporation

MERIT AWARD
Newspaper 600 Lines or
Less: Single

ART DIRECTOR
Tony Calcao

WRITER
Bill Wright

PHOTOGRAPHER
Tricia Chang

CLIENT
Vermont Ginseng

AGENCY
Crispin Porter & Bogusky/
Miami

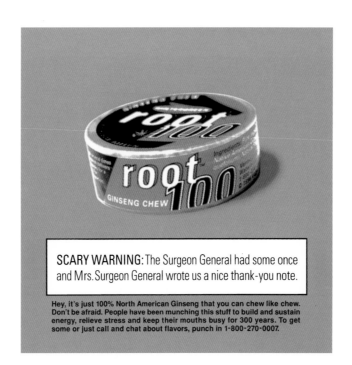

SCARY WARNING: The Surgeon General had some once
and Mrs. Surgeon General wrote us a nice thank-you note.

Hey, it's just 100% North American Ginseng that you can chew like chew.
Don't be afraid. People have been munching this stuff to build and sustain
energy, relieve stress and keep their mouths busy for 300 years. To get
some or just call and chat about flavors, punch in 1-800-270-0007.

AGENCY
DGWB Advertising/
Irvine

WRITER
Ed Crayton

CLIENT
Duke's Barber Shop

MERIT AWARD
Newspaper 600 Lines
or Less: Single

ART DIRECTOR
Barrett Whitfield

The Virgin Cola Company
Los Angeles, CA

MERIT AWARD
Newspaper 600 Lines
or Less: Single

ART DIRECTOR
Nairb Arotrot

WRITER
Grant Holland

CLIENT
Virgin Cola USA

AGENCY
Ground Zero/
Marina del Rey

Douglas Ivester
President and CEO
The Coca-Cola Company
One Coca-Cola Plaza
Atlanta, GA 30313

Dear Doug,

In case you haven't heard, we're launching Virgin Cola in the United States. Inevitably, this means both Virgin Cola and Coca-Cola will have to spend millions of dollars on advertising, celebrity endorsements, and those pesky promotions designed to undercut one another.

You know as well as I do how messy and expensive it can get battling for market share. So instead, I'd like to propose a simple solution: let's arm wrestle. Winner takes all. The loser promises to never sell his cola in the United States again. I think you'll agree that this arrangement will save us both a lot of headaches. Give me a buzz, and let's set up a date and time as soon as possible.

Cheers,

Richard Branson
Chairman of Virgin

MERIT AWARD
Newspaper 600 Lines
or Less: Single

ART DIRECTOR
Ari Merkin

WRITER
Ari Merkin

CLIENT
5th Avenue Stamp Gallery

AGENCY
Hampel Stefanides/
New York

THE JERRY GARCIA STAMP.

LICK AT YOUR OWN RISK.

Perhaps you should just sniff the glue instead. After all, this
stamp is a collector's item. And right now, each sheet is
only $12.95. To order, call 1 (800) 607-2799. Or just stop by
535 Fifth Avenue for a visit. You'll find it well worth the trip.

MERIT AWARD
Newspaper 600 Lines
or Less: Single

ART DIRECTOR
Ari Merkin

WRITER
Ari Merkin

CLIENT
5th Avenue Stamp Gallery

AGENCY
Hampel Stefanides/
New York

YOU SHOULD SEE
THE **OTHER** STAMP.

The other four, to be exact. Which means you get exactly
what you'd expect from a Rocky commemorative: sequals.
The series is just $19.95. So call 1 (800) 607-2799 and get
all five sheets in mint condition. Even if their subject isn't.

GOOD THINGS ABOUT THE LOCKOUT #34

NBA
Central Division

	W	L	Pct.
Charlotte	0	0	.000
Chicago	0	0	.000
Milwaukee	0	0	.000
Indiana	0	0	.000
Detroit	0	0	.000
Atlanta	0	0	.000

IT'S DECEMBER, AND WE'RE STILL TIED WITH CHICAGO.

We're trying to remain optimistic. We hope you are too.

MERIT AWARD
Newspaper 600 Lines
or Less: Single

ART DIRECTORS
John Boone
Adam Roth

WRITER
David Oakley

CLIENT
Charlotte Hornets

AGENCY
The Martin Agency/
Charlotte

WHICH CAME FIRST

THE SPICE GIRLS

OR THE MUTE BUTTON?

106.5 THE END

MERIT AWARD
Newspaper 600 Lines
or Less: Single

ART DIRECTOR
John Boone

WRITER
David Oakley

CLIENT
WEND 106.5

AGENCY
The Martin Agency/
Charlotte

MERIT AWARD
Newspaper 600 Lines
or Less: Single

ART DIRECTOR
John Boone

WRITER
David Oakley

CLIENT
WEND 106.5

AGENCY
The Martin Agency/
Charlotte

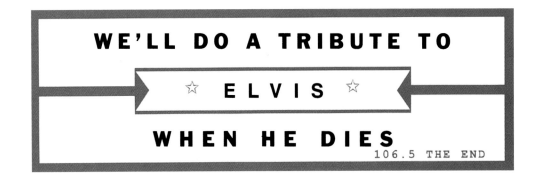

MERIT AWARD
Newspaper 600 Lines
or Less: Single

ART DIRECTOR
John Boone

WRITER
David Oakley

CLIENT
WEND 106.5

AGENCY
The Martin Agency/
Charlotte

MERIT AWARD
Newspaper 600 Lines
or Less: Single

ART DIRECTOR
Flint Cohen

WRITER
Oliver Albrecht

PHOTOGRAPHER
Frank Short

CLIENT
Pacific Termite

AGENCY
matthews/mark/
San Diego

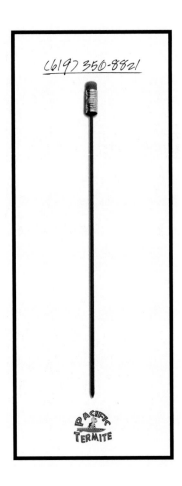

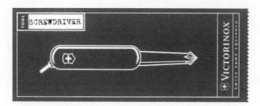

MERIT AWARD
Newspaper 600 Lines
or Less: Single

ART DIRECTOR
Greg Bokor

WRITER
Jim Garaventi

PHOTOGRAPHER
Bruce Peterson

CLIENT
Swiss Army Brands

AGENCY
Mullen Advertising/
Wenham

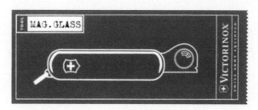

MERIT AWARD
Newspaper 600 Lines
or Less: Single

ART DIRECTOR
Greg Bokor

WRITER
Jim Garaventi

PHOTOGRAPHER
Bruce Peterson

CLIENT
Swiss Army Brands

AGENCY
Mullen Advertising/
Wenham

MERIT AWARD
Newspaper 600 Lines
or Less: Single

ART DIRECTOR
Ian Grais

WRITER
Alan Russell

PHOTOGRAPHER
Anthony Redpath

CLIENT
TV Twelve

AGENCY
Palmer Jarvis DDB/
Vancouver

MERIT AWARD
Newspaper 600 Lines
or Less: Single

ART DIRECTOR
Ian Grais

WRITER
Alan Russell

PHOTOGRAPHER
Anthony Redpath

CLIENT
TV Twelve

AGENCY
Palmer Jarvis DDB/
Vancouver

**NEW DEALERSHIP
NOW OPEN AT**

**28° 13' 30" S
28° 18' 20" E**

LAND ROVER

HOCHLAND

MERIT AWARD
Newspaper 600 Lines
or Less: Single

ART DIRECTOR
Jan Jacobs

WRITER
Clare McNally

CLIENT
Land Rover

AGENCY
TBWA Hunt Lascaris/
Johannesburg

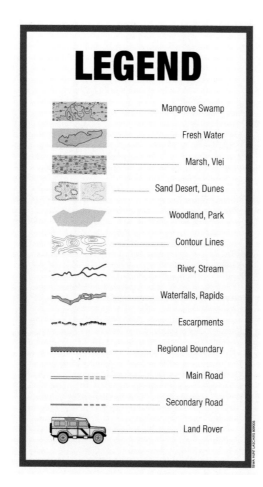

LEGEND

Mangrove Swamp

Fresh Water

Marsh, Vlei

Sand Desert, Dunes

Woodland, Park

Contour Lines

River, Stream

Waterfalls, Rapids

Escarpments

Regional Boundary

Main Road

Secondary Road

Land Rover

MERIT AWARD
Newspaper 600 Lines
or Less: Single

ART DIRECTOR
Jan Jacobs

WRITER
Clare McNally

ILLUSTRATORS
Andrew Falkson
Janine Wittrowski

CLIENT
Land Rover

AGENCY
TBWA Hunt Lascaris/
Johannesburg

MERIT AWARD
Newspaper 600 Lines
or Less: Campaign

ART DIRECTORS
John Boone
Adam Roth

WRITER
David Oakley

CLIENT
Charlotte Hornets

AGENCY
The Martin Agency/
Charlotte

GOOD THINGS ABOUT THE LOCKOUT #16

THE HORNETS ARE UNDEFEATED.

We're trying to remain optimistic. We hope you are too.

GOOD THINGS ABOUT THE LOCKOUT #22

NO ONE HAS SCORED ON US YET.

We're trying to remain optimistic. We hope you are too.

GOOD THINGS ABOUT THE LOCKOUT #47

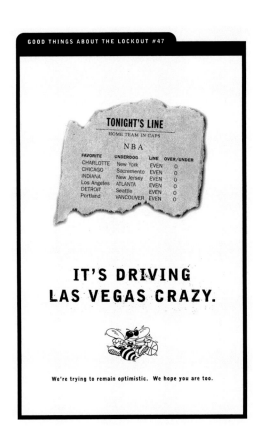

IT'S DRIVING LAS VEGAS CRAZY.

We're trying to remain optimistic. We hope you are too.

GOOD THINGS ABOUT THE LOCKOUT #61

MASE DIDN'T FOUL OUT LAST NIGHT.

We're trying to remain optimistic. We hope you are too.

MERIT AWARD
Newspaper 600 Lines
or Less: Campaign

ART DIRECTORS
John Boone
Adam Roth

WRITER
David Oakley

CLIENT
Charlotte Hornets

AGENCY
The Martin Agency/
Charlotte

MERIT AWARD
Newspaper 600 Lines
or Less: Campaign

ART DIRECTOR
Ng Pei Pei

WRITER
Andy Greenaway

PHOTOGRAPHER
John Clang

CLIENT
Mattel

AGENCY
Ogilvy & Mather/
Singapore

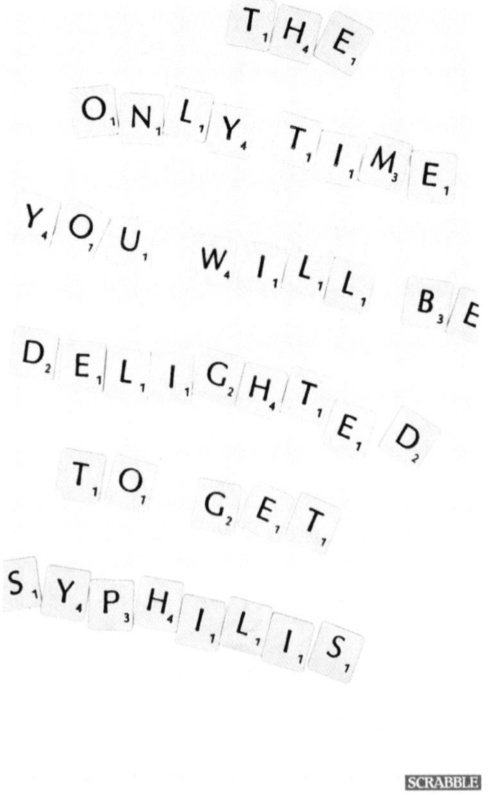

THE ONLY TIME YOU WILL BE DELIGHTED TO GET SYPHILIS

SCRABBLE

ONE OF THE FEW OCCASIONS WHEN CELIBACY IS BETTER THAN SEX

SCRABBLE

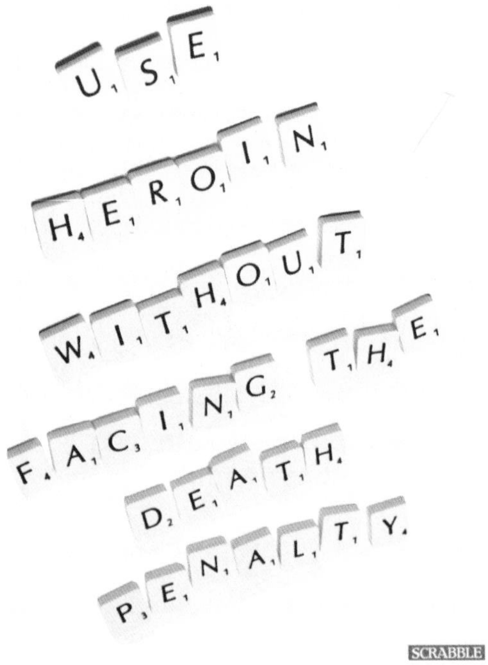

USE HEROIN WITHOUT FACING THE DEATH PENALTY

SCRABBLE

This is what's left after an $8,000 cremation.

This is what's left after a $2,000 cremation.

When you're gone, you're gone. **No Frills** FUNERALS & CREMATIONS   For information call 9247 6895.

This is what you're buried under in a $25,000 funeral.

This is what you're buried under in a $2,000 funeral.

When you're gone, you're gone. **No Frills** FUNERALS & CREMATIONS   For information call 9247 6895.

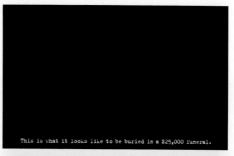

This is what it looks like to be buried in a $25,000 funeral.

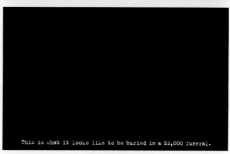

This is what it looks like to be buried in a $2,000 funeral.

When you're gone, you're gone. **No Frills** FUNERALS & CREMATIONS   For information call 9247 6895.

MERIT AWARD
Newspaper 600 Lines
or Less: Campaign

ART DIRECTOR
Steve Carlin

WRITER
Jay Furby

PHOTOGRAPHER
Gary Richardson

CLIENT
No Frills Funerals

AGENCY
Saatchi & Saatchi/
Sydney

MERIT AWARD
Magazine B/W Full Page
or Spread: Single

ART DIRECTOR
Jon Wyville

WRITER
Kara Goodrich

PHOTOGRAPHER
Walker Evans

CLIENT
Checkered Past Records

AGENCY
Arian Lowe & Travis/
Chicago

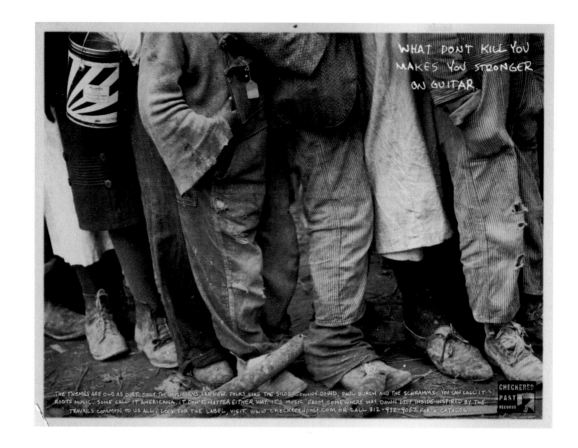

MERIT AWARD
Magazine B/W Full Page
or Spread: Single

ART DIRECTOR
Mark Martin

WRITER
Chris Rickaby

PHOTOGRAPHER
Alex Telfer

CLIENT
House of Hardy

AGENCY
Robson Brown/
Newcastle Upon Tyne

A car like this comes around
only twice in a lifetime.

Drivers wanted:

© 1998 Volkswagen. 1-800 DRIVE VW or WWW.VW.COM

If you were really good in a past life,
you come back as something better.

Drivers wanted:

© 1998 Volkswagen. 1-800 DRIVE VW or WWW.VW.COM

The engine's in the front,
but its heart's in the same place.

Drivers wanted:

© 1998 Volkswagen. 1-800 DRIVE VW or WWW.VW.COM

MERIT AWARD
Magazine Color Full Page
or Spread: Single

ART DIRECTOR
Lance Paull

WRITERS
Josh Caplan
Robert Hamilton

CLIENT
Volkswagen

AGENCY
Arnold Communications/
Boston

If you sold your soul in the 80s,
here's your chance to buy it back.

© 1998 Volkswagen. 1-800-DRIVE-VW or WWW.VW.COM

Drivers wanted.

MERIT AWARD
Magazine Color Full Page
or Spread: Single

ART DIRECTOR
Lance Paull

WRITERS
Ron Lawner
Lance Jenson

CLIENT
Volkswagen

AGENCY
Arnold Communications/
Boston

Lime.

Also comes in red, black, silver, white, dark blue, and bright blue. And of course, a lemon yellow. **Drivers wanted.**

© 1998 Volkswagen. 1-800-DRIVE-VW or WWW.VW.COM. Some colors available by order only.

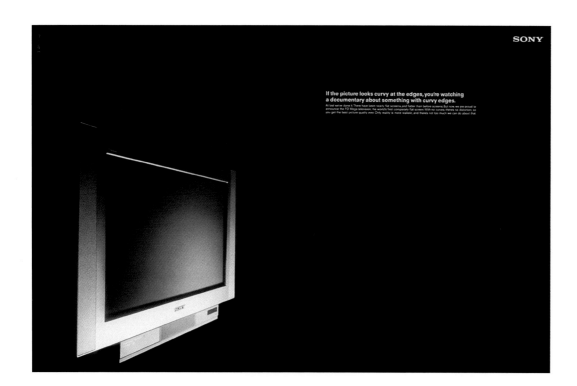

MERIT AWARD
Magazine Color Full Page
or Spread: Single

ART DIRECTOR
Richard Flintham

WRITER
Andy McCleod

PHOTOGRAPHER
Jenny van Sommers

CLIENT
Sony

AGENCY
BMP DDB/London

MERIT AWARD
Magazine Color Full Page
or Spread: Single

ART DIRECTOR
Dave Dye

WRITER
Sean Doyle

ILLUSTRATOR
Grundy Northedge

CLIENT
Volkswagen Group UK

AGENCY
BMP DDB/London

MERIT AWARD
Magazine Color Full Page
or Spread: Single

ART DIRECTOR
Neil Dawson

WRITER
Clive Pickering

PHOTOGRAPHER
Paul Reas

CLIENT
Volkswagen Group UK

AGENCY
BMP DDB/London

MERIT AWARD
Magazine Color full Page
or Spread: Single

ART DIRECTOR
Dave Dye

WRITER
Sean Doyle

ILLUSTRATOR
Jeff Fisher

CLIENT
Volkswagen Group UK

AGENCY
BMP DDB/London

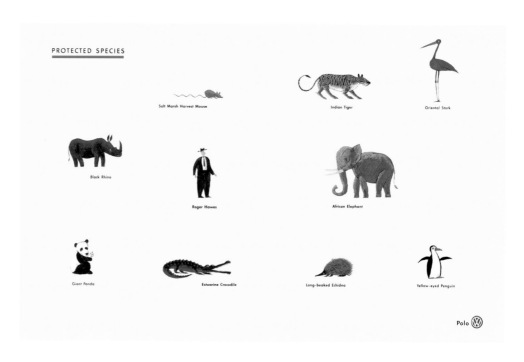

MERIT AWARD
Magazine Color Full Page
or Spread: Single

ART DIRECTOR
Andrew Fraser

WRITER
Andrew Fraser

PHOTOGRAPHER
Paul Reas

CLIENT
Volkswagen Group UK

AGENCY
BMP DDB/London

MERIT AWARD
Magazine Color Full Page
or Spread: Single

ART DIRECTOR
Neil Dawson

WRITER
Clive Pickering

PHOTOGRAPHER
Paul Reas

CLIENT
Volkswagen Group UK

AGENCY
BMP DDB/London

MERIT AWARD
Magazine Color Full Page
or Spread: Single

ART DIRECTOR
Dave Masterman

WRITER
Ed Edwards

ILLUSTRATOR
Typo Fads

PHOTOGRAPHER
Kevin Summers

CLIENT
Volkswagen Group UK

AGENCY
BMP DDB/London

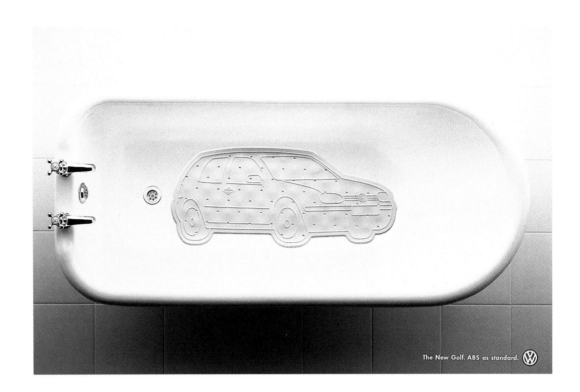

MERIT AWARD
Magazine Color Full Page
or Spread: Single)

ART DIRECTOR
Dave Dye

WRITER
Sean Doyle

ILLUSTRATOR
Christopher Wormell

CLIENT
Volkswagen Group UK

AGENCY
BMP DDB/London

"My older brother has a Harley. Mom told me his name is Dave."

When someone gets out into the dust and the wind and the big, wide-open country with a Harley-Davidson motorcycle thundering in their grip, there's no possible way of telling how far things will go. All we can say for sure is, the road is infinite. For the location of the Harley dealer near you, call 1-800-443-2153 or visit us at www.harley-davidson.com. The Legend Rolls On.

MERIT AWARD
Magazine Color Full Page
or Spread: Single

ART DIRECTOR
Paul Asao

WRITER
Jim Nelson

PHOTOGRAPHER
Olaf Veitman

CLIENT
Harley-Davidson

AGENCY
Carmichael Lynch/
Minneapolis

RESERVED RESERVED RESERVED RESERVED DON'T EVEN THINK ABOUT IT RESERVED

A Harley-Davidson motorcycle stands for something. We know it. You know it. And everyone else knows it, too. Ninety-five years on the road have seen to that. So there's no need to explain it. Once you've got a Harley of your own, all you need to do is enjoy it. For the dealer nearest you, call 1-800-443-2153 or visit us at www.harley-davidson.com. The Legend Rolls On.

MERIT AWARD
Magazine Color Full Page
or Spread: Single

ART DIRECTOR
Paul Asao

WRITER
Jim Nelson

PHOTOGRAPHER
Shawn Michienzi

CLIENT
Harley-Davidson

AGENCY
Carmichael Lynch/
Minneapolis

CARE OF GARMENT: SANDBLAST FREQUENTLY BEHIND 18 WHEELERS. BEAT CLEAN WITH CROWBAR.

Built to take what the road throws you. Snap-down collar won't flap. Rotated shoulders for comfort. Premium leather. Harley-Davidson MotorClothes riding leathers. Only at your dealer. 1-800-588-2743.

MERIT AWARD
Magazine Color Full Page
or Spread: Single

ART DIRECTOR
Glenn Gray

WRITER
Tom Camp

PHOTOGRAPHER
Shawn Michienzi

CLIENT
Harley-Davidson
MotorClothes

AGENCY
Carmichael Lynch/
Minneapolis

MERIT AWARD
Magazine Color Full Page
or Spread: Single

ART DIRECTOR
Jim Amadeo

WRITER
Spencer Deadrick

PHOTOGRAPHER
Scott Goodwin

CLIENT
InterNutria

AGENCY
Clarke Goward
Advertising/Boston

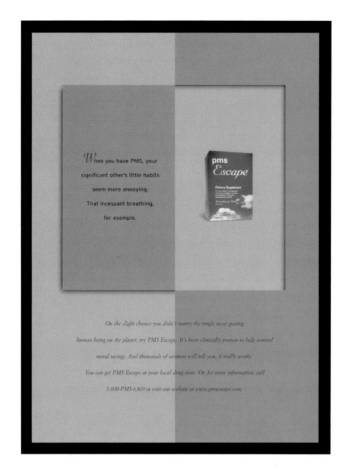

MERIT AWARD
Magazine Color Full Page
or Spread: Single

ART DIRECTOR
Jim Amadeo

WRITER
Spencer Deadrick

PHOTOGRAPHER
Scott Goodwin

CLIENT
InterNutria

AGENCY
Clarke Goward
Advertising/Boston

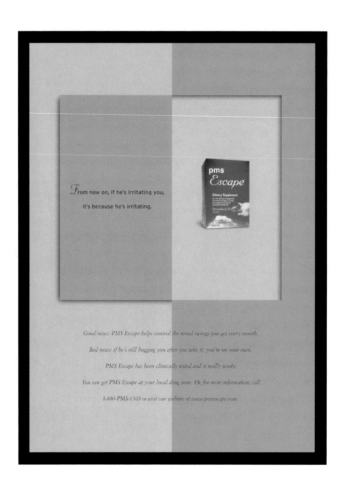

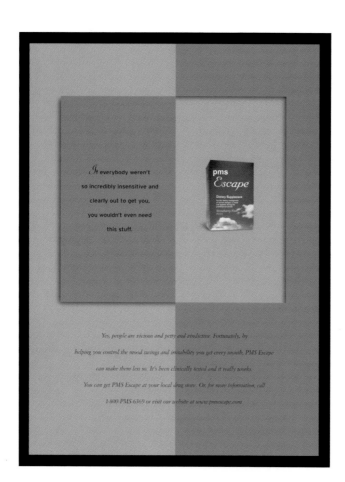

MERIT AWARD
Magazine Color Full Page
or Spread: Single

ART DIRECTOR
Jim Amadeo

WRITER
Spencer Deadrick

PHOTOGRAPHER
Scott Goodwin

CLIENT
InterNutria

AGENCY
Clarke Goward
Advertising/Boston

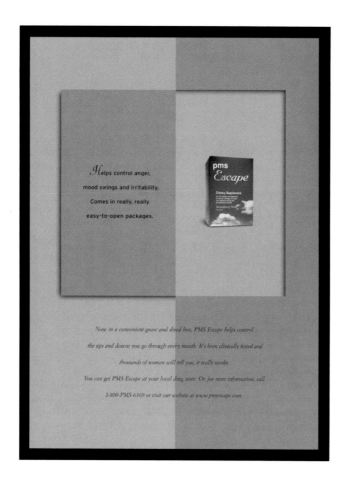

MERIT AWARD
Magazine Color Full Page
or Spread: Single

ART DIRECTOR
Jim Amadeo

WRITER
Spencer Deadrick

PHOTOGRAPHER
Scott Goodwin

CLIENT
InterNutria

AGENCY
Clarke Goward
Advertising/Boston

MERIT AWARD
Magazine Color Full Page
or Spread: Single

ART DIRECTOR
Bob Barrie

WRITER
Dean Buckhorn

PHOTOGRAPHER
Cynthia Johnson

CLIENT
TIME

AGENCY
Fallon McElligott/
Minneapolis

The world's most interesting magazine.

MERIT AWARD
Magazine Color Full Page
or Spread: Single

ART DIRECTOR
Bob Barrie

WRITER
Dean Buckhorn

PHOTOGRAPHER
John Stanmeyer

CLIENT
TIME

AGENCY
Fallon McElligott/
Minneapolis

Always the truth.

Occasionally, the awful truth.

The world's most interesting magazine.

MERIT AWARD
Magazine Color Full Page
or Spread: Single

ART DIRECTOR
Bob Barrie

WRITER
Dean Buckhorn

PHOTOGRAPHER
Charles Wenzelberg

CLIENT
TIME

AGENCY
Fallon McElligott/
Minneapolis

On occasion, the story we tell

may pale next to the story

you'll tell your grandkids.

The world's most interesting magazine.

If there's a story in there,

we'll find it.

The world's most interesting magazine.

MERIT AWARD
Magazine Color Full Page
or Spread: Single

ART DIRECTOR
Bob Barrie

WRITER
Dean Buckhorn

PHOTOGRAPHER
Joe Skipper

CLIENT
TIME

AGENCY
Fallon McElligott/
Minneapolis

824 words on the X-Games.

(And only two of them were "dude.")

The world's most interesting magazine.

MERIT AWARD
Magazine Color Full Page
or Spread: Single

ART DIRECTOR
Bob Barrie

WRITER
Dean Buckhorn

PHOTOGRAPHER
Denis Poroy

CLIENT
TIME

AGENCY
Fallon McElligott/
Minneapolis

Make sense of anything.

Almost.

The world's most interesting magazine.

MERIT AWARD
Magazine Color Full Page
or Spread: Single

ART DIRECTOR
Bob Barrie

WRITER
Dean Buckhorn

PHOTOGRAPHER
Sygma

CLIENT
TIME

AGENCY
Fallon McElligott/
Minneapolis

MERIT AWARD
Magazine Color Full Page
or Spread: Single

ART DIRECTOR
Jeremy Postaer

WRITER
Brad Roseberry

PHOTOGRAPHERS
National Geographic Stock
Heimo

CLIENT
Bell Sports

AGENCY
Goodby Silverstein &
Partners/San Francisco

MERIT AWARD
Magazine Color Full Page
or Spread: Single

ART DIRECTOR
Paul Hirsch

WRITER
John Denberg

PHOTOGRAPHER
Steve Bonini

CLIENT
Nike

AGENCY
Goodby Silverstein &
Partners/San Francisco

YOU COULD GET MAULED BY A BEAR AND DIE.
YOU COULD GET BIT BY A SNAKE AND DIE.
YOU COULD FALL OFF A CLIFF AND DIE.
YOU COULD GET GORED BY A BISON AND DIE.
YOU COULD GET STRUCK BY LIGHTNING AND DIE.
YOU COULD GET SHOT BY A HUNTER AND DIE.
YOU COULD GET ATTACKED BY FIRE ANTS AND DIE.

OR YOU COULD STAY HOME ON THE COUCH,
EAT POTATO CHIPS AND DIE.

L ke y ur b ain, the n w L nd Rov r autom tic lly adj sts to anyth ng.

Introducing the most technologically advanced Land Rover ever.
When it came to creating the all-new Discovery Series II, we didn't leave anything out.
Whether you're looking under the hood or around the cabin, you'll find something new.
Or something improved.

Or something reengineered.
Or something redesigned.
You'll even come across technological innovations not found in other SUVs. Like the newly available Active Cornering Enhancement. A feature that uses computer software and an advanced hydraulic system to create an extraordinarily un-SUV-like ride.
Even in turns as sharp as th.

Suffice it to say that there's not a more streetwise 4x4.
But what are brains without brawn?
Thanks to four-wheel electronic traction control, all-terrain ABS, and permanent four-wheel drive, there's almost no off-road problem the new Discovery can't solve.
We've even rethought its braking system. It now comes equipped with

electronic brake force distribution.
A feature that is designed to balance front and rear braking for increased driver control. In all conditions.
And while the new Discovery adjusts to practically anything outside, no adjustments are necessary inside.
Its larger interior caters to you and your family with such conveniences as ergonomically designed seats,

three-point safety belts for everyone, and optional forward-facing rear seats.

Moreover, this new Land Rover helps put your mind at ease. There are side impact beams and a rugged 14-gauge steel chassis.
So call 1-800-FINE 4WD for your local retailer.
And with a starting MSRP of $34,775* there's one thing we suspect you won't be doing.
Thinking twice.

DISCOVERY SERIES II $34,775*

*Always use your seatbelts. SRS/airbags alone do not provide sufficient protection.

BGH Silent Air

MERIT AWARD
Magazine Color Full Page
or Spread: Single

ART DIRECTOR
Mike Proctor

WRITER
Ian Cohen

CLIENT
Diadora

AGENCY
Hammerquist &
Halverson/Seattle

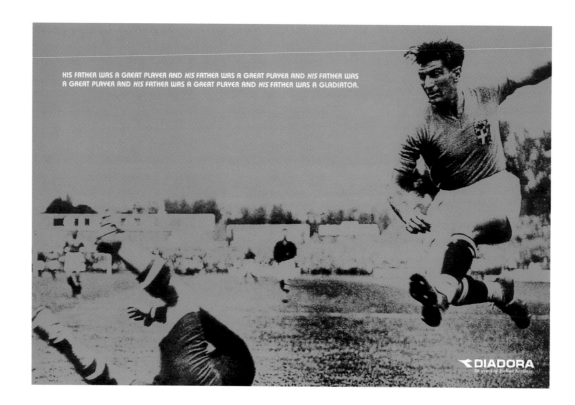

MERIT AWARD
Magazine Color Full Page
or Spread: Single

ART DIRECTOR
Miguel Coimbra

WRITER
Ricardo Adolfo

PHOTOGRAPHER
Chico Prata

CLIENT
Lego

AGENCY
J. Walter Thompson
Publicidade/Alges

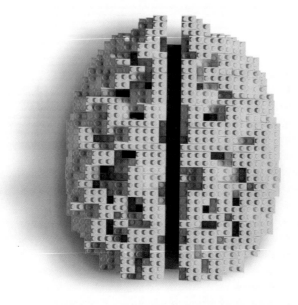

MERIT AWARD
Magazine Color Full Page
or Spread: Single

ART DIRECTOR
Marcus Fernandez

WRITER
Brian Millar

PHOTOGRAPHER
Alan McPhail

CLIENT
Gold's Gym Franchising

AGENCY
JACK/Venice

MERIT AWARD
Magazine Color Full Page
or Spread: Single

ART DIRECTOR
Tony Davidson

WRITER
Kim Papworth

PHOTOGRAPHER
Nick Georghiou

CLIENT
Adidas

AGENCY
Leagas Delaney/London

MERIT AWARD
Magazine Color Full Page
or Spread: Single

ART DIRECTOR
Dustin Smith

WRITER
Brendon Duffy

PHOTOGRAPHER
Tony D'Orio

CLIENT
Callard & Bowser-Suchard

AGENCY
Leo Burnett/Chicago

MERIT AWARD
Magazine Color Full Page
or Spread: Single

ART DIRECTOR
Jason Ross

WRITER
Paul Ruta

PHOTOGRAPHER
John Clang

CLIENT
British Airways

AGENCY
M+C Saatchi/Singapore

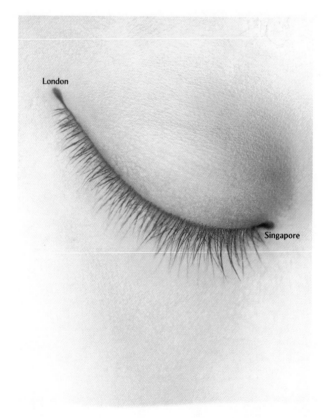

MERIT AWARD
Magazine Color Full Page
or Spread: Single

ART DIRECTOR
Jim Henderson

WRITER
Tom Kelly

PHOTOGRAPHERS
Gary Kufner
Curtis Johnson

CLIENT
Coleman

AGENCY
Martin/Williams
Advertising/Minneapolis

MERIT AWARD
Magazine Color Full Page
or Spread: Single

ART DIRECTOR
Jim Henderson

WRITER
Tom Kelly

PHOTOGRAPHERS
Douglas Walker
Curtis Johnson

CLIENT
Coleman

AGENCY
Martin/Williams
Advertising/Minneapolis

MERIT AWARD
Magazine Color Full Page
or Spread: Single

ART DIRECTORS
Mark Walker
Tom Moyer

WRITERS
Brett Craig
Tom Page

PHOTOGRAPHER
Craig Saruwatari

CLIENT
FreeStyle

AGENCY
The M1 Agency/
Santa Monica

MERIT AWARD
Magazine Color Full Page
or Spread: Single

ART DIRECTOR
Monica Taylor

WRITER
Dylan Lee

PHOTOGRAPHER
Geoff Stein

CLIENT
Swiss Army Brands

AGENCY
Mullen Advertising/
Wenham

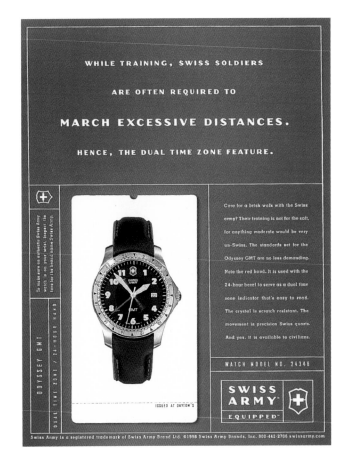

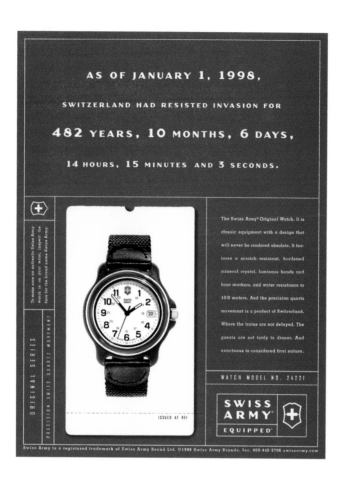

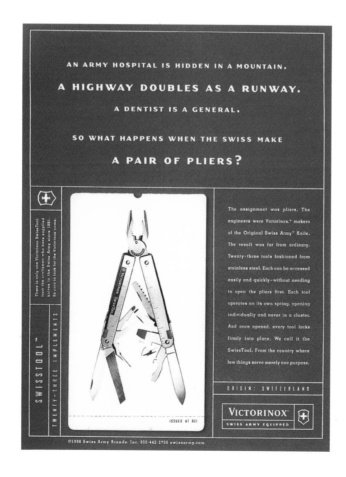

MERIT AWARD
Magazine Color Full Page
or Spread: Single

ART DIRECTOR
Monica Taylor

WRITER
Dylan Lee

PHOTOGRAPHER
Geoff Stein

CLIENT
Swiss Army Brands

AGENCY
Mullen Advertising/
Wenham

MERIT AWARD
Magazine Color Full Page
or Spread: Single

ART DIRECTOR
Monica Taylor

WRITER
Dylan Lee

PHOTOGRAPHER
Geoff Stein

CLIENT
Swiss Army Brands

AGENCY
Mullen Advertising/
Wenham

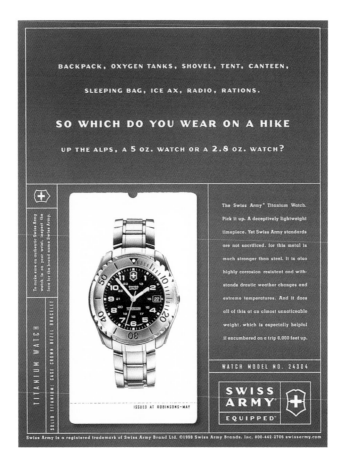

MERIT AWARD
Magazine Color Full Page
or Spread: Single

ART DIRECTOR
Monica Taylor

WRITER
Dylan Lee

PHOTOGRAPHER
Geoff Stein

CLIENT
Swiss Army Brands

AGENCY
Mullen Advertising/
Wenham

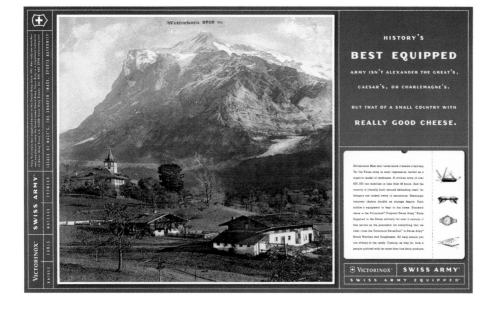

MERIT AWARD
Magazine Color Full Page
or Spread: Single

ART DIRECTOR
Monica Taylor

WRITER
Dylan Lee

PHOTOGRAPHER
Geoff Stein

CLIENT
Swiss Army Brands

AGENCY
Mullen Advertising/
Wenham

MERIT AWARD
Magazine Color Full Page
or Spread: Single

ART DIRECTOR
Monica Taylor

WRITER
Dylan Lee

PHOTOGRAPHER
Geoff Stein

CLIENT
Swiss Army Brands

AGENCY
Mullen Advertising/
Wenham

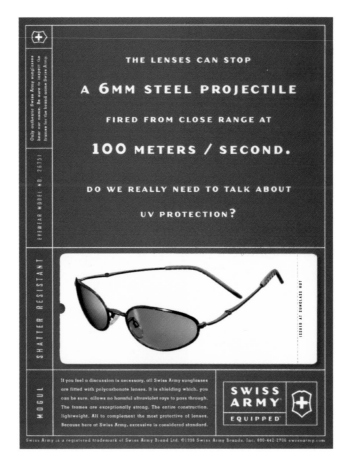

MERIT AWARD
Magazine Color Full Page
or Spread: Single

ART DIRECTOR
Monica Taylor

WRITER
Dylan Lee

PHOTOGRAPHER
Geoff Stein

CLIENT
Swiss Army Brands

AGENCY
Mullen Advertising/
Wenham

MERIT AWARD
Magazine Color Full Page
or Spread: Single

ART DIRECTOR
Sarel Esterhuizen

WRITERS
Mark Winkler
Joshua Bryer

PHOTOGRAPHER
Larry J. Pierce

CLIENT
Volkswagen

AGENCY
Ogilvy & Mather/
Cape Town

MERIT AWARD
Magazine Color Full Page
or Spread: Single)

ART DIRECTOR
Ben Bradley

WRITER
Graham Kelly

PHOTOGRAPHER
Roy Cheong

CLIENT
Mattel

AGENCY
Ogilvy & Mather/
Singapore

MERIT AWARD
Magazine Color Full Page
or Spread: Single

ART DIRECTOR
Torsten Rieken

WRITER
Jan Ritter

PHOTOGRAPHER
Gerd George

CLIENT
Deutsche Angelgeräte
Silstar

AGENCY
Springer & Jacoby
Werbung GmbH/
Hamburg

MERIT AWARD
Magazine Color Full Page
or Spread: Single

ART DIRECTOR
Sara Riesgo

WRITER
Raymond Hwang

CLIENT
ABC

AGENCY
TBWA/Chiat/Day/
Playa del Rey

If TV's so
bad for you,
why is there
one in every
hospital room?

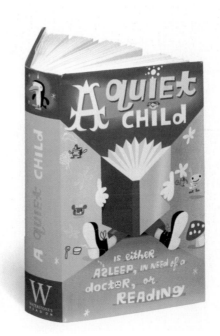

MERIT AWARD
Magazine Color Full Page
or Spread: Single

ART DIRECTOR
Paul Belford

WRITER
Nigel Roberts

ILLUSTRATOR
J. Otto Seibold

PHOTOGRAPHER
Laurie Haskell

CLIENT
Waterstone's Booksellers

AGENCY
TBWA GGT Simons
Palmer/London

MERIT AWARD
Magazine Color Full Page
or Spread: Single

ART DIRECTOR
Ross Ventress

WRITER
Tracey Funke

CLIENT
Hi Rise

AGENCY
TBWA Hunt Lascaris/
Johannesburg

MERIT AWARD
Magazine Color Full Page
or Spread: Single

ART DIRECTOR
Jan Jacobs

WRITER
Clare McNally

PHOTOGRAPHER
Martin Taylor

CLIENT
Land Rover

AGENCY
TBWA Hunt Lascaris/
Johannesburg

MERIT AWARD
Magazine Color Full Page
or Spread: Single

ART DIRECTOR
Philip Ireland

WRITER
Catherine Thomson

PHOTOGRAPHER
Annecke Grobler

CLIENT
Wonderbra

AGENCY
TBWA Hunt Lascaris/
Johannesburg

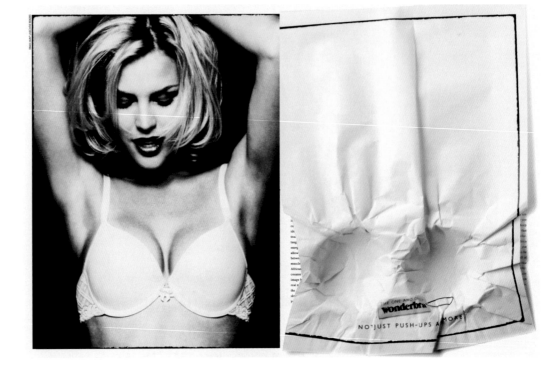

MERIT AWARD
Magazine Color Full Page
or Spread: Single

ART DIRECTOR
Gustavo Taretto

WRITER
Gabriel Vazquez

PHOTOGRAPHER
Ackerman

CLIENT
Gatic SA

AGENCY
Vega Olmos Ponce/
Buenos Aires

MERIT AWARD
Magazine Color Full Page
or Spread: Single

ART DIRECTOR
Andy Fackrell

WRITER
Kash Sree

PHOTOGRAPHER
Pete Seaward

CLIENT
Nike International

AGENCY
Wieden & Kennedy/
Portland

MERIT AWARD
Magazine B/W Full Page or
Spread: Campaign

ART DIRECTOR
Jon Wyville

WRITER
Kara Goodrich

PHOTOGRAPHER
Walker Evans

CLIENT
Checkered Past Records

AGENCY
Arian Lowe & Travis/
Chicago

MERIT AWARD
Magazine B/W Full Page or
Spread: Campaign

ART DIRECTOR
John Doyle

WRITER
Dave O'Hare

PHOTOGRAPHER
R.J. Muna

CLIENT
Aspen Skiing Company

AGENCY
Publicis & Hal Riney/
San Francisco

MERIT AWARD
Magazine Color Full Page
or Spread: Campaign

ART DIRECTOR
Paul Renner

WRITER
Carl Loeb

PHOTOGRAPHER
Steve Belkowitz

CLIENT
Converse

AGENCY
Arnold Communications/
Boston

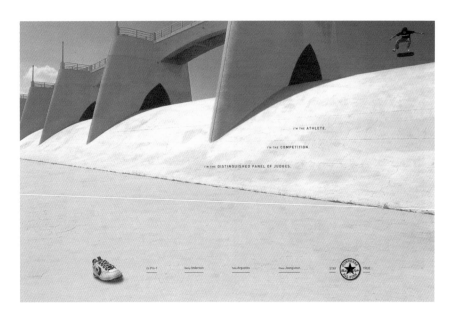

Digitally remastered.

Drivers wanted. Ⓥ

©1998 Volkswagen. 1-800 DRIVE VW or WWW.VW.COM

MERIT AWARD
Magazine Color Full Page
or Spread: Campaign

ART DIRECTORS
Will Uronis
Lance Paull

WRITERS
David Weist
Mark Moll
Lance Jensen

CLIENT
Volkswagen

AGENCY
Arnold Communications/
Boston

Beetle 2.0

Drivers wanted. Ⓥ

©1998 Volkswagen. 1-800 DRIVE VW or WWW.VW.COM

Reverse engineered from UFOs.

Drivers wanted. Ⓥ

©1998 Volkswagen. 1-800 DRIVE VW or WWW.VW.COM

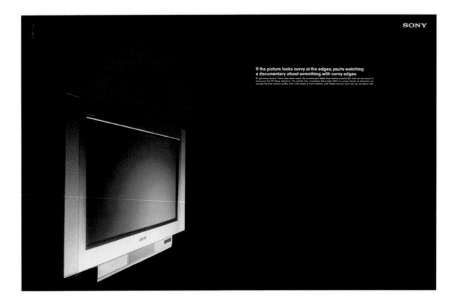

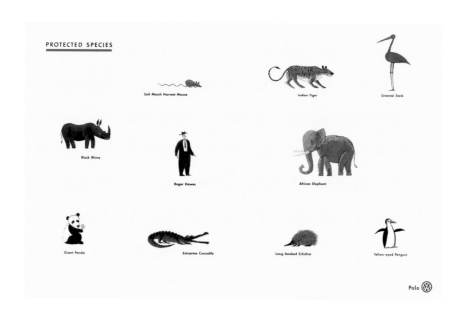

MERIT AWARD
Magazine Color Full Page
or Spread: Campaign

ART DIRECTOR
Dave Dye

WRITER
Sean Doyle

ILLUSTRATOR
Grundy Northedge

CLIENT
Volkswagen Group UK

AGENCY
BMP DDB/London

MERIT AWARD
Magazine Color Full Page
or Spread: Campaign

ART DIRECTOR
Paul Asao

WRITER
Jim Nelson

PHOTOGRAPHERS
Shawn Michienzi
Olaf Veitman

CLIENT
Harley-Davidson

AGENCY
Carmichael Lynch/
Minneapolis

THEY HAVE CUSTOM
HARDWARE.
THEY HAVE STEEL TOES.
THEY FREQUENT
THE NIGHTMARES OF
SMALL, FLUFFY
POODLES.

Built to take the heat from a 65 mph buzzsaw called the road. Soles are stitched, not glued. Heels have nine nails up,ten nails down for durability. Harley-Davidson® MotorClothes® boots. Only at your dealer. 1-800-588-2743.

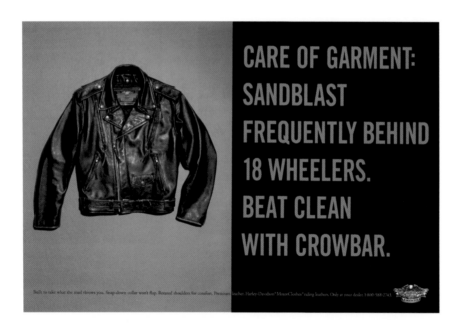

CARE OF GARMENT:
SANDBLAST
FREQUENTLY BEHIND
18 WHEELERS.
BEAT CLEAN
WITH CROWBAR.

Built to take what the road throws you. Snap-down collar won't flap. Rotated shoulders for comfort. Premium leather. Harley-Davidson® MotorClothes® riding leathers. Only at your dealer. 1-800-588-2743.

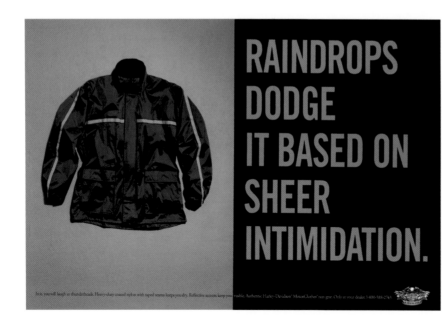

RAINDROPS
DODGE
IT BASED ON
SHEER
INTIMIDATION.

First, you will laugh at thunderheads. Heavy-duty coated nylon with taped seams keeps you dry. Reflective accents keep you visible. Authentic Harley-Davidson® MotorClothes® rain gear. Only at your dealer. 1-800-588-2743.

MERIT AWARD
Magazine Color Full Page
or Spread: Campaign

ART DIRECTOR
Glenn Gray

WRITER
Tom Camp

PHOTOGRAPHER
Shawn Michienzi

CLIENT
Harley-Davidson
MotorClothes

AGENCY
Carmichael Lynch/
Minneapolis

MERIT AWARD
Magazine Color Full Page
or Spread: Campaign

ART DIRECTOR
Bob Barrie

WRITER
Dean Buckhorn

PHOTOGRAPHERS
Denis Poroy
Frank Driggs
John Giles
Richard Drew
Quest

CLIENT
TIME

AGENCY
Fallon McElligott/
Minneapolis

824 words on the X-Games.

(And only two of them were "dude.")

The world's most interesting magazine.

The genuine article.

The world's most interesting magazine.

We'll let you know   if Ireland can   also wage peace.

The world's most interesting magazine.

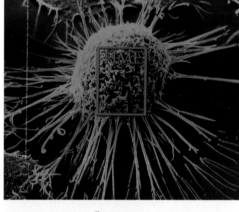

The war on cancer.

Magnified 1000x.

The world's most interesting magazine.

Buy low.

Sell high.

Read fast.

The world's most interesting magazine.

MERIT AWARD
Magazine Color Full Page
or Spread: Campaign

ART DIRECTOR
Jeremy Postaer

WRITER
Brad Roseberry

PHOTOGRAPHERS
National Geographic
Heimo
George Hall

CLIENT
Bell Sports

AGENCY
Goodby Silverstein &
Partners/San Francisco

MERIT AWARD
Magazine Color Full Page
or Spread: Campaign

ART DIRECTOR
Joel Clement

WRITER
Harold Einstein

PHOTOGRAPHER
Eugene Richards

CLIENT
Hewlett-Packard

AGENCY
Goodby Silverstein &
Partners/San Francisco

MERIT AWARD
Magazine Color Full Page
or Spread: Campaign

ART DIRECTOR
Sean Farrell

WRITER
Sharon Tao

PHOTOGRAPHER
Heimo

CLIENT
Nike

AGENCY
Goodby Silverstein &
Partners/San Francisco

MERIT AWARD
Magazine Color Full Page
or Spread: Campaign

ART DIRECTOR
Scott O'Leary

WRITER
Roger Baldacci

PHOTOGRAPHER
Peggy Sirota

CLIENT
Blue Cross Blue Shield
of Massachusetts

AGENCY
Holland Mark Martin
Edmund/Boston

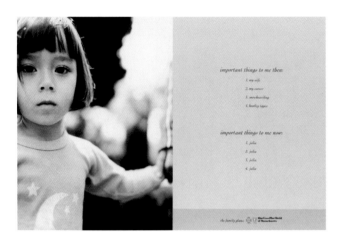

CLIENT
Tanner Krolle

AGENCY
Leagas Delaney/London

WRITER
Mark Goodwin

PHOTOGRAPHERS
Hans Gissinger
Giles Revell

MERIT AWARD
Magazine Color Full Page
or Spread: Campaign

ART DIRECTOR
Tiger Wnek-Savage

MERIT AWARD
Magazine Color Full Page
or Spread: Campaign

ART DIRECTORS
Mark Faulkner
Noel Haan
Dustin Smith

WRITERS
Steffan Postaer
Kit Cramer

PHOTOGRAPHER
Tony D'Orio

CLIENT
Callard Bowser-Suchard

AGENCY
Leo Burnett/Chicago

MERIT AWARD
Magazine Color Full Page
or Spread: Campaign

ART DIRECTOR
Jim Henderson

WRITER
Tom Kelly

PHOTOGRAPHERS
Douglas Walker
Robin Hood
Gary Kufner
Brian Bailey
Curtis Johnson

CLIENT
Coleman

AGENCY
Martin/Williams
Advertising/Minneapolis

MERIT AWARD
Magazine Color Full Page
or Spread: Campaign

ART DIRECTOR
Monica Taylor

WRITER
Dylan Lee

PHOTOGRAPHER
Geoff Stein

CLIENT
Swiss Army Brands

AGENCY
Mullen Advertising/
Wenham

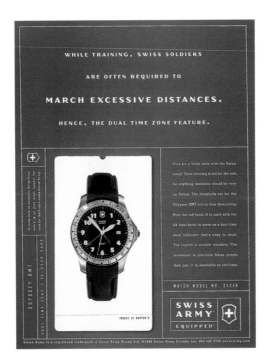

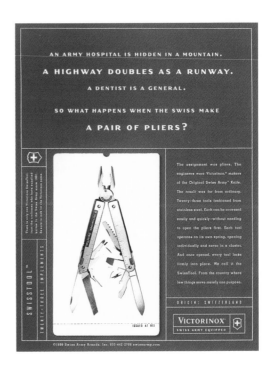

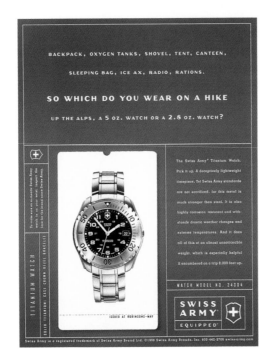

If TV's so
bad for you,
why is there
one in every
hospital room?

abc

Without a TV,
how would
you know
where to put
the sofa?

abc

Before TV,
two World Wars.
After TV, zero.

MERIT AWARD
Magazine Color Full Page
or Spread: Campaign

ART DIRECTORS
John Shirley
Sara Riesgo

WRITERS
Rich Siegel
Raymond Hwang

CLIENT
ABC

AGENCY
TBWA/Chiat/Day/
Playa del Rey

MERIT AWARD
Magazine Color Full Page
or Spread: Campaign

ART DIRECTOR
Paul Belford

WRITER
Nigel Roberts

ILLUSTRATORS
J. Otto Seibold
J.P.
Paul Belford
Mick Brownfield

PHOTOGRAPHER
Laurie Haskell

CLIENT
Waterstone's Booksellers

AGENCY
TBWA GGT Simons
Palmer/London

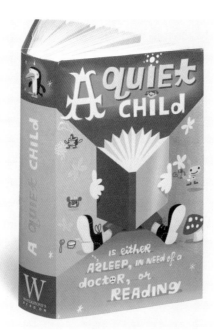

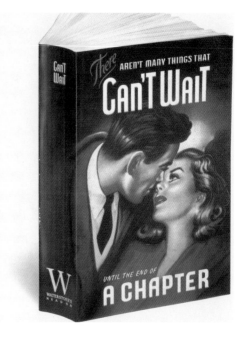

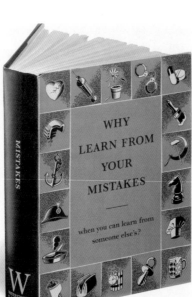

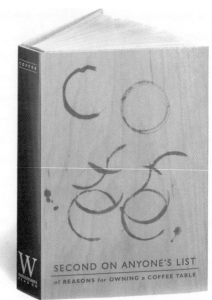

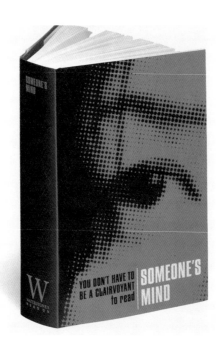

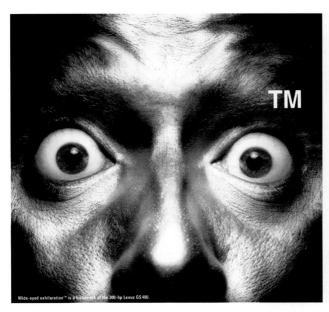

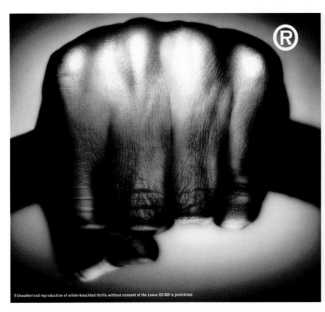

MERIT AWARD
Magazine Color Full Page
or Spread: Campaign

ART DIRECTOR
Greg Wells

WRITER
Eric Walker

PHOTOGRAPHERS
Bob Carey
Michael Ruppert

CLIENT
Lexus

AGENCY
Team One Advertising/
El Segundo

MERIT AWARD
Magazine Color Full Page
or Spread: Campaign

ART DIRECTORS
Jeff Williams
Alicia Johnson
Hal Wolverton

WRITERS
Jeff Kling
Ned McNeilage

PHOTOGRAPHERS
Terry Richardson
Michel Haddi
Melodie McDaniel

CLIENT
Miller Brewing Company

AGENCY
Wieden & Kennedy/
Portland

CLIENT
Nike International

AGENCY
Wieden & Kennedy/
Portland

WRITER
Kash Sree

PHOTOGRAPHER
Pete Seaward

MERIT AWARD
Magazine Color Full Page
or Spread: Campaign

ART DIRECTOR
Andy Fackrell

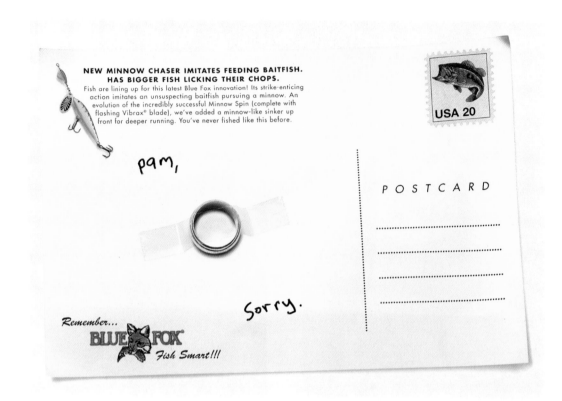

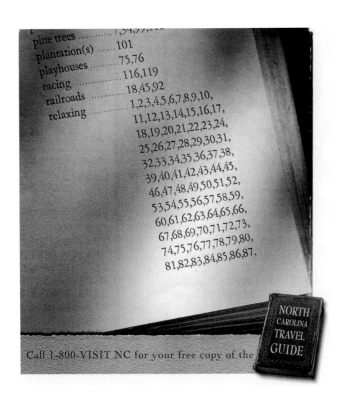

MERIT AWARD
Magazine B/W or Color
Less Than a Page: Single

ART DIRECTOR
Doug Pedersen

WRITER
Curtis Smith

PHOTOGRAPHER
Pat Staub

CLIENT
North Carolina Travel
& Tourism

AGENCY
Loeffler Ketchum
Mountjoy/Charlotte

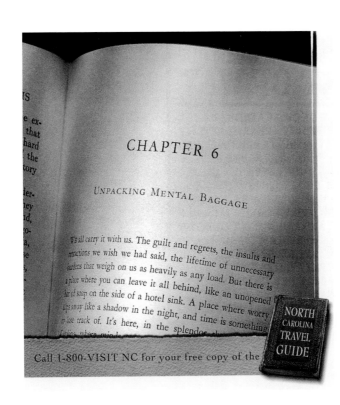

MERIT AWARD
Magazine B/W or Color
Less Than a Page: Single

ART DIRECTOR
Doug Pedersen

WRITER
Curtis Smith

PHOTOGRAPHER
Pat Staub

CLIENT
North Carolina Travel
& Tourism

AGENCY
Loeffler Ketchum
Mountjoy/Charlotte

MERIT AWARD
Magazine B/W or Color
Less Than a Page:
Campaign

ART DIRECTOR
Jon Wyville

WRITER
David Register

CLIENT
Checkered Past Records

AGENCY
Pagano Schenck & Kay/
Boston

MUSIC
FOR AN ACID RAINY DAY

SOULED AMERICAN IS ABOUT AS AMERICAN AS BASEBALL, APPLE PIE AND LETHAL INJECTION. WITH DRONING UNNATURAL SOUNDS AND EERILY BEAUTIFUL VOCALS, "FROZEN" IS MOOD MUSIC THAT'S GUARANTEED TO LEAVE YOU IN A BAD MOOD. SEND $13 TO CHECKERED PAST RECORDS. 1456 N. DAYTON ST. SUITE 205 CHICAGO, IL 60622 PHONE: (312) 932-9057 FAX: (312) 932-9063 WEB: WWW.CHECKEREDPAST.COM

SONGS
THAT WILL STICK IN YOUR HEAD LIKE AN ICE PICK

ONE MAN'S MISERY IS ANOTHER MAN'S MUSIC. JOHNNY DOWD'S WRONG SIDE OF MEMPHIS IS SOMETHING DARKER THAN BLUES. IT'S BONE-CHILLING REALITY. FROM THE FIRST NOTE, YOU'LL BE DRAWN TO THESE HAUNTING TALES OF LIFE AND ALL THAT'S WRONG WITH IT. TAKE A RIDE WITH JOHNNY AND YOU MAY NEVER COME BACK. SEND $13 TO CHECKERED PAST RECORDS. 1456 N. DAYTON ST. SUITE 205 CHICAGO, IL 60622 PHONE: (312) 932-9057 FAX: (312) 932-9063 WEB: WWW.CHECKEREDPAST.COM

UPLIFTING
IN A "GLAD I'M NOT YOU" SORT OF WAY

ONCE AGAIN, HADACOL PROVES THAT SOMETIMES NOTHING'S MORE SOOTHING THAN THE SOUND OF PAIN. WITH VENOMOUS LYRICS AND KICKIN' GUITAR LICKS, THESE GOOD OL' BOYS FROM MISSOURI WILL HAVE YOU HUMMING ALONG TO THEIR TALES OF REBELLION AND ANGST IN NO TIME. FOR THEIR LATEST RELEASE SEND $13 TO CHECKERED PAST RECORDS. 1456 NORTH DAYTON STREET SUITE 205 CHICAGO, ILLINOIS 60622 PHONE: (312) 932-9057 FAX: (312) 932-9063 WEB: WWW.CHECKEREDPAST.COM

MERIT AWARD
Outdoor: Single

ART DIRECTOR
John Gorse

WRITER
Jeremy Carr

CLIENT
The Economist

AGENCY
Abbott Mead
Vickers.BBDO/London

The pregnant pause.
Make sure
you're not the father.

The Economist

MERIT AWARD
Outdoor: Single

ART DIRECTOR
Guy Moore

WRITER
Tony Malcolm

CLIENT
The Economist

AGENCY
Abbott Mead
Vickers.BBDO/London

MERIT AWARD
Outdoor: Single

ART DIRECTOR
Michael Durban

WRITER
Tony Strong

CLIENT
The Economist

AGENCY
Abbott Mead
Vickers.BBDO/London

MERIT AWARD
Outdoor: Single

ART DIRECTOR
Tim Delaney

WRITER
Jim Newcombe

CLIENT
Ameritech/
1-800 Conference

AGENCY
Ammirati Puris Lintas/
Chicago

MERIT AWARD
Outdoor: Single

ART DIRECTOR
Lance Paull

WRITER
Stuart D'Rozario

PHOTOGRAPHER
Bill Cash

CLIENT
Volkswagen

AGENCY
Arnold Communications/
Boston

MERIT AWARD
Outdoor: Single

ART DIRECTOR
Dave Masterman

WRITER
Ed Edwards

ILLUSTRATOR
Typo Fads

CLIENT
Volkswagen Group UK

AGENCY
BMP DDB/London

MERIT AWARD
Outdoor: Single

ART DIRECTORS
Mark Schruntek
Dan Kelleher

WRITERS
Dan Kelleher
Mark Schruntek

PHOTOGRAPHER
Craig Cutler

CLIENT
Sauza Conmemorativo

AGENCY
Cliff Freeman and
Partners/New York

MERIT AWARD
Outdoor: Single

ART DIRECTORS
Rossana Bardales
Sally Overheu

WRITERS
Sally Overheu
Rossana Bardales

PHOTOGRAPHER
Criag Cutler

CLIENT
Sauza Conmemorativo

AGENCY
Cliff Freeman and
Partners/New York

MERIT AWARD
Outdoor: Single

ART DIRECTOR
Adrian An

WRITER
Ben Osbourne

CLIENT
Good in Bed

AGENCY
DDB/Sydney

MERIT AWARD
Outdoor: Single

ART DIRECTOR
Peter Holmes

WRITER
Peter Holmes

CLIENT
The Weather Network

AGENCY
Holmes & Lee/Toronto

MERIT AWARD
Outdoor: Single

ART DIRECTOR
Miguel Coimbra

WRITER
Ricardo Adolfo

PHOTOGRAPHER
Chico Prata

CLIENT
Lego

AGENCY
J. Walter Thompson
Publicidade/Alges

MERIT AWARD
Outdoor: Single

ART DIRECTOR
Rich Kohnke

WRITER
Dave Hanneken

ILLUSTRATOR
Jim McDonald

PHOTOGRAPHER
Dave Gilo

CLIENT
The Welk Resort

AGENCY
Kohnke Hanneken/
Milwaukee

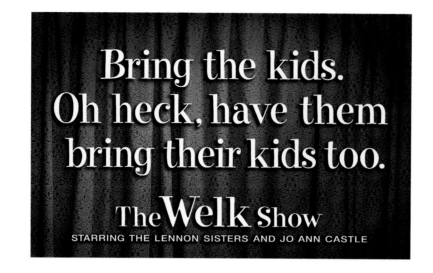

MERIT AWARD
Outdoor: Single

ART DIRECTOR
Steve Mapp

WRITER
Reed Woodson

CLIENT
Adidas

AGENCY
Leagas Delaney/
San Francisco

MERIT AWARD
Outdoor: Single

ART DIRECTOR
Myles Lord

WRITER
Brent Liebenberg

CLIENT
IMAX

AGENCY
Lowe Bull Calvert Pace/
Cape Town

MERIT AWARD
Outdoor: Single

ART DIRECTOR
John Boone

WRITER
David Oakley

CLIENT
WEND 106.5

AGENCY
The Martin Agency/
Charlotte

MERIT AWARD
Outdoor: Single

ART DIRECTOR
John Boone

WRITER
David Oakley

CLIENT
WEND 106.5

AGENCY
The Martin Agency/
Charlotte

MERIT AWARD
Outdoor: Single

ART DIRECTORS
Greg Bokor
Gerard Caputo

WRITER
Jim Garaventi

PHOTOGRAPHER
Susie Cushner

CLIENT
Swiss Army Brands

AGENCY
Mullen Advertising/
Wenham

MERIT AWARD
Outdoor: Single

ART DIRECTORS
Greg Bokor
Gerard Caputo

WRITER
Jim Garaventi

PHOTOGRAPHER
Susie Cushner

CLIENT
Swiss Army Brands

AGENCY
Mullen Advertising/
Wenham

MERIT AWARD
Outdoor: Single

ART DIRECTORS
Greg Bokor
Gerard Caputo

WRITER
Jim Garaventi

PHOTOGRAPHER
Shawn Michienzi

CLIENT
Swiss Army Brands

AGENCY
Mullen Advertising/
Wenham

CLIENT
Guinness Asia Pacific

AGENCY
Ogilvy & Mather/
Singapore

WRITER
Andy Greenaway

ILLUSTRATOR
The Lounge

PHOTOGRAPHER
Shaun Pettigrew

MERIT AWARD
Outdoor: Single

ART DIRECTOR
Eugene Cheong

MERIT AWARD
Outdoor: Single

ART DIRECTOR
Ian Grais

WRITER
Alan Russell

PHOTOGRAPHER
Anthony Redpath

CLIENT
TV Twelve

AGENCY
Palmer Jarvis DDB/
Vancouver

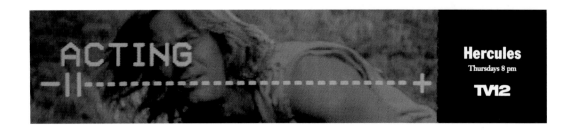

MERIT AWARD
Outdoor: Single

ART DIRECTOR
Ian Grais

WRITER
Alan Russell

PHOTOGRAPHER
Anthony Redpath

CLIENT
TV Twelve

AGENCY
Palmer Jarvis DDB/
Vancouver

MERIT AWARD
Outdoor: Single

ART DIRECTOR
Ian Grais

WRITER
Alan Russell

PHOTOGRAPHER
Anthony Redpath

CLIENT
TV Twelve

AGENCY
Palmer Jarvis DDB/
Vancouver

MERIT AWARD
Outdoor: Single

ART DIRECTOR
Ian Grais

WRITER
Alan Russell

PHOTOGRAPHER
Anthony Redpath

CLIENT
TV Twelve

AGENCY
Palmer Jarvis DDB/
Vancouver

CLIENT
Toyota

WRITER
Jay Furby

MERIT AWARD
Outdoor: Single

AGENCY
Saatchi & Saatchi/
Sydney

PHOTOGRAPHER
Simon Harsent

ART DIRECTOR
Paul Bennell

MERIT AWARD
Outdoor: Single

ART DIRECTOR
Sara Riesgo

WRITER
Raymond Hwang

CLIENT
ABC

AGENCY
TBWA/Chiat/Day/
Playa del Rey

MERIT AWARD
Outdoor: Single

ART DIRECTOR
John Shirley

WRITER
Rich Siegel

CLIENT
ABC

AGENCY
TBWA/Chiat/Day/
Playa del Rey

MERIT AWARD
Outdoor: Single

ART DIRECTOR
Sara Riesgo

WRITER
Raymond Hwang

CLIENT
ABC

AGENCY
TBWA/Chiat/Day/
Playa del Rey

MERIT AWARD
Outdoor: Single

ART DIRECTOR
Alan Lewus

WRITER
Alan Lewus

PHOTOGRAPHER
Janyon Boshoff

CLIENT
Nashua

AGENCY
TBWA Hunt Lascaris/
Johannesburg

MERIT AWARD
Outdoor: Campaign

ART DIRECTORS
Mark Schruntek
Dan Kelleher
Taras Wayner

WRITERS
Adam Chasnow
Michelle Roufa
Dan Kelleher
Mark Schruntek

PHOTOGRAPHER
Craig Cutler

CLIENT
Sauza Conmemorativo

AGENCY
Cliff Freeman and
Partners/New York

MERIT AWARD
Outdoor: Campaign

ART DIRECTORS
Mark Schruntek
Dan Kelleher
Taras Wayner

WRITERS
Adam Chasnow
Michelle Roufa
Dan Kelleher
Mark Schruntek

PHOTOGRAPHER
Craig Cutler

CLIENT
Sauza Conmemorativo

AGENCY
Cliff Freeman and
Partners/New York

MERIT AWARD
Outdoor: Campaign

ART DIRECTORS
Matt Vescovo
David Angelo
Taras Wayner
Rossana Bardales
Sally Overheu

WRITERS
Tina Hall
Michelle Roufa
Kevin Roddy
Sally Overheu
Rossana Bardales

PHOTOGRAPHER
Craig Cutler

CLIENT
Sauza Conmemorativo

AGENCY
Cliff Freeman and
Partners/New York

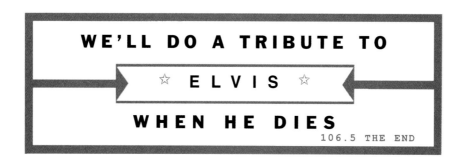

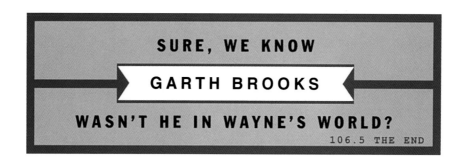

MERIT AWARD
Outdoor: Campaign

ART DIRECTOR
John Boone

WRITER
David Oakley

CLIENT
WEND 106.5

AGENCY
The Martin Agency/
Charlotte

MERIT AWARD
Outdoor: Campaign

ART DIRECTOR
Eugene Cheong

WRITER
Andy Greenaway

ILLUSTRATOR
The Lounge

PHOTOGRAPHER
Shaun Pettigrew

CLIENT
Guinness Asia Pacific

AGENCY
Ogilvy & Mather/
Singapore

CLIENT
TV Twelve

AGENCY
Palmer Jarvis DDB/
Vancouver

WRITER
Alan Russell

PHOTOGRAPHER
Anthony Redpath

MERIT AWARD
Outdoor: Campaign

ART DIRECTOR
Ian Grais

MERIT AWARD
Guerilla Advertising

ART DIRECTOR
Brad Emmett

WRITERS
Sal DeVito
Dave Brenner

CLIENT
Daffy's

AGENCY
DeVito/Verdi/New York

MERIT AWARD
Guerilla Advertising

ART DIRECTOR
Kevin Smith

WRITER
Greg Hahn

CLIENT
The Firm

AGENCY
Fallon McElligott/
Minneapolis

Wrigley Field 9-98 When Maggie told me
how much she saves at Skylab Imaging,
my arm moved, and I missed
Sosa hitting #62.

REDEEM THIS FOR:
a free 2nd set of color prints
at time of processing
—or—
a free roll of AGFA 200 27 exp film
—or—
one free 35mm color 5x7 print

"Lost snapshots" were placed in public areas in Minneapolis.
Finders can redeem "coupon" for Skylab offers.

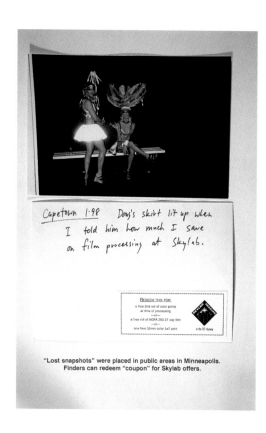

Capetown 1-98 Doug's skirt lit up when
I told him how much I save
on film processing at Skylab.

REDEEM THIS FOR:
a free 2nd set of color prints
at time of processing
—or—
a free roll of AGFA 200 27 exp film
—or—
one free 35mm color 5x7 print

"Lost snapshots" were placed in public areas in Minneapolis.
Finders can redeem "coupon" for Skylab offers.

Mpls 10-98 Dawn is happy now that she can
afford the dental work — thanks to all
the money she saves at Skylab.

REDEEM THIS FOR:
a free 2nd set of color prints
at time of processing
—or—
a free roll of AGFA 200 27 exp film
—or—
one free 35mm color 5x7 print

"Lost snapshots" were placed in public areas in Minneapolis.
Finders can redeem "coupon" for Skylab offers.

MERIT AWARD
Guerilla Advertising

ART DIRECTOR
Joe Sweet

WRITER
Joe Sweet

PHOTOGRAPHER
Joe Sweet

CLIENT
Skylab Imaging

AGENCY
Fallon McElligott/
Minneapolis

MERIT AWARD
Guerilla Advertising

ART DIRECTOR
Joe Sweet

WRITER
Joe Sweet

PHOTOGRAPHER
Joe Sweet

CLIENT
Skylab Imaging

AGENCY
Fallon McElligott/
Minneapolis

MERIT AWARD
Guerilla Advertising

ART DIRECTOR
Joe Sweet

WRITER
Joe Sweet

PHOTOGRAPHER
Joe Sweet

CLIENT
Skylab Imaging

AGENCY
Fallon McElligott/
Minneapolis

MERIT AWARD
Guerilla Advertising

ART DIRECTOR
Wade Koniakowski

WRITER
Phil Glist

CLIENT
Gold's Gym Franchising

AGENCY
JACK/Venice

MERIT AWARD
Guerilla Advertising

ART DIRECTOR
Theo Ferreira

WRITER
Alistair Morgan

CLIENT
Virgin Atlantic

AGENCY
Net#Work/
Johannesburg

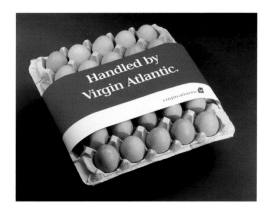

MERIT AWARD
Guerilla Advertising

ART DIRECTOR
Glenn Jameson

WRITER
Nigel Corbett

ILLUSTRATOR
Keren McLennen

CLIENT
Work and Income NZ

AGENCY
The New Colenso/
Wellington

BBDO/Guerrero Ortega. Very, very persuasive advertising.

MERIT AWARD
Trade B/W Full Page
or Spread: Single

ART DIRECTOR
Simon Yung

WRITER
David Guerrero

PHOTOGRAPHER
Neal Oshima

CLIENT
BBDO/Guerrero Ortega

AGENCY
BBDO/Guerrero
Ortega/Salcedo Village

JOKES THAT APPEAL TO 99.9% OF THE WORLD
or
HUMOR FOR IDIOTS.

Let's face it: when you're a moron, finding something to laugh at is not a problem. The brain of an idiot will laugh at the mere sight of a plunger. But when you're cursed with superhuman, demigodian intelligence, it becomes more and more difficult to appease your immense brain. It is like bringing gifts before Pharaoh: if you offer your brain anything less than the Hope Diamond it might throw you to the lions. Such is the curse of having eye-melting brilliance. Which is why we recommend occasionally taking your brain on a descent into the teeming masses of the great unwashed. There's no quicker way to make your brain realize how magnificently utopian its existence really is than by forcing it to rub neurons with the common rabble in some seedy waterfront dive.

COMEDIC SLUMMING

Walk down any street and you will soon find yourself surrounded by insipid cretins. Do not, under any circumstances, tell any jokes about electromagnetic induction or the half-life of antineutrinos. Instead, pick out someone in the crowd who is different; making fun of the unfortunate is a guaranteed laugh riot. Simply identify someone who is not blending in perfectly and call attention to his defect by pointing and shouting things like, "Hey fatso! You're really fat, fat boy!" or "Hey, old blind woman! You're really blind, old blind woman!" Soon you will have a crowd around you cheering you on, ready to laugh at any idiotic thing you say. They will lift you up on their shoulders and parade you around the city, begging you to make fun of someone else's deformity.

Every once in awhile you can throw in a side-splitting observation such as, "Hey, look at that plunger!" Soon all the cretins will want to have sex with you, which is a good time to leave.

IDIOT SEX

Idiots are everywhere. Every idiot is like a little idiot factory, churning out more and more idiots all the time. This, despite the fact that whenever idiots are naked they tend to point and laugh at each other, leaving little time for sex. Because there are so damn many of them, a few inevitably manage to assume positions of power, becoming leaders of countries or directors of movies like *Titanic* or denying funding for altruistic causes such as the Dublin Nuclear Humor Testing Facility or, even more appallingly, deciding that *The Wacky Electromagnetic Induction Hour* starring Rick Dublin would not make a good replacement for *Seinfeld*. Those of you who can use the telephone without injuring yourself are invited to call us at 213-960-3522 (L.A.) or 612-332-8864 (Mpls.).

DUBLIN
PRODUCTIONS

MERIT AWARD
Trade B/W Full Page
or Spread: Single

ART DIRECTOR
Steve Mitchell

WRITER
Doug Adkins

CLIENT
Dublin Productions

AGENCY
Hunt Adkins/Minneapolis

MERIT AWARD
Trade Color Full Page
or Spread: Single

ART DIRECTOR
Jim Amadeo

WRITER
Spencer Deadrick

PHOTOGRAPHER
Scott Goodwin

CLIENT
InterNutria

AGENCY
Clarke Goward
Advertising/Boston

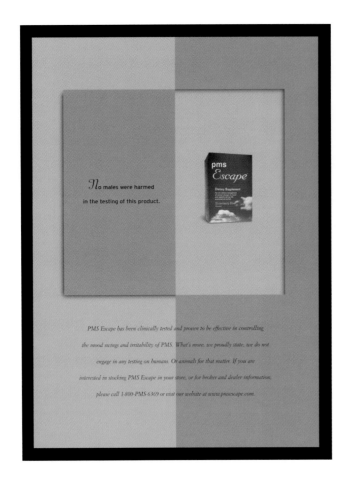

MERIT AWARD
Trade Color Full Page
or Spread: Single

ART DIRECTOR
Danny Boone

WRITER
Rob McPherson

CLIENT
Nikon

AGENCY
Fallon McElligott/
Minneapolis

A bomb explodes.
Ten thousand miles away,
you feel the impact.

The world's most interesting magazine.

Rumors fly.
The truth arrives at a more reliable pace.

The world's most interesting magazine.

Was it show biz?
Was it science?
Yes.

The world's most interesting magazine.

MERIT AWARD
Trade Color Full Page
or Spread: Single

ART DIRECTOR
Bob Barrie

WRITER
Dean Buckhorn

PHOTOGRAPHER
Khalil Senosi

CLIENT
TIME

AGENCY
Fallon McElligott/
Minneapolis

MERIT AWARD
Trade Color Full Page
or Spread: Single

ART DIRECTOR
Bob Barrie

WRITER
Dean Buckhorn

PHOTOGRAPHER
Jeff Slocomb

CLIENT
TIME

AGENCY
Fallon McElligott/
Minneapolis

MERIT AWARD
Trade Color Full Page
or Spread: Single

ART DIRECTOR
Bob Barrie

WRITER
Dean Buckhorn

PHOTOGRAPHER
Mark M. Lawrence

CLIENT
TIME

AGENCY
Fallon McElligott/
Minneapolis

MERIT AWARD
Trade Color Full Page
or Spread: Single

ART DIRECTOR
Jimmy Bonner

WRITER
Denzil Strickland

PHOTOGRAPHERS
Jim Arndt
Kelli Coggins

CLIENT
Twin Eagles
Cattle Company

AGENCY
FGI/Chapel Hill

MERIT AWARD
Trade Color Full Page
or Spread: Single

ART DIRECTOR
Jimmy Bonner

WRITER
Denzil Strickland

PHOTOGRAPHERS
Jim Arndt
Kelli Coggins

CLIENT
Twin Eagles
Cattle Company

AGENCY
FGI/Chapel Hill

MERIT AWARD
Trade Color Full Page
or Spread: Single

ART DIRECTOR
Steve Mitchell

WRITER
Doug Adkins

PHOTOGRAPHER
Rick Dublin

CLIENT
Dublin Productions

AGENCY
Hunt Adkins/Minneapolis

MERIT AWARD
Trade Color Full Page
or Spread: Single

ART DIRECTOR
Steve Mitchell

WRITER
Doug Adkins

PHOTOGRAPHER
Rick Dublin

CLIENT
Dublin Productions

AGENCY
Hunt Adkins/Minneapolis

MERIT AWARD
Trade Color Full Page
or Spread: Single

ART DIRECTOR
Steve Mitchell

WRITER
Doug Adkins

PHOTOGRAPHER
Rick Dublin

CLIENT
Dublin Productions

AGENCY
Hunt Adkins/Minneapolis

NO ANIMALS WERE HARMED IN THE
MAKING OF THIS PRODUCT. YET.

Boker's Folding Hunter No. 2006

The highly prized red bone handle fits your hand. The 440C stainless blade fits your hunt.
FOR A FREE CATALOG OF OVER 200 KNIVES, 1.800.992.6537, WWW.BOKERUSA.COM
OR WRITE TO US AT BOKER USA, INC., 1550 BALSAM ST. LAKEWOOD, CO 80215

BÖKER
BAUMWERK·SOLINGEN
TRUSTED SINCE 1869.

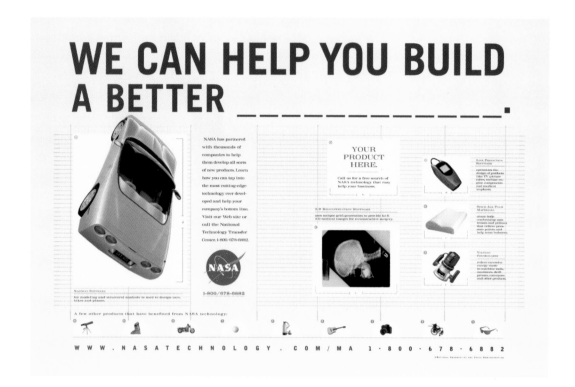

THERE ARE LOTS OF STUPID WAYS
TO REACH BRITISH COLUMBIANS.

Stupid Way #31: Avalanche-Assisted Direct Mail

Thankfully, there's a smarter way to reach British Columbians. Namely, book your ads with The Vancouver Sun and The Province. With over 1,249,000 readers a week, circulation and subscriptions are up in both papers and more people are signing up every day. In fact, our combined daily readership is 910,000 and has shown steady growth over the past three years. And with good reason. Our new printing presses deliver our very best four-colour reproduction yet, with sharp, crystal-clear images every time. And besides, who wants to waste their media dollars on Saint-Bernards and rescue teams?

THE INTELLIGENT CHOICE

THERE ARE LOTS OF STUPID WAYS
TO REACH BRITISH COLUMBIANS.

Stupid Way #27: Air Crash Survivor Transit Shelters (ACSTS)

You don't have to be an intellectual to figure out that it's just plain smart to book your ads in The Vancouver Sun and The Province. With the power of both papers, you'll reach a combined 910,000 readers on any given weekday. In fact, readership in The Province has risen 10 percent over the last two years, while The Sun, on the other hand, has 526,000 daily readers and counting. Plus, our new printing presses deliver our finest four-colour reproduction ever—which is a fact you may or may not appreciate if you happen to find yourself in a rapidly descending aircraft.

THE INTELLIGENT CHOICE

MERIT AWARD
Trade Color Full Page
or Spread: Single

ART DIRECTOR
Mark Mizgala

WRITER
James Lee

ILLUSTRATORS
Margo Davies Leclair
Visual Sense

CLIENT
Pacific Press

AGENCY
Palmer Jarvis DDB/
Vancouver

MERIT AWARD
Trade Color Full Page
or Spread: Single

ART DIRECTOR
Mark Mizgala

WRITER
James Lee

ILLUSTRATORS
Margo Davies Leclair
Visual Sense

CLIENT
Pacific Press

AGENCY
Palmer Jarvis DDB/
Vancouver

MERIT AWARD
Trade Color Full Page
or Spread: Single

ART DIRECTOR
Mark Mizgala

WRITER
James Lee

ILLUSTRATORS
Margo Davies Leclair
Visual Sense

CLIENT
Pacific Press

AGENCY
Palmer Jarvis DDB/
Vancouver

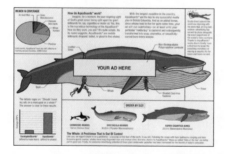

IT COMES IN A NICE SHADE OF BLUE.

JUST LIKE THE SKY USED TO.

THE ELECTRIC CAR IS HERE.

1.800.25ELECTRIC or www.gmev.com

MERIT AWARD
Trade Color Full Page
or Spread: Single

ART DIRECTOR
Mike Mazza

WRITER
Jack Harding

PHOTOGRAPHER
R.J. Muna

CLIENT
EV1/General Motors

AGENCY
Publicis & Hal Riney/
San Francisco

Bloods

Robaire and Hogshead

Crips

We've moved to a neighborhood that works as late as we do.

Now in Venice, Robaire and Hogshead, a freelance creative department, 905 Electric Ave. Loft C Venice, CA 90291 phone 310.452.6222 fax 452.0022 rohog@gts.net

MERIT AWARD
Trade Color Full Page
or Spread: Single

ART DIRECTORS
John Domas
Jean Robaire

WRITERS
Dave Holloway
Sally Hogshead

CLIENT
Robaire and Hogshead

AGENCY
Robaire and Hogshead/
Venice

MERIT AWARD
Trade Color Full Page
or Spread: Single

ART DIRECTOR
Jean Robaire

WRITER
Sally Hogshead

CLIENT
Michael Ruppert
Photography

AGENCY
Robaire and Hogshead/
Venice

MERIT AWARD
Trade Color Full Page
or Spread: Single

ART DIRECTOR
Jeff Labbe

WRITERS
Bob Moore
Ian Reichenthal

PHOTOGRAPHERS
Elliott Moore
Sally Schoolmaster
Stock

CLIENT
Ann Sacks

AGENCY
Wieden & Kennedy/
Portland

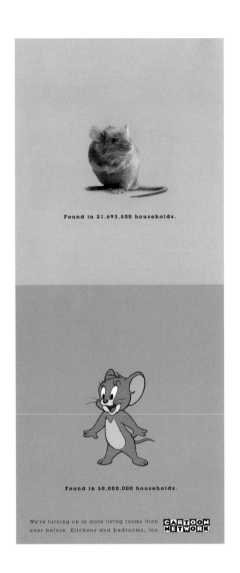

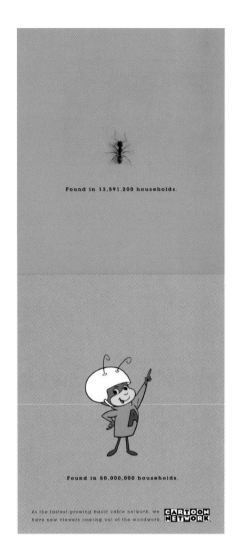

MERIT AWARD
Trade B/W or Color
Any Size: Campaign

ART DIRECTORS
Taras Wayner
Rossana Bardales

WRITER
Adam Chasnow

CLIENT
FOX Sports

AGENCY
Cliff Freeman and
Partners/New York

THE TRUTH BEHIND TV DEMOGRAPHICS:

While forecasting the audience of adult viewers for our seven hour block of Super Bowl Pregame programming, we discovered that other networks have been counting this hermaphrodite as both a male and female viewer. At FOX, we find this misleading tactic reprehensible. That's because we know we'll deliver more adults, 18-34 and 18-49, than the NBA, NHL and MLB combined.* Besides, our researchers easily concluded that this is indeed a woman. The pouty lips were a dead giveaway.

The FOX Super Bowl Pregame block of programming, January 31, 1999, 11:00 am to 6:18 pm ET. For more information contact Jim Burnette, Senior Vice President of Sales, at 212-556-2431.

THE TRUTH BEHIND TV DEMOGRAPHICS:

Some networks have been known to count Alexander and Daniel as two separate viewers to inflate their ratings estimates. During the seven hour block of Super Bowl Pregame programming, FOX will deliver more adult viewers, 18-34 and 18-49, than the four networks' average during Primetime.* And you can be sure each and every one of them will have their own brain stem.

The FOX Super Bowl Pregame block of programming, January 31, 1999, 11:00 am to 6:18 pm ET. For more information contact Jim Burnette, Senior Vice President of Sales, at 212-556-2431.

THE TRUTH BEHIND TV DEMOGRAPHICS:

Ray has a disorder which causes him to randomly assume multiple identities across a variety of demographic profiles. Some networks might pad their ratings estimates by counting Ray as many as 23 times. During the seven hour block of Super Bowl Pregame programming, FOX will only count Ray when he's fully medicated, making him just one of over 89 million adults, 18-49,* you'll reach.

The FOX Super Bowl Pregame block of programming, January 31, 1999, 11:00 am to 6:18 pm ET. For more information contact Jim Burnette, Senior Vice President of Sales, at 212-556-2431.

Yes, but can he beat out Margaret Thatcher? There are people whose ideas and beliefs have undeniably shaped our lives and our future. As the millennium draws near, TIME Magazine will announce the TIME 100. The definitive list of the most influential men and women of the past 100 years. Who will it be? Look for our six special issues and six CBS prime time shows. "Leaders and Revolutionaries" on newsstands April 6.

If anyone could buy our vote, it would probably be him. As the 20th century draws to a close, TIME Magazine will announce The TIME 100. The definitive list of the 100 individuals whose ideas and works have shaped our past and will continue to influence our future. Who will make the cut? Who won't? Look for our six special issues and six CBS prime time shows. "Leaders and Revolutionaries" on newsstands April 6.

Obviously, it's not a popularity contest. Over the past 100 years, there have been individuals who have irreversibly shaped our lives and our future. As the new millennium draws near, TIME Magazine presents the TIME 100. The definitive list of the 100 most influential people of the century. Who will make the list? Who will be left off? Look for our six special issues and the six provocative CBS prime time programs.

Each reinvention of herself will be considered equally. There are certain people whose words and actions have influenced our lives and our culture. As the 20th century draws to a close, TIME Magazine will present The TIME 100. The definitive list of the century's 100 most influential people. Who will make the cut? Look for six special issues and six CBS prime time programs. "Artists and Entertainers" on newsstands June 1.

MERIT AWARD
Trade B/W or Color
Any Size: Campaign

ART DIRECTOR
Bob Barrie

WRITER
Dean Buckhorn

PHOTOGRAPHERS
John Rooney
George Lange
Cinergi Pictures
Entertainment

CLIENT
TIME 100

AGENCY
Fallon McElligott/
Minneapolis

MERIT AWARD
Trade B/W or Color
Any Size: Campaign

ART DIRECTOR
John Liegey

WRITER
Dean Buckhorn

ILLUSTRATORS
Dave Danz
Mike McMillen

PHOTOGRAPHER
Tony Martin

CLIENT
VCU Adcenter

AGENCY
Fallon McElligott/
Minneapolis

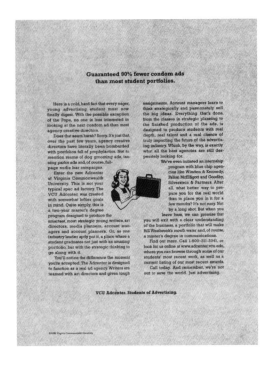

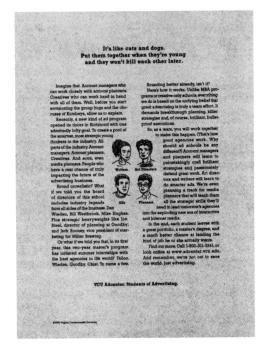

MERIT AWARD
Trade B/W or Color
Any Size: Campaign

ART DIRECTOR
Jimmy Bonner

WRITER
Denzil Strickland

PHOTOGRAPHERS
Jim Arndt
Kelli Coggins

CLIENT
Twin Eagles
Cattle Company

AGENCY
FGI/Chapel Hill

MERIT AWARD
Trade B/W or Color
Any Size: Campaign

ART DIRECTOR
Guy Shelmerdine

WRITER
Steve O'Brien

PHOTOGRAPHERS
Bruce Dale
Tim Page
Henri Cartier Bresson

CLIENT
Fahrenheit Films

AGENCY
Ground Zero/
Santa Monica

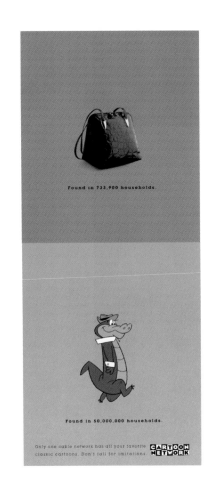

MERIT AWARD
Trade B/W or Color
Any Size: Campaign

ART DIRECTOR
Joe Paprocki

WRITER
Ron Huey

PHOTOGRAPHER
Dave Keisgan

CLIENT
Cartoon Network

AGENCY
Huey/Paprocki/Atlanta

MERIT AWARD
Trade B/W or Color
Any Size: Campaign

ART DIRECTOR
Steve Mitchell

WRITER
Doug Adkins

PHOTOGRAPHER
Rick Dublin

CLIENT
Dublin Productions

AGENCY
Hunt Adkins/Minneapolis

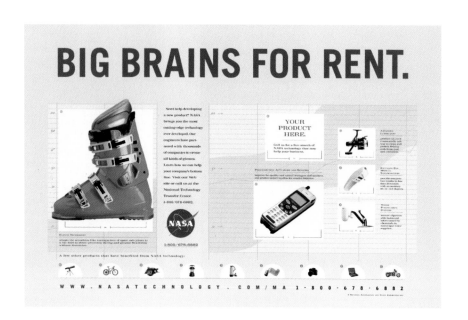

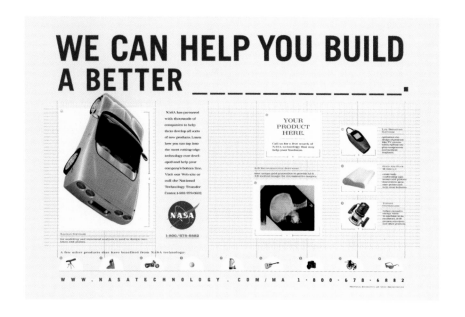

MERIT AWARD
Trade B/W or Color
Any Size: Campaign

ART DIRECTOR
Noel Ritter

WRITER
Raymond McKinney

PHOTOGRAPHER
Kip Dawkins

CLIENT
NASA

AGENCY
The Martin Agency/
Richmond

MERIT AWARD
Trade B/W or Color
Any Size: Campaign

ART DIRECTOR
Paul Laffy

WRITERS
Ben Resnikoff
Edward Boches

CLIENT
Money Magazine

AGENCY
Mullen Advertising/
Wenham

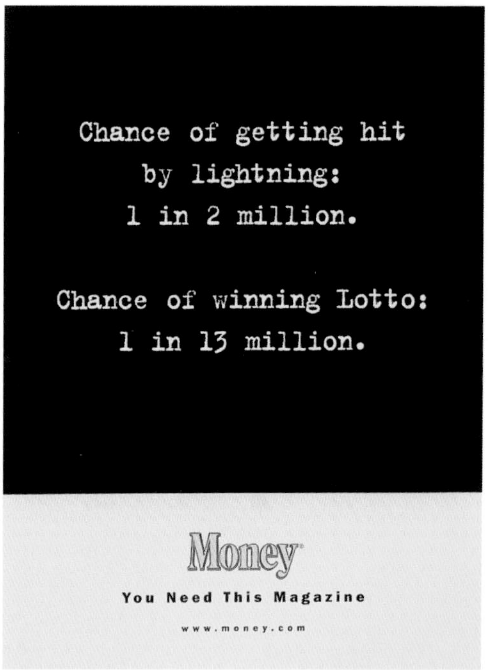

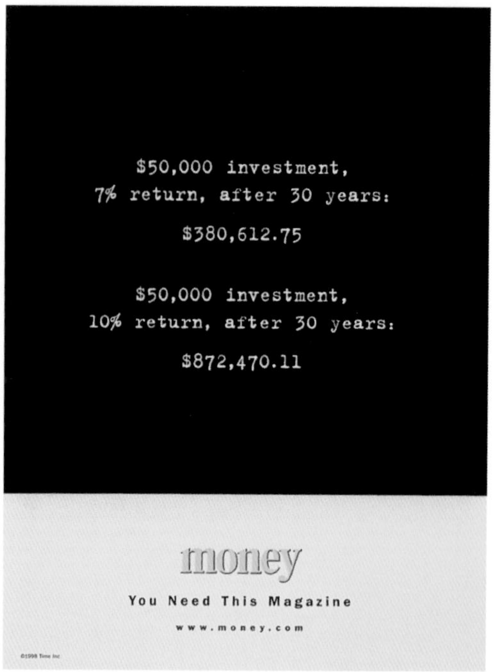

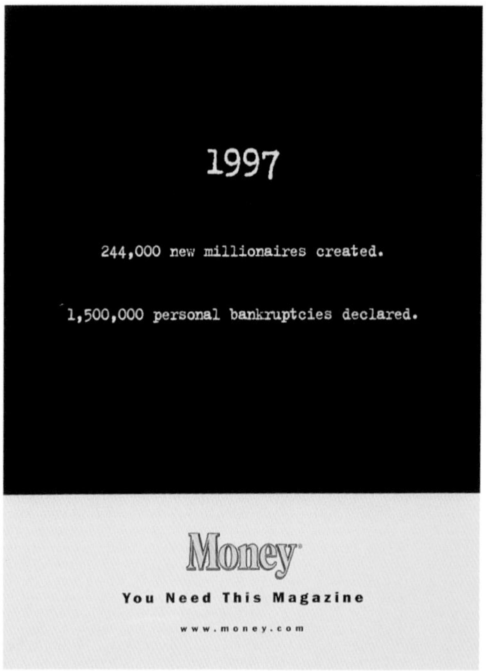

Chance of getting hit
by lightning:
1 in 2 million.

Chance of winning Lotto:
1 in 13 million.

Money
You Need This Magazine
www.money.com

$50,000 investment,
7% return, after 30 years:
$380,612.75

$50,000 investment,
10% return, after 30 years:
$872,470.11

money
You Need This Magazine
www.money.com

1997

244,000 new millionaires created.

1,500,000 personal bankruptcies declared.

Money
You Need This Magazine
www.money.com

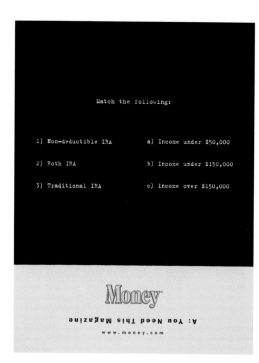

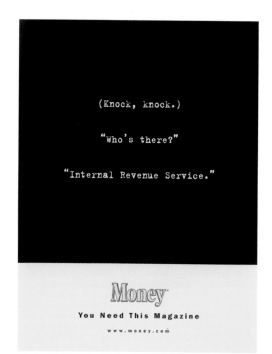

Taxpayer Relief Act of 1997
SEC.408A. ROTH IRAS

DEFINITIONS

(i) adjusted gross income shall be determined in the same manner as under section 219(g)(3), except that any amount included in gross income under subsection (d)(3) shall not be taken into account and the deduction under section 219 shall be taken into account, and

(ii) the applicable dollar amount is—

(I) in the case of a taxpayer filing a joint return, $150,000,

(II) in the case of any other taxpayer (other than a married individual filing a separate return), $95,000, and

(III) in the case of a married individual filing a separate return, zero.

Money
You Need This Magazine
www.money.com

Match the following:

1) Non-deductible IRA   a) Income under $50,000

2) Roth IRA   b) Income under $150,000

3) Traditional IRA   c) Income over $150,000

Money
A: You Need This Magazine
www.money.com

(Knock, knock.)

"Who's there?"

"Internal Revenue Service."

Money
You Need This Magazine
www.money.com

MERIT AWARD
Trade B/W or Color
Any Size: Campaign

ART DIRECTOR
Paul Laffy

WRITERS
Edward Boches
Ben Resnikoff

CLIENT
Money Magazine

AGENCY
Mullen Advertising/
Wenham

MERIT AWARD
Trade B/W or Color
Any Size: Campaign

ART DIRECTOR
Jean Robaire

WRITER
Sally Hogshead

CLIENT
Michael Ruppert
Photography

AGENCY
Robaire and Hogshead/
Venice

TIME TO SWITCH TO TOSHIBA PROFESSIONAL LIGHTING.

AVAILABLE EXCLUSIVELY AT NOVENA LIGHTING, BLK 206, TOA PAYOH NORTH, #01-1215, S'PORE 310206. TEL: 255-7845 FAX: 253-2435.

TIME TO SWITCH TO TOSHIBA PROFESSIONAL LIGHTING.

AVAILABLE EXCLUSIVELY AT NOVENA LIGHTING, BLK 206, TOA PAYOH NORTH, #01-1215, S'PORE 310206. TEL: 255-7845 FAX: 253-2435.

MERIT AWARD
Trade B/W or Color
Any Size: Campaign

ART DIRECTOR
Gregory Yeo

WRITER
Justin Lim

ILLUSTRATORS
Yau Digital Imaging
Felix Wang

PHOTOGRAPHER
Eric Seow

CLIENT
Novena Lighting

AGENCY
TBWA/Singapore

TIME TO SWITCH TO TOSHIBA PROFESSIONAL LIGHTING.

AVAILABLE EXCLUSIVELY AT NOVENA LIGHTING, BLK 206, TOA PAYOH NORTH, #01-1215, S'PORE 310206. TEL: 255-7845 FAX: 253-2435.

MERIT AWARD
Trade B/W or Color
Any Size: Campaign

ART DIRECTOR
Jeff Labbe

WRITERS
Bob Moore
Ian Reichenthal

PHOTOGRAPHERS
Elliott Moore
Sally Schoolmaster

CLIENT
Ann Sacks

AGENCY
Wieden & Kennedy/
Portland

MERIT AWARD
Collateral: Brochures

ART DIRECTORS
Clif Wong
Lance Paull

WRITER
Lance Jensen

CLIENT
Volkswagen

AGENCY
Arnold Communications/
Boston

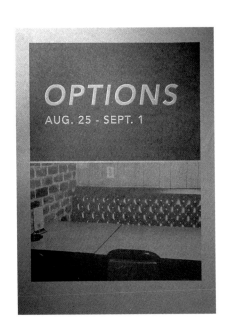

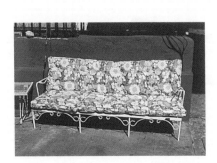

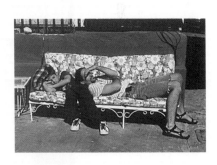

CLIENT
Mohawk Paper Mills

AGENCY
Cahan & Associates/
San Francisco

DESIGNERS
Kevin Roberson
Bob Dinetz

PHOTOGRAPHERS
Bob Dinetz
Kevin Roberson

ART DIRECTOR
Bill Cahan

WRITERS
Kevin Roberson
Bob Dinetz

ILLUSTRATOR
Riccardo Vecchio

MERIT AWARD
Collateral: Brochures

MERIT AWARD
Collateral: Brochures

ART DIRECTOR
James Victore

WRITER
Sally Hogshead

CLIENT
Portfolio Center

AGENCY
Portfolio Center

MERIT AWARD
Collateral: Brochures

ART DIRECTOR
Scott MacGregor

WRITER
Michael McKay

PHOTOGRAPHER
Smith/Nelson

CLIENT
Advertising Club
of Los Angeles/
Belding Awards

AGENCY
TBWA/Chiat/Day/
Playa del Rey

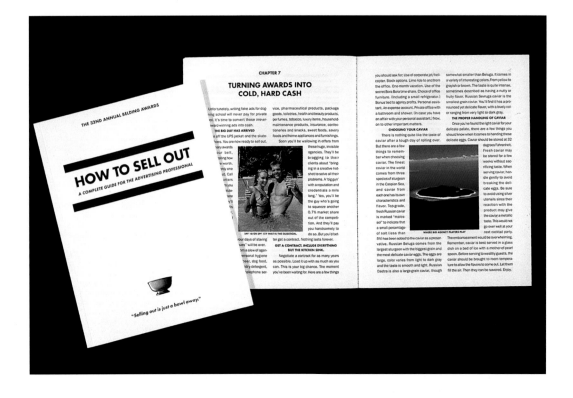

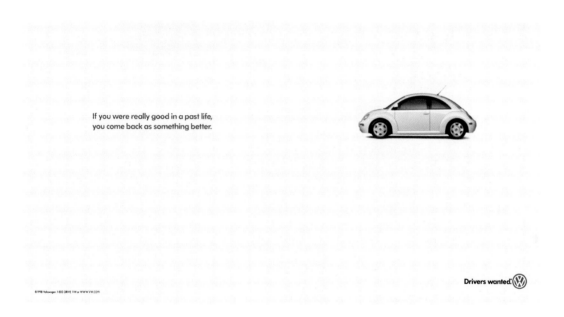

If you were really good in a past life,
you come back as something better.

©1998 Volkswagen. 1-800 DRIVE VW or WWW.VW.com

Drivers wanted. VW

MERIT AWARD
Collateral Direct Mail:
Single

ART DIRECTOR
Dana Neibert

WRITERS
Ming Lai
Craig Evans

CLIENT
San Diego Convention
& Visitors Bureau

AGENCY
Di Zinno Thompson/
San Diego

MERIT AWARD
Collateral Direct Mail:
Single

ART DIRECTOR
Dawn McCarthy

WRITER
Dean Buckhorn

PHOTOGRAPHER
Kim Puliti

CLIENT
Minneapolis Art Directors/
Copywriters Club

AGENCY
Fallon McElligott/
Minneapolis

MERIT AWARD
Collateral Direct Mail:
Single

ART DIRECTOR
Brock Davis

WRITER
Brock Davis

PHOTOGRAPHER
Curtis Johnson

CLIENT
Curtis Johnson and
Associates

AGENCY
Hunt Adkins/Minneapolis

MERIT AWARD
Collateral Direct Mail:
Single

ART DIRECTOR
Mike Kubat

WRITER
Doug Adkins

DESIGNER
Mike Kubat

PHOTOGRAPHERS
Bill Phelps
Patrick Fox

CLIENT
Domtar Papers

AGENCY
Hunt Adkins/Minneapolis

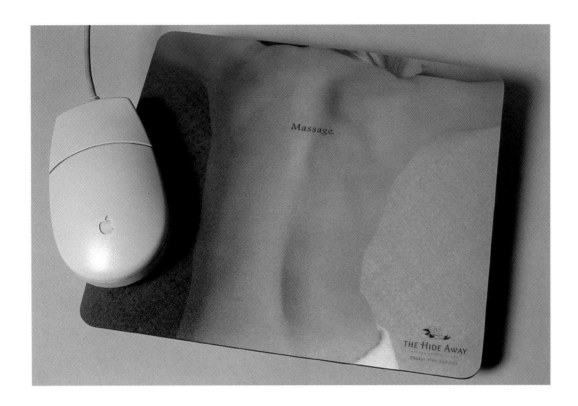

MERIT AWARD
Collateral Direct Mail:
Single

ART DIRECTOR
Kevin Ng

WRITER
Simon Kornberg

PHOTOGRAPHER
Kevin Orpin

CLIENT
The Hide Away Herbal
Aromatic Spa

AGENCY
Leo Burnett/Hong Kong

MERIT AWARD
Collateral Direct Mail:
Single

ART DIRECTOR
Don Shelford

WRITER
Andy Carrigan

PHOTOGRAPHER
Don Shelford

CLIENT
Triangle Brick

AGENCY
McKinney & Silver/
Raleigh

**WHY DO PEOPLE ASSUME
BRICKS ARE STUPID.
BRICKS AREN'T STUPID.**

You may not even realize you're saying it. Most people don't. But when you see something a little odd or stupid, like a dog chasing a moving car tire for the umpteenth time, you tend to think, "Dumb as a brick." Right? (It's okay, this poking fun at brick is a natural phenomenon as there's something kind of funny about an object that just sits there.) But consider for a moment if you were building a new home. Or putting a wall at the end of your driveway. Or building a barbecue pit in your backyard. Brick lasts up to 40% longer than many other building materials. It withstands annoying natural occurrences like hurricanes, fires and insects. Brick even withstands a few occurrences that

aren't so natural. Like a drunk driver plowing into your new brick wall. How dumb are bricks now? Truth is, there's nothing stronger or more lasting than brick. Did you know that just three bricks have the strength to support an entire Boeing 747 aircraft? Now that may not get your new home built quicker. But it sure tells you where your construction stands if Hurricane Henrietta decides she's going to blow through town. Of course, there's one advantage to brick we haven't mentioned: brick gives your home a more classic look. Ever notice what stands out when you're driving through one of those quaint, postcard towns? Brick. Not to mention these homes have been standing for over a hundred years. Many of them twice that. Do you have any idea what these homes

are worth? Even if you don't live in a Charleston or Williamsburg, brick increases the value of your home significantly because it's what people admire most when they're looking to buy. Right down to the brick fireplace. (A brick garage is equally appealing to families with teens who play the drums. Brick is also soundproof, you see.) Of course, all this neat and tidy information wouldn't be complete without telling you that brick is also fuel efficient. Brick insulates in winter and cools in summer. So you can expect lower heating and air conditioning bills in your home for say, oh, a hundred years. After all, that's the life expectancy of just one dumb brick.

Triangle Brick
800-672-8547

MERIT AWARD
CollateraL Direct Mail:
Campaign

ART DIRECTORS
Lance Paull
Karl Weld

WRITERS
Lance Jensen
David Weist

PHOTOGRAPHER
Bill Cash

CLIENT
Volkswagen

AGENCY
Arnold Communications/
Boston

Less flower. More power.

Drivers wanted. VW

© 1998 Volkswagen. 1 800 DRIVE VW or WWW.VW.COM

MERIT AWARD
Collateral Direct Mail:
Campaign

ART DIRECTOR
Lance Paull

WRITER
Dana Satterwhite

PHOTOGRAPHER
Bill Cash

CLIENT
Volkswagen

AGENCY
Arnold Communications/
Boston

Tell your folks they raised tuition.

How to cruise through history.

MERIT AWARD
Collateral Direct Mail:
Campaign

ART DIRECTOR
Greg Rowan

WRITER
Randy Stein

PHOTOGRAPHER
Greg Rowan

CLIENT
Slickity Jim's

AGENCY
BBDO/Vancouver

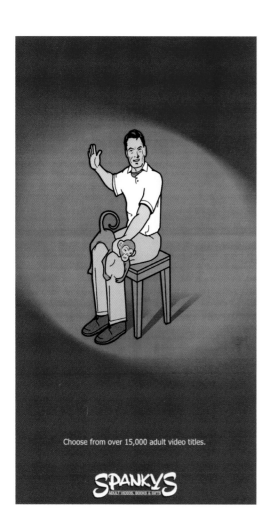

Choose from over 15,000 adult video titles.

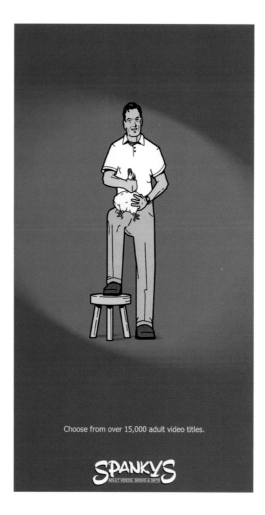

Choose from over 15,000 adult video titles.

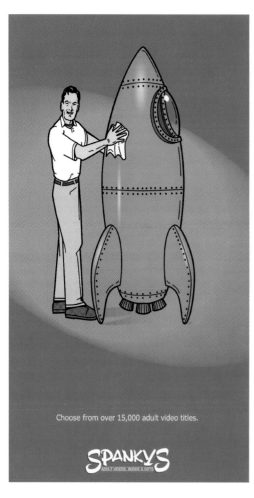

Choose from over 15,000 adult video titles.

Choose from over 15,000 adult video titles.

MERIT AWARD
Collateral Direct Mail:
Campaign

ART DIRECTOR
Dave Lugin

WRITER
Debbie Lugin

ILLUSTRATOR
Dave Lugin

CLIENT
Spanky's

AGENCY
Dal Design/Seal Beach

MERIT AWARD
Collateral: Point of
Purchase and In-Store

ART DIRECTORS
Mark Cohen
Michael Cohen

WRITERS
Mark Cohen
Michael Cohen

ILLUSTRATOR
Paul Burton

CLIENT
Wing Zone

AGENCY
Bayless & Partners/Atlanta

MERIT AWARD
Collateral: Point of
Purchase and In-Store

ART DIRECTOR
Jeff Terwilliger

WRITER
Michael Hart

ILLUSTRATOR
Brad Palm

PHOTOGRAPHER
Joe Michl
Perry Hanson

CLIENT
Caribou Coffee

AGENCY
Carmichael Lynch/
Minneapolis

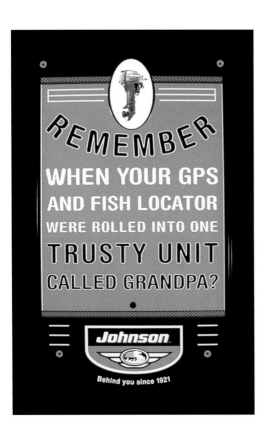

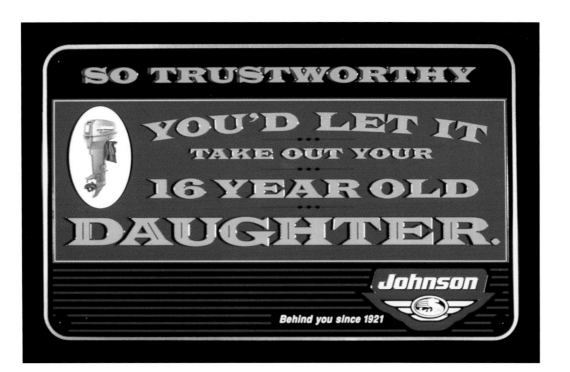

MERIT AWARD
Collateral: Point of
Purchase and In-Store

ART DIRECTOR
Glenn Gray

WRITER
Steve Casey

CLIENT
Outboard Marine
Corporation

AGENCY
Carmichael Lynch/
Minneapolis

MERIT AWARD
Collateral: Point of
Purchase and In-Store

ART DIRECTOR
Glenn Gray

WRITER
Steve Casey

CLIENT
Outboard Marine
Corporation

AGENCY
Carmichael Lynch/
Minneapolis

MERIT AWARD
Collateral: Point of
Purchase and In-Store

ART DIRECTOR
Glenn Gray

WRITER
Steve Casey

CLIENT
Outboard Marine
Corporation

AGENCY
Carmichael Lynch/
Minneapolis

MERIT AWARD
Collateral: Point of
Purchase and In-Store

ART DIRECTOR
Jerome Marucci

WRITERS
Michael Herlehy
Nick Pipitone
Jerome Marucci

ILLUSTRATOR
Jerome Marucci

PHOTOGRAPHER
Tim Waite

CLIENT
Kist Bottling Company

AGENCY
The Consortium/
Milwaukee

MERIT AWARD
Collateral: Point of
Purchase and In-Store

ART DIRECTOR
Jerome Marucci

WRITERS
Michael Herlehy
Nick Pipitone
Jerome Marucci

ILLUSTRATOR
Jerome Marucci

PHOTOGRAPHER
Tim Waite

CLIENT
Kist Bottling Company

AGENCY
The Consortium/
Milwaukee

MERIT AWARD
Collateral: Point of
Purchase and In-Store

ART DIRECTOR
Goh Wee Kim

WRITER
Farrokh Madon

ILLUSTRATOR
Yau Digital Imaging

PHOTOGRAPHER
Eric Seow

CLIENT
Koning

AGENCY
Galaxy/Singapore

MERIT AWARD
Collateral: Point of
Purchase and In-Store

ART DIRECTOR
Goh Wee Kim

WRITER
Farrokh Madon

ILLUSTRATOR
Yau Digital Imaging

PHOTOGRAPHER
Eric Seow

CLIENT
Koning

AGENCY
Galaxy/Singapore

MERIT AWARD
Collateral: Point of
Purchase and In-Store

ART DIRECTOR
Ng Tian It

WRITER
Troy Lim

PHOTOGRAPHERS
Poon
One-Twenty-One

CLIENT
The Tricon Restaurants

AGENCY
INK/Singapore

MERIT AWARD
Collateral: Point of
Purchase and In-Store

ART DIRECTORS
Greg Bokor
Gerard Caputo

WRITERS
Jim Garaventi

PHOTOGRAPHER
Russ Quackenbush

CLIENT
Swiss Army Brands

AGENCY
Mullen Advertising/
Wenham

MERIT AWARD
Collateral: Point of
Purchase and In-Store

ART DIRECTORS
Greg Bokor
Gerard Caputo

WRITER
Jim Garaventi

PHOTOGRAPHER
Shawn Michienzi

CLIENT
Swiss Army Brands

AGENCY
Mullen Advertising/
Wenham

MERIT AWARD
Collateral: Point of
Purchase and In-Store

ART DIRECTORS
Greg Bokor
Gerard Caputo

WRITER
Jim Garaventi

PHOTOGRAPHER
Russ Quackenbush

CLIENT
Swiss Army Brands

AGENCY
Mullen Advertising/
Wenham

MERIT AWARD
Collateral: Point of
Purchase and In-Store

ART DIRECTOR
Steve Sandstrom

WRITERS
Buddy T. Ramstedder
Steve Sandstrom

CLIENT
Miller Brewing Company

AGENCY
Sandstrom Design/
Portland

MERIT AWARD
Collateral: Point of
Purchase and In-Store

ART DIRECTORS
Tyson Brown
Kenny Sink

WRITER
Scott Corbett

PHOTOGRAPHER
Stretch Ledford

CLIENT
Whistler Radar Detectors

AGENCY
SMC/Richmond

MERIT AWARD
Collateral: Point of
Purchase and In-Store

ART DIRECTORS
Erich Funke
Stuart Walsh

WRITERS
Stuart Walsh
Erich Funke

PHOTOGRAPHER
Michael Meyersfeld

CLIENT
Wonderbra

AGENCY
TBWA Hunt Lascaris/
Johannesburg

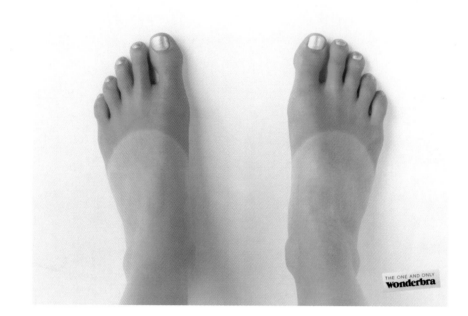

MERIT AWARD
Collateral: Point of
Purchase and In-Store

ART DIRECTOR
Cory Noonan

WRITER
Jonathan Schoenberg

PHOTOGRAPHER
Ethan Hill

CLIENT
Urban Angler

AGENCY
TDA Adversing & Design/
Longmont

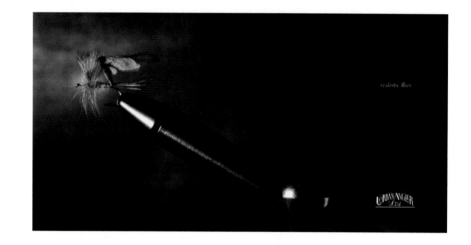

MERIT AWARD
Collateral: Point of
Purchase and In-Store

ART DIRECTOR
Shawn Brown

WRITER
Eran Thomson

ILLUSTRATOR
Todd Dengler

PHOTOGRAPHER
Vic Cotto

CLIENT
Pinehurst Candles

AGENCY
West & Vaughan/
Durham

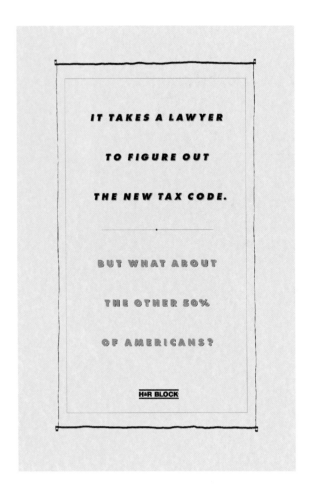

IT TAKES A LAWYER

TO FIGURE OUT

THE NEW TAX CODE.

BUT WHAT ABOUT

THE OTHER 50%

OF AMERICANS?

H&R BLOCK

MERIT AWARD
Collateral: Point of
Purchase and In-Store

ART DIRECTOR
Greg Nygard

WRITER
John Matejczyk

CLIENT
H&R Block

AGENCY
Young & Rubicam/
Chicago

MERIT AWARD
Collateral: Self-Promotion

ART DIRECTOR
K.V. Sridhar

WRITER
Pushpinder Singh

CLIENT
Chaitra Leo Burnett

AGENCY
Chaitra Leo Burnett/
Mumbai

The penis mightier than the sword.

Chaitra Leo Burnett urgently requires a proof-reader. Fax your resume to Manohar at 3802800.

MERIT AWARD
Collateral: Self-Promotion

ART DIRECTORS
Franklin Tipton
Richard Walker
Paul Bruce
Libby Brockhoff

WRITERS
Franklin Tipton
Ben Mooge
Mark Waites

ILLUSTRATOR
Hugh Beattie

PHOTOGRAPHER
Paul Baker

CLIENT
Mother

AGENCY
Mother/London

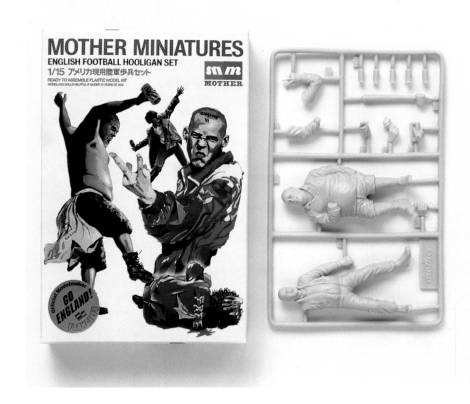

MERIT AWARD
Collateral: Self-Promotion

ART DIRECTOR
Daryl Gardiner

WRITER
Miles Markovich

PHOTOGRAPHER
Leon Behar

CLIENT
Palmer Jarvis DDB

AGENCY
Palmer Jarvis DDB/
Vancouver

MERIT AWARD
Collateral: Self-Promotion

ART DIRECTOR
Mark Hesse

WRITER
Heather Vincent

PHOTOGRAPHER
Brad Stringer

CLIENT
Palmer Jarvis DDB

AGENCY
Palmer Jarvis DDB/
Vancouver

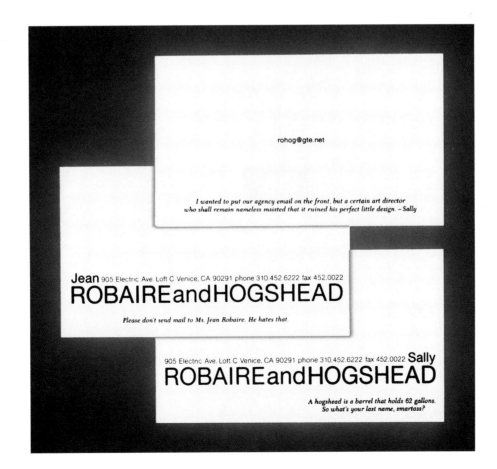

MERIT AWARD
Collateral: Self-Promotion

ART DIRECTORS
Ellen Steinberg
Jean Robaire

WRITER
Sally Hogshead

CLIENT
Robaire and Hogshead

AGENCY
Robaire and Hogshead/
Venice

MERIT AWARD
Collateral: Self-Promotion

ART DIRECTORS
John Domas
Jean Robaire

WRITERS
Dave Holloway
Sally Hogshead

CLIENT
Robaire and Hogshead

AGENCY
Robaire and
Hogshead/Venice

MERIT AWARD
Collateral: Self-Promotion

ART DIRECTOR
Steve Sandstrom

WRITERS
Matt Elhardt
Jim Haven
Austin Howe
Peter Wegner

CLIENT
Sandstrom Design

AGENCY
Sandstrom Design/Portland

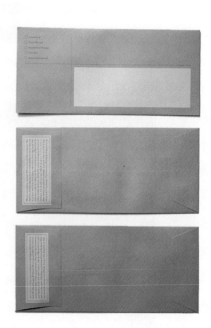

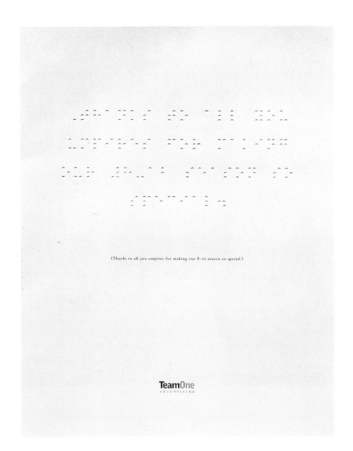

MERIT AWARD
Collateral: Self-Promotion

ART DIRECTOR
Kyle Marcella

WRITER
Suzanne Steele

CLIENT
Team One Advertising

AGENCY
Team One Advertising/
El Segundo

MERIT AWARD
Collateral: Posters

ART DIRECTOR
Bradley Wood

WRITER
Ryan Ebner

CLIENT
Valor Tours

AGENCY
Butler Shine & Stern/
Sausalito

MERIT AWARD
Collateral: Posters

ART DIRECTOR
Sean Farrell

WRITER
Colin Nissan

PHOTOGRAPHERS
Cheryl Clegg
Stock

CLIENT
Eastpak

AGENCY
Clarke Goward
Advertising/Boston

MERIT AWARD
Collateral: Posters

ART DIRECTOR
Tomas Lorente

WRITER
Carlos Domingos

ILLUSTRATOR
Monica Kornfeld

PHOTOGRAPHER
Archive Image

CLIENT
Folha de São Paulo
Newspaper

AGENCY
DM9 DDB Publicidade/
São Paulo

MERIT AWARD
Collateral: Posters

ART DIRECTOR
Tomas Lorente

WRITER
Carlos Domingos

ILLUSTRATOR
Monica Kornfeld

PHOTOGRAPHER
Archive Image

CLIENT
Folha de São Paulo
Newspaper

AGENCY
DM9 DDB Publicidade/
São Paulo

Folha de S.Paulo Newspaper. Illustrating life with words for 77 years.

MERIT AWARD
Collateral: Posters

ART DIRECTOR
Tomas Lorente

WRITER
Carlos Domingos

ILLUSTRATOR
Monica Kornfeld

PHOTOGRAPHER
Archive Image

CLIENT
Folha de São Paulo
Newspaper

AGENCY
DM9 DDB Publicidade/
São Paulo

MERIT AWARD
Collateral: Posters

ART DIRECTOR
Tomas Lorente

WRITER
Carlos Domingos

ILLUSTRATOR
Monica Kornfeld

PHOTOGRAPHER
Archive Image

CLIENT
Folha de São Paulo
Newspaper

AGENCY
DM9 DDB Publicidade/
São Paulo

Folha de S.Paulo Newspaper. Illustrating life with words for 77 years.

MERIT AWARD
Collateral: Posters

ART DIRECTOR
Tomas Lorente

WRITER
Carlos Domingos

ILLUSTRATOR
Monica Kornfeld

PHOTOGRAPHER
Archive Image

CLIENT
Folha de São Paulo
Newspaper

AGENCY
DM9 DDB Publicidade/
São Paulo

Folha de S. Paulo Newspaper. Illustrating life with words for 77 years.

MERIT AWARD
Collateral: Posters

ART DIRECTOR
Pedro Cappeletti

WRITER
Jader Rossetto

PHOTOGRAPHER
Manolo Moran

CLIENT
Parmalat

AGENCY
DM9 DDB Publicidade/
São Paulo

Parmalat
Fortified Milk.
It gives you
more energy.

MERIT AWARD
Collateral: Posters

ART DIRECTOR
Joseph Tay

WRITER
Allan Tay

PHOTOGRAPHERS
Teo Studio
Procolor

CLIENT
Dunlop Singapore

AGENCY
Doris Soh & Associates/
Singapore

MERIT AWARD
Collateral: Posters

ART DIRECTOR
Steve Sage

WRITER
Tom Rosen

CLIENT
BMW of North America

AGENCY
Fallon McElligott/
Minneapolis

MERIT AWARD
Collateral: Posters

ART DIRECTORS
Jim Carroll
Andrea McAdams

WRITERS
Jim Carroll
Andrea McAdams

PHOTOGRAPHER
Robert Ammirati

CLIENT
Diet Center

AGENCY
JMC Creative/Brooklyn

MERIT AWARD
Collateral: Posters

ART DIRECTOR
Braden Bickle

WRITER
Braden Bickle

PHOTOGRAPHER
Darnell McCown

CLIENT
Mt. Hood
Snowboard Camp

AGENCY
Levenson & Hill/Dallas

MERIT AWARD
Collateral: Posters

ART DIRECTOR
Doug Pedersen

WRITER
Curtis Smith

PHOTOGRAPHER
Jim Arndt

CLIENT
Biltmore Estate

AGENCY
Loeffler Ketchum
Mountjoy/Charlotte

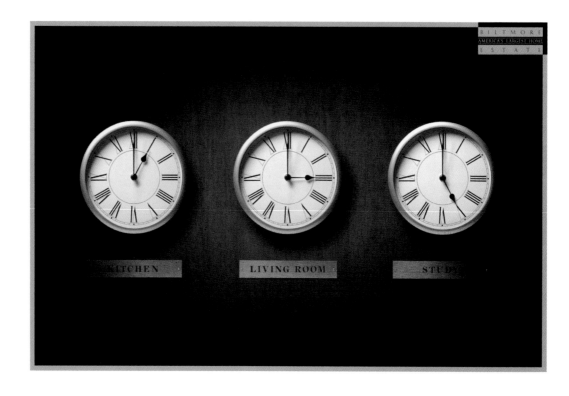

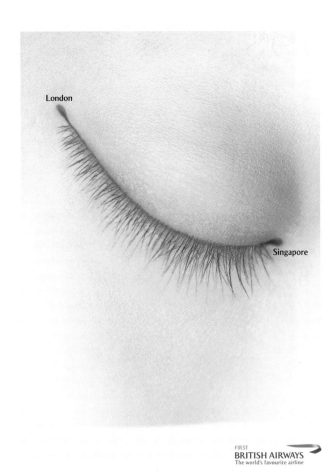

MERIT AWARD
Collateral: Posters

ART DIRECTOR
Jason Ross

WRITER
Paul Ruta

PHOTOGRAPHER
John Clang

CLIENT
British Airways

AGENCY
M+C Saatchi/Singapore

MERIT AWARD
Collateral: Posters

ART DIRECTORS
Noel Ritter
Jonathan Mackler

WRITER
Kerry Feuerman

PHOTOGRAPHER
Clint Clemens

CLIENT
Saab Cars

AGENCY
The Martin Agency/
Richmond

MERIT AWARD
Collateral: Posters

ART DIRECTOR
Rich Pryce-Jones

WRITER
David Chiavegato

PHOTOGRAPHER
Paul Weeks

CLIENT
Nearly Naked Lingerie

AGENCY
Palmer Jarvis DDB/
Toronto

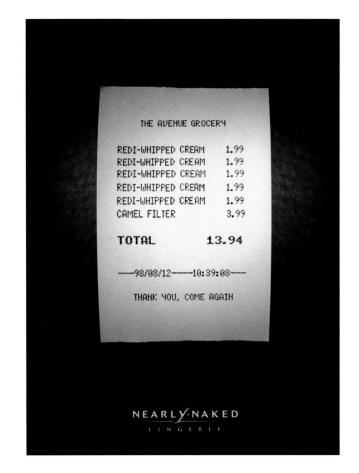

MERIT AWARD
Collateral: Posters

ART DIRECTOR
Ian Grais

WRITER
Alan Russell

PHOTOGRAPHER
Anthony Redpath

CLIENT
TV Twelve

AGENCY
Palmer Jarvis DDB/
Vancouver

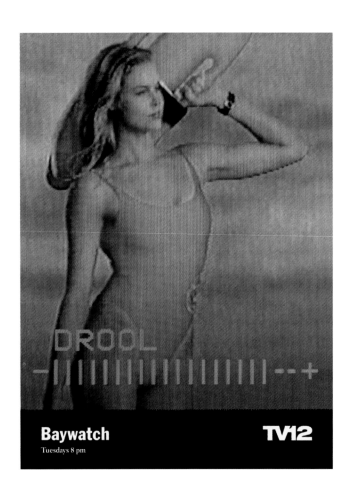

MERIT AWARD
Collateral: Posters

ART DIRECTOR
Ian Grais

WRITER
Alan Russell

PHOTOGRAPHER
Anthony Redpath

CLIENT
TV Twelve

AGENCY
Palmer Jarvis DDB/
Vancouver

MERIT AWARD
Collateral: Posters

ART DIRECTOR
Hernan Barra

WRITERS
Gastón Bigio
Pablo Buffagni

ILLUSTRATOR
Hernan Sanchez

PHOTOGRAPHER
Hernan Churba

CLIENT
McDonald's

AGENCY
Rainuzzo DDB/
Buenos Aires

MERIT AWARD
Public Service/Political
Newspaper or Magazine:
Single

ART DIRECTOR
John Horton

WRITER
Richard Foster

PHOTOGRAPHER
Andrea Modica

CLIENT
Amnesty International

AGENCY
Abbott Mead
Vickers.BBDO/London

MERIT AWARD
Public Service/Political
Newspaper or Magazine:
Single

ART DIRECTOR
Alex Burnard

WRITER
Scott Linnen

PHOTOGRAPHERS
Brad Miller
Louis Jay

CLIENT
Florida Tobacco Pilot
Program

AGENCY
Crispin Porter &
Bogusky/Miami

MERIT AWARD
Public Service/Political
Newspaper or Magazine:
Single

ART DIRECTORS
Abi Aron Spencer
Aaron Eiseman

WRITERS
Aaron Eiseman
Abi Aron Spencer

PHOTOGRAPHER
Henry Leutwyler

CLIENT
Pro-Choice Public
Education Project

AGENCY
DeVito/Verdi/New York

MERIT AWARD
Public Service/Political
Newspaper or Magazine:
Single

ART DIRECTOR
Pedro Cappeletti

WRITER
Jader Rossetto

PHOTOGRAPHER
Alexandre Catan

CLIENT
São Paulo Museum of Art

AGENCY
DM9 DDB Publicidade/
São Paulo

MERIT AWARD
Public Service/Political
Newspaper or Magazine:
Single

ART DIRECTOR
Kevin Daley

WRITER
Craig Johnson

PHOTOGRAPHER
Russ Quackenbush

CLIENT
Massachusetts Society
for Prevention of
Cruelty to Children

AGENCY
Greenberg Seronick
O'Leary & Partners/Boston

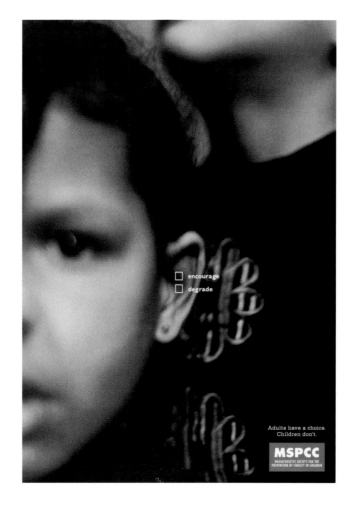

MERIT AWARD
Public Service/Political
Newspaper or Magazine:
Single

ART DIRECTOR
Kevin Daley

WRITER
Craig Johnson

PHOTOGRAPHER
Russ Quackenbush

CLIENT
Massachusetts Society
for Prevention of Cruelty
to Children

AGENCY
Greenberg Seronick
O'Leary & Partners/Boston

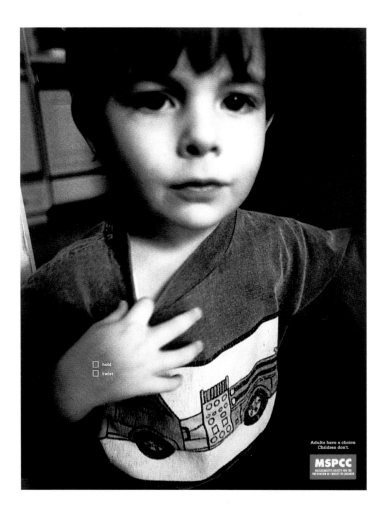

MERIT AWARD
Public Service/Political
Newspaper or Magazine:
Single

ART DIRECTOR
Kevin Daley

WRITER
Craig Johnson

PHOTOGRAPHER
Russ Quackenbush

CLIENT
Massachusetts Society
for Prevention of Cruelty
to Children

AGENCY
Greenberg Seronick
O'Leary & Partners/Boston

MERIT AWARD
Public Service/Political
Newspaper or Magazine:
Single

ART DIRECTOR
Greg Rowan

WRITER
Bob Hall

CLIENT
USS Hornet Museum

AGENCY
JWT West/San Francisco

MERIT AWARD
Public Service/Political
Newspaper or Magazine:
Single

ART DIRECTOR
Doug Pedersen

WRITERS
Curtis Smith
Mike Duckworth

PHOTOGRAPHER
Jim Arndt

CLIENT
Outward Bound/
North Carolina

AGENCY
Loeffler Ketchum
Mountjoy/Charlotte

MERIT AWARD
Public Service/Political
Newspaper or Magazine:
Single

ART DIRECTOR
Christopher Gyorgy

WRITER
Joe Alexander

PHOTOGRAPHERS
David Breashears
Robert Schaver
Gordon Wiltsie

CLIENT
Science Museum
of Virginia

AGENCY
The Martin Agency/
Richmond

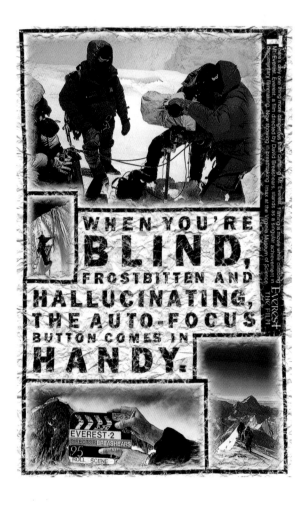

MERIT AWARD
Public Service/Political
Newspaper or Magazine:
Single

ART DIRECTOR
Christopher Gyorgy

WRITER
Joe Alexander

PHOTOGRAPHERS
Ken Kamler
Robert Schaver

CLIENT
Science Museum
of Virginia

AGENCY
The Martin Agency/
Richmond

MERIT AWARD
Public Service/Political
Newspaper or Magazine:
Single

ART DIRECTOR
Christopher Gyorgy

WRITER
Joe Alexander

PHOTOGRAPHERS
Neal Beidleman
Robert Schaver
David Breashears
Sumiyo Tsuzuki

CLIENT
Science Museum
of Virginia

AGENCY
The Martin Agency/
Richmond

MERIT AWARD
Public Service/Political
Newspaper or Magazine:
Single

ART DIRECTOR
Kelly Pon

WRITER
Eugene Cheong

ILLUSTRATOR
Procolor

PHOTOGRAPHER
Simon Taplin

CLIENT
Singapore National
Heart Foundation

AGENCY
Ogilvy & Mather/
Singapore

AIDS: 241. Bacon and Eggs: 30,039.

The Human Immunodeficiency Virus claimed its first Singaporean victim in April 1987.

Today, ten years on, the death toll from this dreadful, and so far, incurable microbe stands at 241.

Without belittling the tragedy of AIDS, we would like to direct your attention to a pestilence whose relentless killing power exceeds that of HIV's by 125 times.

Over this similar ten-year period, a terrible scourge has deprived our society of an entire generation of people carrying away an incredible 30,039 men and women.

The grim reaper, in question, is none other than coronary heart disease. It's the nation's number two killer; second to cancer, only because malignancy isn't really a single illness, but rather a group of afflictions.

Coronary heart disease is, clearly, an epidemic.

What troubles us is the lackadaisical 'we've-all-got-to-go-someday' mindset that Singaporeans seem to have adopted towards the disease.

This nonchalance contrasts sharply with our vigilance against the HIV virus.

We practice safe sex, never safe eating. We curb one appetite whilst blithely indulging the other.

We behave as if death via heart attack is somehow less final than death via AIDS.

If we sound upset, it's because we know as a medical fact that the average person needn't be a heart attack victim.

Yet, like a lamb to the slaughter, one in four succumbs.

Nobody is ever fated to have a heart attack. It's the little choices we make everyday, a hamburger here, an extra egg there, that eventually snowball into the 'big one'.

The American Surgeon General concurs: "For the two out of three adults who do not smoke and do not drink excessively, one personal choice seems to influence long-term health prospects more than any other: what we eat."

What then should we eat to keep our ticker in the pink?

In a word, less.

Less fat. And less cholesterol.

Let's begin with the 'F' word. Fats are divided into two main groups, called saturated and unsaturated.

Doctors unanimously agree that saturated fat is the main culprit responsible for raising cholesterol level in your blood.

Olive, safflower and canola oils are mostly unsaturated. However, palm and coconut oils are mostly saturated, as are meat and dairy derived oil.

But it's wise to cut down on all fatty food.

Aim at reducing your total fat intake to 30%, or less, of your daily energy intake. (To give you a yardstick: a third of Singaporeans exceeds this 30% limit.)

It makes a huge difference if you spread less butter or margarine and eat less fried and creamy foods.

When eating out at hawker centers, order noodle soup instead of the 'dry' version. And don't gulp down all the gravy because that's where the fat is.

Munch a fruit rather than crisps, crackers and other tidbits. They contain surprising amounts of 'hidden' fat.

Now, on to cholesterol.

You probably know a bit about the subject, but we thought there are a few things worth revisiting. (After all, it's a fairly human trait to forget.)

This waxy fat-like substance is manufactured by the liver and is, suffice to say, essential for life.

There's a little hitch though.

Our high-saturated-fat diet stimulates the liver to produce more cholesterol than the body actually needs, and this excess ends up choking our arteries.

So the last thing our body needs is for us to swallow more of the stuff.

Dietary cholesterol is found only in animal foods. Organ meats, cuttlefish, fish roe and egg yolk are particularly high in cholesterol. Eat them sparingly or, better yet, not at all.

Most of these changes you'd have to agree are easy ones.

Furthermore, they'll have a positive effect no matter how you've lived your life till now.

Until very recently, the narrowing of the arteries or atherosclerosis was thought to be an unavoidable process.

However, research now indicates that atherosclerosis can be stopped, and occasionally even reversed by lowering cholesterol in the blood through dietary changes.

As we've said, you don't have to be a victim of coronary heart disease.

Unlike AIDS, there is a cure for heart attack.

You.

SINGAPORE NATIONAL HEART FOUNDATION

It's the exact
opposite of
selling your soul
to get to the top.

PEACE CORPS
How far are you willing to go to make a difference?
· ·
www.peacecorps.gov · 1-800-424-8580

MERIT AWARD
Public Service/Political
Newspaper or Magazine:
Single

ART DIRECTOR
Dave Dickey

WRITER
Mark Wegwerth

ILLUSTRATOR
Procolor

PHOTOGRAPHER
Kyle Johnson-MacPherson

CLIENT
Peace Corps

AGENCY
Periscope/Minneapolis

With all due respect,
taking a $125,000
job on Wall Street
is not "going out into
the real world."

PEACE CORPS
How far are you willing to go to make a difference?
· ·
www.peacecorps.gov · 1-800-424-8580

MERIT AWARD
Public Service/Political
Newspaper or Magazine:
Single

ART DIRECTOR
Dave Dickey

WRITER
Mark Wegwerth

ILLUSTRATOR
Procolor

PHOTOGRAPHER
Kyle Johnson-MacPherson

CLIENT
Peace Corps

AGENCY
Periscope/Minneapolis

MERIT AWARD
Public Service/Political
Newspaper or Magazine:
Single

ART DIRECTOR
Mark Mason

WRITERS
Mark Legward
Mark Mason

ILLUSTRATOR
Wesley Lewis

CLIENT
Saatchi & Saatchi

AGENCY
Saatchi & Saatchi/
Cape Town

(Callers responding to this number received the following message.)

Hi, man... you ready for some hot cock... cause I got 12 inches of dick just waiting to shoot its load into your tight ass... You wanna come over here and spread that butt for me oh... yeah... that's good... you like my big dick in your ass... man.

If this was more than just a phone call buddy, ask yourself: would you have checked if I was wearing a condom.

MERIT AWARD
Public Service/Political
Newspaper or Magazine:
Single

ART DIRECTOR
Colin Jones

WRITER
Mike McKenna

PHOTOGRAPHER
Graham Cornthwaite

CLIENT
Department of Health/COI

AGENCY
Saatchi & Saatchi/London

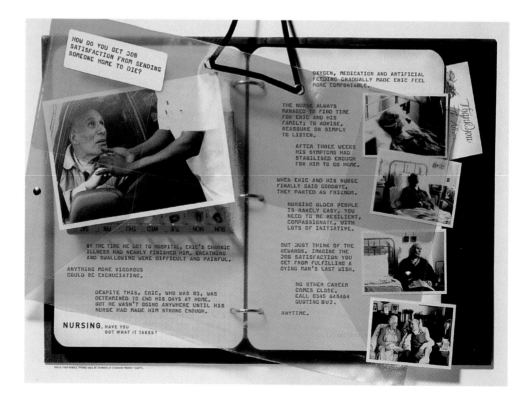

THERE ARE NO CALORIES IN A STEADY DIET OF PROPAGANDA

THE CHILDREN OF NORTH KOREA RECEIVE 110 CALORIES A DAY. THIS IS STARVATION LEVEL. CAUGHT BETWEEN A U.N. EMBARGO AND A POVERTY-STRICKEN GOVERNMENT, THE SURVIVAL OF AN ENTIRE GENERATION IS AT STAKE. BUT THERE ARE EFFORTS TO HELP.

Half a bowl of rice. That's the daily ration for every North Korean. Exactly 110 calories.

When you consider that the human body requires a daily minimum of 1600 calories just for basic maintenance, it doesn't take a genius to see the problem.

Desperation has driven many into the parks and fields to forage for bark, roots, even blades of grass. Needless to say, none of these substitutes contain a shred of nutrition. Worse still, they are highly toxic.

The people of North Korea are in the grip of a famine that will have devastating consequences for generations to come.

Three years of savage floods have been followed by the worst drought this century. The most recent harvests have failed yet again. Three-quarters of the corn crop has been destroyed, livestock are dying, the rice crop is negligible.

On top of that, the economy has stagnated, water and sewage systems have broken down, and the medical system is collapsing. Hospitals report catastrophic increases in patients suffering from intestinal problems and respiratory and urinary tract infections.

The highest-ranking North Koreans to defect to the South estimated that 2.5 million North Koreans have died from famine related causes in the last three years. It's a disaster of unimaginable proportions. Yet most of the world community is reluctant to help.

Instead of upholding a long tradition of providing humanitarian aid to those in need, political interests have coloured the global conscience. Thankfully, a few agencies and non-government organizations have answered the call.

The Campaign for Famine Relief in North Korea is one of them, working to bring this disaster to the attention of the international community.

We fully support direct aid to the people of North Korea. The U.N. World Food Programme and other humanitarian groups are now in a position to be able to monitor food and medical supplies from entry to point of distribution.

We also believe in the long-term rehabilitation of North Korean agriculture through the supply of seeds and research materials, as well as arranging agricultural study tours abroad for North Korean farmers and scientists.

Some have argued that North Korea can stop the famine simply by purchasing grain on the international market. But the economy is crumbling. North Korea has no international credit rating, it cannot purchase commodities. Even if it could, the currency is not exchangeable.

Others maintain that providing aid to North Korea only serves to prolong the status quo.

FAMINE IS FAR MORE DANGEROUS TO REGIONAL SECURITY. IT IS HIGHLY DESTABILISING AND UNPREDICTABLE. DESPERATE PEOPLE WILL TAKE DESPERATE MEASURES. ALREADY THERE ARE REPORTS OF VAST POPULATION MIGRATION TOWARDS THE SOUTH, VILLAGERS VAINLY SEARCHING FOR FOOD. SUCH ACTIONS ARE BOUND TO BE VIEWED AS PROVOCATIVE; ON BOTH SIDES OF THE BORDER. WHATEVER ONE'S POLITICAL BELIEFS, FOOD IS NOT A WEAPON. FAMINE ONLY BREEDS CHAOS, NOT DEMOCRACY. IF PROPERLY MANAGED AND REGULATED, FOOD RELIEF CAN SET THE STAGE FOR PEACE AND CO-OPERATION: WITNESS ETHIOPIA AND ANGOLA.

THE POLITICAL DEBATE CANNOT BE AVOIDED. QUESTIONS MUST BE ASKED AND ANSWERED. BUT THEY SHOULD NOT BE ALLOWED TO BLOCK INTERNATIONAL EFFORTS AIMED AT PREVENTING THE DEATHS OF MILLIONS OF INNOCENT MEN, WOMEN AND CHILDREN. RIGHT NOW, THE CAMPAIGN FOR FAMINE RELIEF IN NORTH KOREA URGES YOU TO WRITE TO HIS EXCELLENCY MR. KOFI ANNAN, SECRETARY-GENERAL OF THE UNITED NATIONS, SHOWING YOUR SUPPORT FOR THE U.N. WORLD FOOD PROGRAMME AND REMINDING THOSE INVOLVED THAT A HUNGRY CHILD KNOWS NO POLITICS.

THE CAMPAIGN FOR FAMINE RELIEF IN NORTH KOREA

MERIT AWARD
Public Service/Political
Newspaper or Magazine:
Single

ART DIRECTOR
Ted Royer

WRITER
Rowan Chanen

ILLUSTRATOR
Procolor

PHOTOGRAPHER
Tom Haskell

CLIENT
Campaign for Famine
Relief in North Korea

AGENCY
Saatchi & Saatchi/
Singapore

TED BUNDY. JEFFREY DAHMER. THE BOSTON STRANGLER.
HOW DO YOU THINK THEY GOT THEIR START?

From psychopaths and murderers to child abusers and wife beaters, almost all violent criminals have a history of animal abuse.

Ted Bundy's first victims weren't pretty, dark-haired co-eds. They were cats and dogs.

The Milwaukee Cannibal, Jeffrey Dahmer, was suspected of killing and eating over 17 people. But his murderous career actually began with the killing and torturing of animals.

Albert De Salvo, the Boston Strangler, didn't become a strangler overnight either. As a young man, he experimented with puppies and kittens. He trapped them in orange crates and shot arrows through the boxes.

Ed Kemper, David Berkowitz, James Oliver Huberty – even the teenager who brutally murdered two children in Kobe, Japan, this year was no exception – all of them graduated from abusing animals.

The FBI and law enforcement agencies in many countries recognise this connection.

In fact, the FBI's Behavioural Science Unit uses animal cruelty as one of the factors in assessing the 'threat potential' of dangerous criminals.

Sociologists, psychologists and people who counsel battered women recognise it too.

So why do violent people pick on animals?

Research shows that animal abusers usually grow up in troubled and violent families. Ironically, they may themselves be victims of abuse.

For some, the animals are merely scapegoats. Their anger is really directed against parents, neighbours or society as a whole.

For others, the violence is a means to get attention, to shock people or to terrorize them into submission. By strangling a cat, an abuser demonstrates his power. "This is what I can do. And there's nothing you can do to stop me."

It's also a way of saying "you're next." It is a warning.

But a warning that is frequently ignored by the only people who can help – the witnesses.

Tragically, almost 7 out of 10 cases of animal abuse go unreported. Neighbours look the other way and passers-by quicken their steps.

It is only when we hear of women being attacked on the streets or children murdered on the way home from school, that we begin to take notice. "Who could do such a terrible thing?" we wonder.

If you witness any act of animal cruelty, please call the SPCA or the police. Please remember that the animal may not be the only one in need of help.

Society for the Prevention of
Cruelty to Animals (Hong Kong)
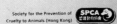

MERIT AWARD
Public Service/Political
Newspaper or Magazine:
Single

ART DIRECTOR
Edmund Choe

WRITER
Jagdish Ramakrishnan

ILLUSTRATOR
Procolor

CLIENT
SPCA/Hong Kong

AGENCY
Saatchi & Saatchi/
Singapore

MERIT AWARD
Public Service/Political
Newspaper or Magazine:
Single

ART DIRECTOR
Francis Wee

WRITER
Calvin Soh

ILLUSTRATOR
Procolor

PHOTOGRAPHER
Shutterbug

CLIENT
Underwater World

AGENCY
Saatchi & Saatchi/
Singapore

Piranhas and other deadly creatures at UNDERWATER WORLD Singapore

MERIT AWARD
Public Service/Political
Newspaper or Magazine:
Single

ART DIRECTOR
Steve Carlin

WRITER
Jay Furby

PHOTOGRAPHER
Michael Corridore

CLIENT
Coalition for Gun Control

AGENCY

Saatchi & Saatchi/
Sydney

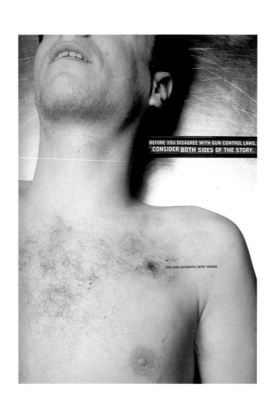

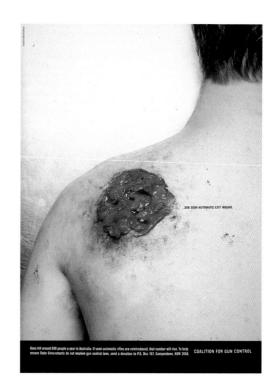

WRITER
Ron Anderson

CLIENT
Gun-Free South Africa

AGENCY
Sonnenberg Murphy Leo Burnett/Johannesburg

MERIT AWARD
Public Service/Political Newspaper or Magazine: Single

ART DIRECTOR
Angus Buchanan

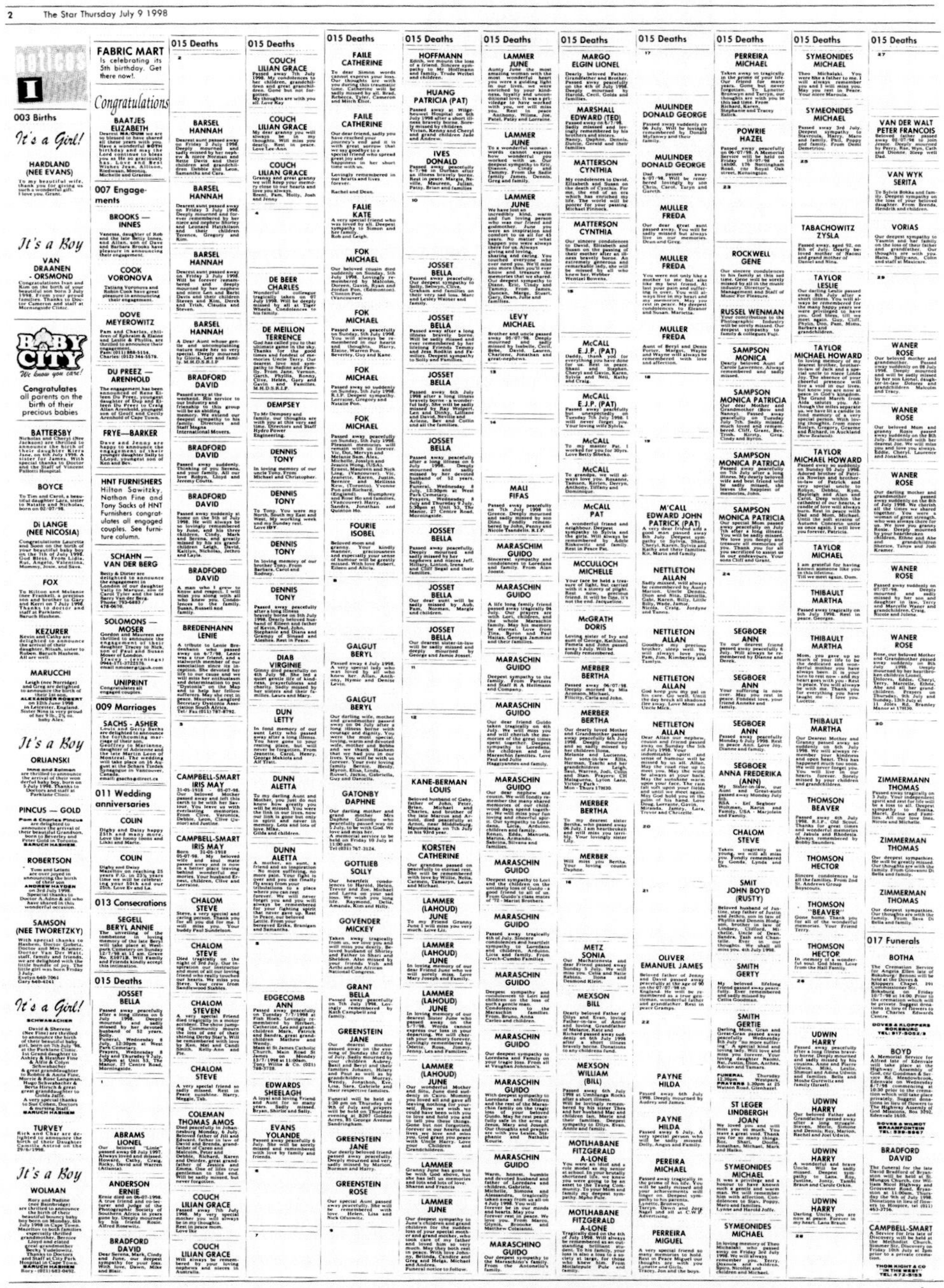
2 The Star Thursday July 9 1998

Notices

003 Births

007 Engagements

009 Marriages

011 Wedding anniversaries

013 Consecrations

015 Deaths

017 Funerals

SAVE THIRTY LIVES A DAY. SUPPORT A GUN-FREE SOUTH AFRICA.

MERIT AWARD
Public Service/Political
Newspaper or Magazine:
Campaign

ART DIRECTOR
Rick Kourchenko

WRITER
Denzil Strickland

CLIENT
Carolina Ballet

AGENCY
FGI/Chapel Hill

Change the outcome. MENTOR. It only takes an hour to change a life. Call 1-877-SERVE-NC
for more information on how you can help, or visit our website at SERVE.NC.STATE.NC.US

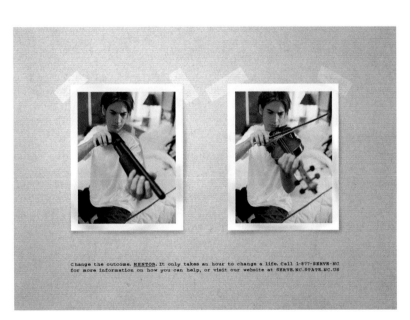

Change the outcome. MENTOR. It only takes an hour to change a life. Call 1-877-SERVE-NC
for more information on how you can help, or visit our website at SERVE.NC.STATE.NC.US

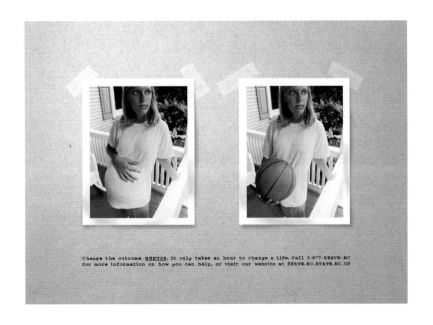

Change the outcome. MENTOR. It only takes an hour to change a life. Call 1-877-SERVE-NC
for more information on how you can help, or visit our website at SERVE.NC.STATE.NC.US

MERIT AWARD
Public Service/Political
Newspaper or Magazine:
Campaign

ART DIRECTOR
Katherine Dymond

WRITER
Ryan Coleman

ILLUSTRATOR
John Gilbert

PHOTOGRAPHER
Stretch Ledford

CLIENT
North Carolina
Promise/Mentoring

AGENCY
McKinney & Silver/
Raleigh

MERIT AWARD
Public Service/Political
Newspaper or Magazine:
Campaign

ART DIRECTOR
Kelly Pon

WRITER
Eugene Cheong

ILLUSTRATOR
Procolor

PHOTOGRAPHER
Simon Taplin

CLIENT
Singapore National Heart
Foundation

AGENCY
Ogilvy & Mather/
Singapore

AIDS: 241. Bacon and Eggs: 30,039.

The Human Immunodeficiency Virus claimed its first Singaporean victim in April 1987.

Today, ten years on, the death toll from this dreadful, and so far, incurable microbe stands at 241.

Without belittling the tragedy of AIDS, we would like to direct your attention to a pestilence whose relentless killing power exceeds that of HIV's by 125 times.

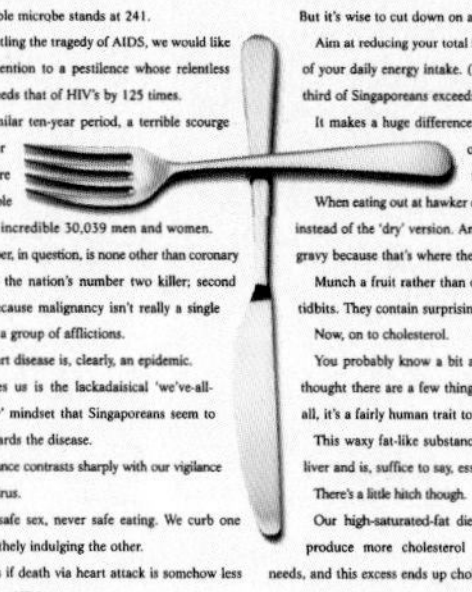

Over this similar ten-year period, a terrible scourge has deprived our society of an entire generation of people carrying away an incredible 30,039 men and women.

The grim reaper, in question, is none other than coronary heart disease. It's the nation's number two killer; second to cancer, only because malignancy isn't really a single illness, but rather a group of afflictions.

Coronary heart disease is, clearly, an epidemic.

What troubles us is the lackadaisical 'we've-all-got-to-go-someday' mindset that Singaporeans seem to have adopted towards the disease.

This nonchalance contrasts sharply with our vigilance against the HIV virus.

We practice safe sex, never safe eating. We curb one appetite whilst blithely indulging the other.

We behave as if death via heart attack is somehow less final than death via AIDS.

If we sound upset, it's because we know as a medical fact that the average person needn't be a heart attack victim.

Yet, like a lamb to the slaughter, one in four succumbs.

Nobody is ever fated to have a heart attack. It's the little choices we make everyday, a hamburger here, an extra egg there, that eventually snowball into the 'big one'.

The American Surgeon General concurs: "For the two out of three adults who do not smoke and do not drink excessively, one personal choice seems to influence long-term health prospects more than any other: what we eat."

What then should we eat to keep our ticker in the pink?

In a word, less.

Less fat. And less cholesterol.

Let's begin with the 'F' word. Fats are divided into two main groups, called saturated and unsaturated.

Doctors unanimously agree that saturated fat is the main culprit responsible for raising cholesterol level in your blood.

Olive, safflower and canola oils are mostly unsaturated. However, palm and coconut oils are mostly saturated, as are meat and dairy derived oil.

But it's wise to cut down on all fatty food.

Aim at reducing your total fat intake to 30%, or less, of your daily energy intake. (To give you a yardstick: a third of Singaporeans exceeds this 30% limit.)

It makes a huge difference if you spread less butter or margarine and eat less fried and creamy foods.

When eating out at hawker centers, order noodle soup instead of the 'dry' version. And don't gulp down all the gravy because that's where the fat is.

Munch a fruit rather than crisps, crackers and other tidbits. They contain surprising amounts of 'hidden' fat.

Now, on to cholesterol.

You probably know a bit about the subject, but we thought there are a few things worth revisiting. (After all, it's a fairly human trait to forget.)

This waxy fat-like substance is manufactured by the liver and is, suffice to say, essential for life.

There's a little hitch though.

Our high-saturated-fat diet stimulates the liver to produce more cholesterol than the body actually needs, and this excess ends up choking our arteries.

So the last thing our body needs is for us to swallow more of the stuff.

Dietary cholesterol is found only in animal foods. Organ meats, cuttlefish, fish roe and egg yolk are particularly high in cholesterol. Eat them sparingly or, better yet, not at all.

Most of these changes you'd have to agree are easy ones.

Furthermore, they'll have a positive effect no matter how you've lived your life up till now.

Until very recently, the narrowing of the arteries or atherosclerosis was thought to be an unavoidable process.

However, research now indicates that atherosclerosis can be stopped, and occasionally even reversed by lowering cholesterol in the blood through dietary changes.

As we've said, you don't have to be a victim of coronary heart disease.

Unlike AIDS, there is a cure for heart attack.

You.

SINGAPORE NATIONAL HEART FOUNDATION

It killed more people in the past 25 years than the 2 World Wars, the Korean War, the Vietnam War, the Iran-Iraq War and the Bosnia-Herzegovina War combined.

Multiplied by 4.

In all, the six major wars of the 20th Century carried away a grand total of 74 million souls.

That, in graphic terms, means every other man, woman and child in the whole of Russia.

The enormity of war, it appears, is dwarfed by the malevolence of low-density lipoprotein.

Known in layman's language as the 'bad' cholesterol, low-density lipoprotein, or LDL, is the villain that creates the plug that blocks the artery that strangles the heart.

WHO estimates that in the last 25 years, it, and it alone, is responsible for 268 million deaths.

So commonly does this waxy, pale yellow substance betray the heart that its treachery is the cause of at least a quarter of all deaths.

If you include other types of cardiovascular diseases like stroke, LDL can be linked to two in every five deaths.

Put it this way, when you die, there's about a 40 per cent chance you'll die this way.

Before you go into a depression, allow us to cheer you up with a fact: you do not have to be a victim of heart attack.

Granted, the threat of heart disease is omnipresent, but it's, by no means, an inevitability.

Doctors agree that for every one per cent drop in blood cholesterol level, the risk of heart attack falls two per cent.

But how on earth do you go about lowering your blood cholesterol level?

By eating less fat and exercising more. You probably know that already, don't you?

What you probably don't know is that you don't have to be a herbivorous triathlon ironman to keep the old ticker in the pink. (So far so good, isn't it?)

Most of the changes you need to make are easy ones.

Moreover, they'll have a positive effect no matter how you've lived your life and abuse your body up till now.

Here are three painless but sure-fire methods of cutting fat and, as a result, cholesterol.

1. Ask yourself if you'd miss those things you eat aimlessly, without really thinking about it. Biscuits, chips, crackers, tidbits. They contain surprising amounts of fat. ('Hidden fat', nutritionists call it.)

2. You needn't go on some crack-pot diet to reduce fats, just be sensible with what you eat. The key words here are reduce, refrain, remove and restrict.

3. Don't make every day a fry-day. Boil, steam and grill, instead. They're healthier, and you get to taste the food, not just the cooking oil.

The heart, as someone once described, is nothing but a bag of muscles. And muscles, we all know, need exercise.

But it doesn't have to be exercise as defined by Jane Fonda. If jogging, cycling or swimming don't appeal, try something a bit simpler. Like walking.

A brisk 30-minute walk three times a week will do wonders for your dear valentine. Even if this is carried out in ten-minute segments throughout the day.

As you can see, it doesn't take all that much to keep your heart in tip-top condition.

Nevertheless, we recognise that even small changes demand some effort. We are, after all, creatures of habit.

Still, we're optimistic, it can be done. That's because, others have done it.

America, as a nation, has been committed to fighting heart diseases aggressively, and there's evidence emerging to indicate that she's been successful.

The death rate in the United States from heart attack is just 42 per cent of what it used to be in 1963.

Clearly, the war against this grim disease can be won.

But first, your heart has to be in it.

SINGAPORE NATIONAL HEART FOUNDATION

Are you digging your own grave?

My, how Singaporeans love to eat.

We're probably the only folks on the planet who'd bring up 'tonight's dinner' as a topic for conversation at lunch.

We pile our plates up so high at 'eat-all-you-can' buffet lunches, perhaps the restaurants should seriously consider erecting height restriction barriers in the premises.

Small wonder, then, one in every four persons on the island is overweight. And, as a whole, the country is growing steadily sideways.

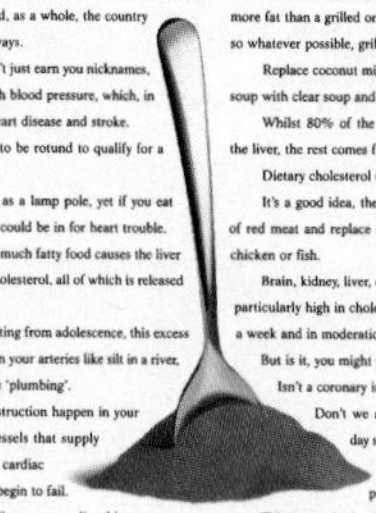

Being too fat doesn't just earn you nicknames, it predisposes you to high blood pressure, which, in turn, lays you open to heart disease and stroke.

Not that you need to be rotund to qualify for a heart attack.

You can be skinny as a lamp pole, yet if you eat too much fatty food you could be in for heart trouble.

You see, eating too much fatty food causes the liver to manufacture excess cholesterol, all of which is released into the blood stream.

Over the years, starting from adolescence, this excess cholesterol accumulates in your arteries like silt in a river, gradually clogging up the 'plumbing'.

Should such an obstruction happen in your coronary arteries (the vessels that supply oxygen-rich blood to the cardiac muscles) your heart will begin to fail.

One in every four Singaporeans dies this way.

Now that we've given you some incentive to cut down on fatty food, allow us to elaborate further.

There are two kinds of fat: saturated and unsaturated.

Doctors are unanimous in their view that saturated fat raises blood cholesterol level; by stimulating your liver to overproduce this waxy fat-like substance.

A lot of people seem to think that all vegetable oils are unsaturated. This is not true. Check the label on the bottle before choosing.

Don't be fooled either, when you see 'No cholesterol' on the label. In the first place, saturated oils are cholesterol-free, however, they are the primary cause of high cholesterol level in your blood.

Olive, safflower, and canola oils are mostly unsaturated. Palm and coconut oils, on the other hand, are mostly saturated, as are meat and dairy derived oil.

It's, nevertheless, prudent to cut down on all fatty food.

Aim at reducing your total fat intake to 30%, or less, of your total calorie consumption.

(One in three, by the way, exceeds this 30% limit.)

It make a huge difference if you spread less butter or margarine, eat less cream cakes and fried foods.

You'll notice that a fried hamburger patty has much more fat than a grilled one. That applies to other foods, too; so whatever possible, grill rather than fry.

Replace coconut milk in curries with skim milk, cream soup with clear soup and salad dressing with low-fat yogurt.

Whilst 80% of the body's cholesterol is produced by the liver, the rest comes from the food we eat.

Dietary cholesterol is found only in animal foods.

It's a good idea, therefore, to reduce the consumption of red meat and replace it with beans or a white meat like chicken or fish.

Brain, kidney, liver, cuttlefish, fish roe and egg yolk are particularly high in cholesterol, so eat these food only once a week and in moderation.

But is it, you might well wonder, worth all the trouble?

Isn't a coronary inevitable, anyway?

Don't we all have to face this affliction one day sooner than we wish?

Until then, why not just sit back, put your feet up and dig in?

This is exactly the thinking we fear, because it puts us at the mercy of a disease that knows no mercy.

The fact is, and this is a medical fact, the average person do not have be a victim of heart attack.

You needn't die of a heart attack if you choose not to.

That's right, you have a say in the matter.

These dietary changes we're recommending will have a positive effect no matter how you've lived your life and abused your body up till now.

Until very recently, the narrowing of the arteries or atherosclerosis was thought to be an unavoidable process.

However, research now indicates that atherosclerosis can be stopped, and occasionally even reversed by lowering cholesterol in the blood through dietary changes.

Do you want to live to a ripe old age?

Well, eat to live, then.

SINGAPORE NATIONAL HEART FOUNDATION

TED BUNDY. JEFFREY DAHMER. THE BOSTON STRANGLER. HOW DO YOU THINK THEY GOT THEIR START?

From psychopaths and murderers to child abusers and wife beaters, almost all violent criminals have a history of animal abuse.

Ted Bundy's first victims weren't pretty, dark-haired co-eds. They were cats and dogs.

The Milwaukee Cannibal, Jeffrey Dahmer, was suspected of killing and eating over 17 people. But his murderous career actually began with the killing and torturing of animals.

Albert De Salvo, the Boston Strangler, didn't become a strangler overnight either. As a young man, he experimented with puppies and kittens. He trapped them in orange crates and shot arrows through the boxes.

Ed Kemper, David Berkowitz, James Oliver Huberty — even the teenager who brutally murdered two children in Kobe, Japan, this year was no exception — all of them graduated from abusing animals.

The FBI and law enforcement agencies in many countries recognise this connection.

In fact, the FBI's Behavioural Science Unit uses animal cruelty as one of the factors in assessing the 'threat potential' of dangerous criminals.

Sociologists, psychologists and people who counsel battered women recognise it too.

So why do violent people pick on animals?

Research shows that animal abusers usually grow up in troubled and violent families. Ironically, they may themselves be victims of abuse.

For some, the animals are merely scapegoats. Their anger is really directed against parents, neighbours or society as a whole.

For others, the violence is a means to get attention, to shock people or to terrorize them into submission. By strangling a cat, an abuser demonstrates his power, "This is what I can do. And there's nothing you can do to stop me."

It's also a way of saying "you're next." It is a warning.

But a warning that is frequently ignored by the only people who can help – the witnesses.

Tragically, almost 7 out of 10 cases of animal abuse go unreported. Neighbours look the other way and passers-by quicken their steps.

It is only when we hear of women being attacked on the streets or children murdered on the way home from school, that we begin to take notice. "Who could do such a terrible thing?" we wonder.

If you witness any act of animal cruelty, please call the SPCA or the police. Please remember that the animal may not be the only one in need of help.

Society for the Prevention of Cruelty to Animals (Hong Kong)   SPCA 香港愛護動物協會

PEOPLE WHO ABUSE ANIMALS ARE CAUGHT SOONER OR LATER. BUT NOT NECESSARILY FOR ABUSING ANIMALS.

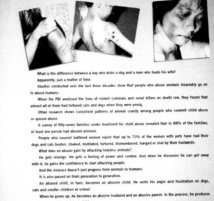

What is the difference between a boy who kicks a dog and a man who beats his wife?

Apparently, just a matter of time.

Studies conducted over the last three decades show that people who abuse animals invariably go on to abuse humans.

When the FBI analysed the lives of violent criminals and serial killers on death row, they found that almost all of them had tortured cats and dogs when they were young.

Other research shows consistent patterns of animal cruelty among people who commit child abuse or spouse abuse.

A survey of fifty-seven families under treatment for child abuse revealed that in 88% of the families, at least one person had abused animals.

People who counsel battered women report that up to 70% of the women with pets have had their dogs and cats beaten, choked, mutilated, tortured, dismembered, hanged or shot by their husbands.

What does an abuser gain by attacking helpless animals?

He gets revenge. He gets a feeling of power and control. And when he discovers he can get away with it, he gains the confidence to start attacking people.

And the violence doesn't just progress from animals to humans.

It is also passed on from generation to generation.

An abused child, in turn, becomes an abusive child. He vents his anger and frustration on dogs, cats and smaller children at school.

When he grows up, he becomes an abusive husband and an abusive parent. In the process, he produces another generation of violent children.

How do you stop this vicious cycle?

Organisations like the Humane Society International stress the importance of correcting abusers early.

Cruelty to animals, whether by a child or an adult, should never be ignored. It is a warning sign.

Not only is it a sign of a mentally disturbed individual, it is also a sign of a troubled family where child and spouse abuse may already be happening.

If you witness any act of animal cruelty, please call the SPCA or the police. Please remember that animals are never the only victims of animal abuse.

Society for the Prevention of Cruelty to Animals (Hong Kong)   SPCA 香港愛護動物協會

IT ISN'T JUST SHAMPOOS AND DRUGS THAT ARE TESTED ON ANIMALS.

Child abuse, wife-beating, murder – recent studies in psychology and criminology reveal that they are all linked to animal abuse.

It turns out that cats and dogs are laboratory rats for human violence. The people who abuse them usually go on to abuse other people.

What does this say about boys who tie tin cans to the tails of kittens and throw stones at mongrels?

It says they are in danger of becoming the kind of men who beat their wives and hurl abuse at their children.

Or worse.

When the FBI analysed the lives of serial killers on death row, they found that almost all of them had tortured animals when they were young.

In 1987, three young boys in Missouri, USA, were charged with the murder of a classmate. All three had engaged in repeated acts of animal mutilation starting several years before the murder.

One boy confessed that he had killed so many cats that he had lost count.

The recent spate of gruesome child murders in Kobe, Japan, started the same way – with animals. Having strangled, hacked and decapitated helpless little kittens, the teenage murderer gained the confidence to attack little school children.

Of course, not all kids who abuse animals will go on to commit sensational crimes. But they can fall into a life-long trap of using violence to solve their problems.

People who counsel battered women and abused children recognise this. So do animal shelters, law enforcement agencies and the courts of many countries.

Unfortunately, the people who actually witness the abuse of animals – family members, neighbours and passers-by – seldom understand its seriousness.

Brenda Spencer fired forty shots at San Diego school children one morning in 1962, fatally wounding two and seriously injuring nine others.

It was only later that neighbours recalled that she had repeatedly tortured dogs and cats, often setting their tails on fire.

Animal cruelty, in itself, is a serious crime. But it's also a warning, a loud alarm bell that goes off before other crimes are committed.

If you witness any act of abuse, call the SPCA or the police. Please remember that the animal may not be the only one in danger.

Society for the Prevention of Cruelty to Animals (Hong Kong)   SPCA 香港愛護動物協會

MERIT AWARD
Public Service/Political
Newspaper or Magazine:
Campaign

ART DIRECTOR

ART DIRECTOR
Edmund Choe

WRITER
Jagdish Ramakrishnan

ILLUSTRATOR
Procolor

PHOTOGRAPHERS
Simon Taplin
Stock

CLIENT
SPCA/Hong Kong

AGENCY
Saatchi & Saatchi/
Singapore

MERIT AWARD
Public Service/Political:
Outdoor and Posters

ART DIRECTOR
Paul Brazier

WRITER
Nick Worthington

CLIENT
DETR Drink Drive

AGENCY
Abbott Mead
Vickers.BBDO/London

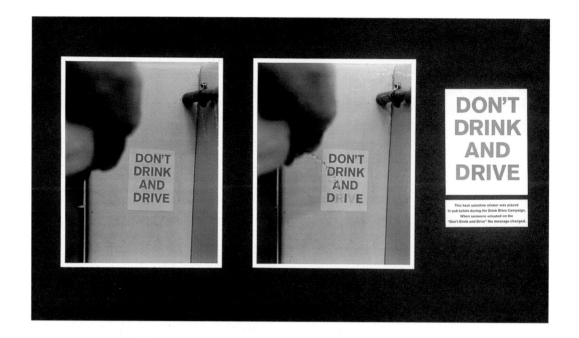

MERIT AWARD
Public Service/Political:
Outdoor and Posters

ART DIRECTOR
Sakol Mongkolkasetarin

WRITERS
Aaron Stern
Dave Knox

ILLUSTRATOR
Sakol Mongkolkasetarin

PHOTOGRAPHER
Peter Samuels

CLIENT
The UFO Museum

AGENCY
Acme Advertising/
San Francisco

HELP CURE SPINAL CORD INJURIES. Send your donation to The Canadian Paraplegic Association, 520 Sutherland Drive, Toronto, ON M4G 3V9. (416) 422-5544. Or visit info@cpaont.org.

MERIT AWARD
Public Service/Political:
Outdoor and Posters

ART DIRECTOR
Bradley Wood

WRITER
Ryan Ebner

ILLUSTRATOR
Bradley Wood

CLIENT
Canadian Paraplegic
Association

AGENCY
Butler Shine & Stern/
Sausalito

MERIT AWARD
Public Service/Political:
Outdoor and Posters

ART DIRECTOR
Bradley Wood

WRITER
Dean Wei

CLIENT
National Jazz Museum

AGENCY
Butler Shine &
Shine/Sausalito

MERIT AWARD
Public Service/Political:
Outdoor and Posters

ART DIRECTOR
Ted Jenkins

WRITER
Bob Volkman

CLIENT
College Football Hall
of Fame

AGENCY
Cramer-Krasselt/Chicago

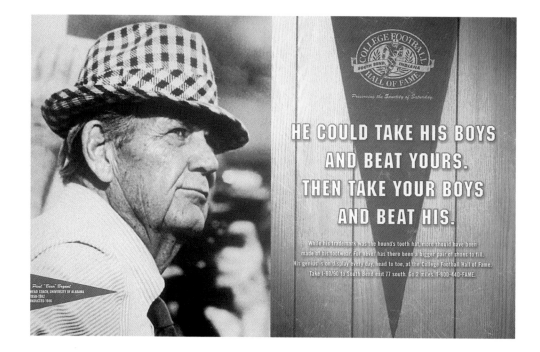

MERIT AWARD
Public Service/Political:
Outdoor and Posters

ART DIRECTOR
Tony Calcao

WRITER
Stefani Zellmer

CLIENT
Florida Tobacco
Pilot Program

AGENCY
Crispin Porter &
Bogusky/Miami

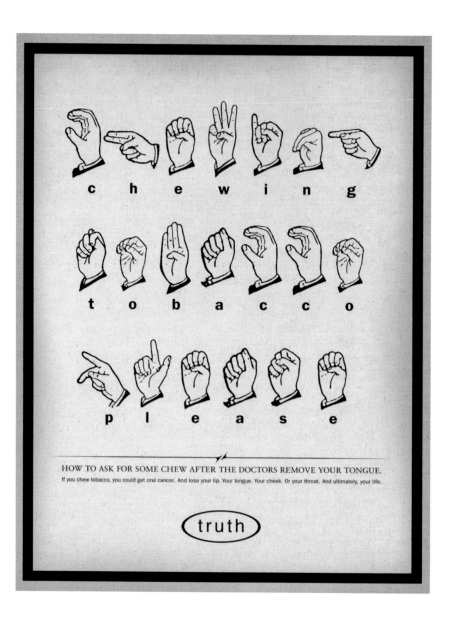

MERIT AWARD
Public Service/Political:
Outdoor and Posters

ART DIRECTOR
Kevin Daley

WRITER
Craig Johnson

PHOTOGRAPHER
Russ Quackenbush

CLIENT
Massachusetts Society for
Prevention of Cruelty
to Children

AGENCY
Greenberg Seronick
O'Leary & Partners/Boston

MERIT AWARD
Public Service/Political:
Outdoor and Posters

ART DIRECTOR
Kevin Daley

WRITER
Craig Johnson

PHOTOGRAPHER
Russ Quackenbush

CLIENT
Massachusetts Society
for Prevention of Cruelty
to Children

AGENCY
Greenberg Seronick
O'Leary & Partners/Boston

MERIT AWARD
Public Service/Political:
Outdoor and Posters

ART DIRECTOR
Lynn Sarnow

WRITERS
Mariella Krause
Karen Schwartz

PHOTOGRAPHER
Dennis Fagan

CLIENT
Parents Anonymous
of Texas

AGENCY
GSD&M/Austin

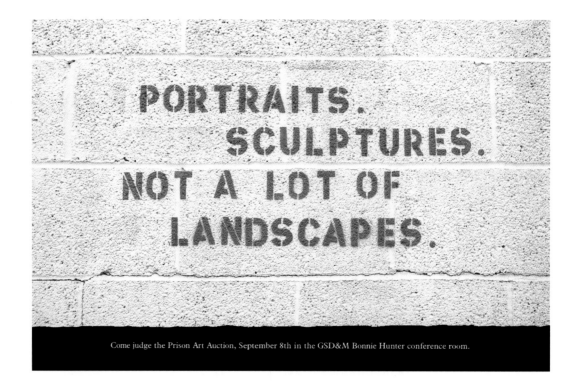

Come judge the Prison Art Auction, September 8th in the GSD&M Bonnie Hunter conference room.

MERIT AWARD
Public Service/Political:
Outdoor and Posters

ART DIRECTOR
Dustin Smith

WRITER
Steffan Postaer

CLIENT
Horizons

AGENCY
Leo Burnett/Chicago

Gosh darn it, just be the best darn Homosexual you can be then.

HORIZONS

CHICAGO'S LESBIAN & GAY COMMUNITY CENTER

773.929.HELP

JOHN KENNEDY'S FINGERPRINT.

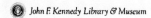

John F. Kennedy Library & Museum

MERIT AWARD
Public Service/Political:
Outdoor and Posters

ART DIRECTOR
Cliff Sorah

WRITER
Joe Alexander

PHOTOGRAPHER
NASA

CLIENT
John F. Kennedy Library
Foundation

AGENCY
The Martin Agency/
Richmond

Homeboys Industries makes hats. And shirts. And jobs so that ex-gang members can leave behind a life of violence and jail. Look for Homeboys apparel at retailers that are willing to make more than a fashion statement.

MERIT AWARD
Public Service/Political:
Outdoor and Posters

ART DIRECTOR
Michael Kadin

WRITER
John Hage

PHOTOGRAPHER
Robert Yager

CLIENT
Home Boy Industries

AGENCY
The Miller Group/
Los Angeles

MERIT AWARD
Public Service/Political:
Outdoor and Posters

ART DIRECTOR
Dave Sakamoto

WRITER
Brad Beerbohm

CLIENT
Lesbian & Gay Rights
Lobby of Texas

AGENCY
RIDE/Austin

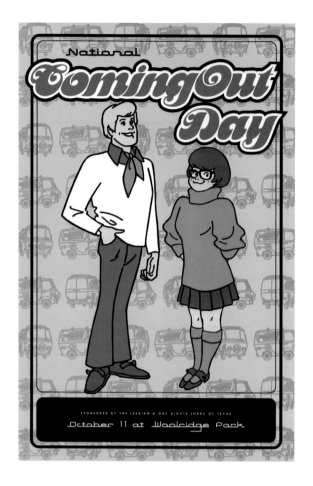

MERIT AWARD
Public Service/Political:
Outdoor and Posters

ART DIRECTOR
Dave Sakamoto

WRITER
Brad Beerbohm

CLIENT
Lesbian & Gay Rights
Lobby of Texas

AGENCY
RIDE/Austin

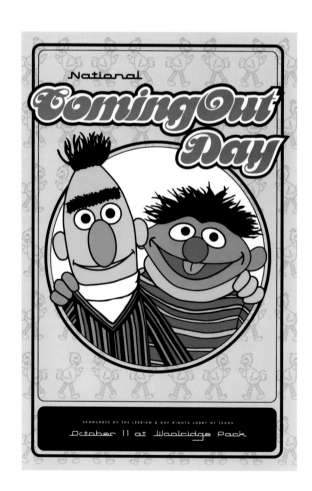

MERIT AWARD
Public Service/Political:
Outdoor and Posters

ART DIRECTOR
Armando Hernandez

WRITER
Armando Hernandez

CLIENT
Little Cuban Museum

AGENCY
Young & Rubicam/Miami

MERIT AWARD
Public Service/Political
Collateral: Brochures and
Direct Mail

ART DIRECTOR
Wade Devers

WRITER
Ted Nelson

PHOTOGRAPHER
Jack Richmond

CLIENT
Friends of Animals

AGENCY
Pagano Schenck & Kay/
Boston

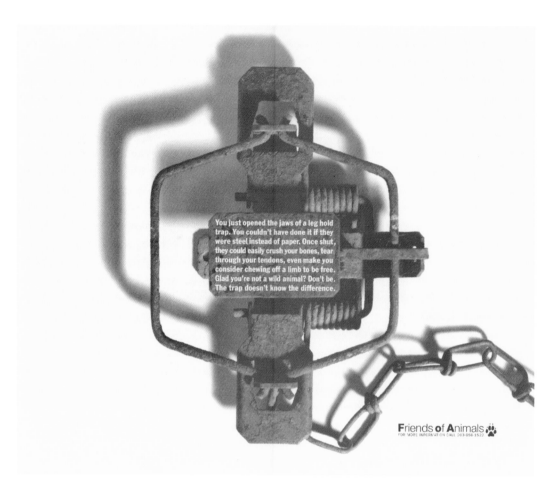

MUSIC: *"Ma Vie En Rose" theme music.*

ANNOUNCER: *Growing up can be tough. Especially when you're the new kid in town. And a transvestite. But when little Ludo's caught trying to marry his father's boss's son, things really go to hell. But, with the help of an imaginary fairy princess, he realizes that when imagination is your passport to adventure, you can be a fairy princess too. At least until your candy-coated neighbors run you out of town on a rail. Critics have agreed, "'Ma Vie en Rose' is a foreign film." Not that there's anything wrong with that.*

SUPER: *Same planet. Different worlds.*

SUPER: *Vancouver International Film Festival.*

SUPER: *Vote for the Air Canada People's Choice Awards.*

MERIT AWARD
Public Service/Political
Television: Single

ART DIRECTOR
Lisa Francilia

WRITER
Dan Scherk

AGENCY PRODUCERS
Camielle Clark
Krista Brydges

**PRODUCTION
COMPANIES**
Coast Mountain
Post Production,
Rainmaker Digital Pictures

CLIENT
The Vancouver
International Film Festival

AGENCY
Bryant Fulton & Shee/
Vancouver

MUSIC: *"State of Dogs" theme music.*

ANNOUNCER: *All dogs go to heaven...except Bassar. Bassar was living a dog's life, scavenging for garbage in the small Mongolian town where he was abandoned...until he got shot.*

SFX: *Gunshot.*

SUPER: *Censored.*

ANNOUNCER: *Now, his spirit's free to roam the earth on a magical adventure where anything can happen. In an all new, three-hour metaphysical allegory the whole family will love. Filled with all new friends and all new songs. You'll go dog wild for "State of Dogs." Until Bassar gets shot.*

SFX: *Gunshot.*

SUPER: *Same planet. Different worlds.*

SUPER: *Vancouver International Film Festival.*

SUPER: *Vote for the Air Canada People's Choice Award.*

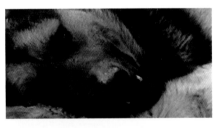

MERIT AWARD
Public Service/
Political Television:
Single

ART DIRECTOR
Lisa Francilia

WRITER
Dan Scherk

AGENCY PRODUCERS
Camielle Clark
Krista Brydges

**PRODUCTION
COMPANIES**
Coast Mountain
Post Production,
Rainmaker Digital Pictures

CLIENT
The Vancouver
International Film Festival

AGENCY
Bryant Fulton & Shee/
Vancouver

MERIT AWARD
Public Service/Political
Television: Single

ART DIRECTOR
Erh Ray

WRITER
Jose Henrique Borghi

AGENCY PRODUCER
Cacilda Oliveira

PRODUCTION COMPANY
Movi & Art

DIRECTOR
Carlos Manga, Jr.

CLIENT
Espaco XXI

AGENCY
DM9 DDB Publicidade/
São Paulo

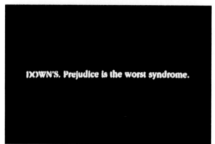

SUPERS: *Jimmy goes to school every day. His friend doesn't.
Jimmy goes swimming every day. His friend doesn't.
Jimmy takes piano lessons. His friend doesn't.*

SUPER: *Hey, this is Jimmy.*
*(The film now reveals that the child who has problems is not the one
with Down's Syndrome.)*

SUPER: *This is his friend. He's homeless.*

SUPER: *Thousands of Brazilian children need your help. Kids with
Down's Syndrome just need your respect.*

SUPER: *Down's. Prejudice is the worst syndrome.*

MERIT AWARD
Public Service/Political
Television: Single

ART DIRECTOR
Viv Walsh

WRITER
Riley Kane

AGENCY PRODUCERS
Kristoffer Knutson
Colleen Shafer

PRODUCTION COMPANY
Menuez Pictures

DIRECTOR
Doug Menuez

CLIENT
Camp Heartland

AGENCY
Fallon McElligott/
Minneapolis

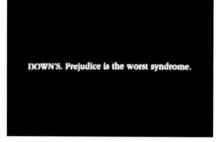

GIRL: *Hi. I have AIDS. Would you hug me? Would you help me go to a
place where people will?*

SUPER: *There's a place where kids with AIDS can get the acceptance
they need.*

SFX: *Nature sounds, crackling campfire.*

SFX: *Kids' laughter trailing away.*

SUPER: *Camp Heartland.*

SUPER: *1-888-724-HOPE. www.campheartland.org*

(A homeless woman is going through a dumpster looking for food. She finds an open can of cat food and starts to eat it.)

SFX: Restaurant ambience. A couple's conversation fading up.
(All dialogue is off camera.)

WOMAN: Oh, this is terrible.

MAN: What's the matter?

WOMAN: This pasta is overcooked, it tastes horrible, I can't eat this.

MAN: We'll send it back. Excuse me waiter, my wife's dinner is overcooked.

WAITER: I'm terribly sorry, ma'am.

WOMAN: I specifically asked for my pasta al dente. This is... I don't know what this is... I can't eat this.

WAITER: I'm very sorry. I'll send it back and get you another.

MAN: What do you have to do to get a decent meal in this town?

WOMAN: Who would eat that?

MAN: Unbelievable... Now we're going to have to wait. My food's going to get cold.

SUPER: Coalition for the Homeless. 964-5900.

MERIT AWARD
Public Service/Political
Television: Single

ART DIRECTOR
Debbie Adjami-Looney

WRITER
Sean Looney

PRODUCTION COMPANY
JGF

DIRECTOR
Jeff Gorman

CLIENT
Coalition for the Homeless

AGENCY
LOONEY²/New York

(A person is picking up dirty clothes out of a garbage can, off the street, out of a shopping cart.)

SFX: Sirens from outside each time the drycleaner's door opens and closes. Bell jingle, cash register, elevator music in background.
(All dialogue is off camera.)

DRYCLEANER: Can I help you, sir?

MAN: Yeah, I need to pick up my shirts.

DRYCLEANER: I'm sorry, sir, those will be done tomorrow.

MAN: Tomorrow? They're supposed to be done today... I need a clean shirt for tonight.

DRYCLEANER: Oh, I'm sorry.

MAN: Oh man, this is unbelievable. I've been wearing these clothes all day. I can't wear them again. Are you sure you can't do it?

DRYCLEANER: No. Tomorrow. I'm sorry.

MAN: Great. This is just great.

SUPER: Coalition for the Homeless. 964-5900.

COALITION FOR THE HOMELESS
964-5900

MERIT AWARD
Public Service/Political
Television: Single

ART DIRECTOR
Debbie Adjami-Looney

WRITER
Sean Looney

PRODUCTION COMPANY
JGF

DIRECTOR
Jeff Gorman

CLIENT
Coalition for the Homeless

AGENCY
LOONEY²/New York

MERIT AWARD
Public Service/
Political Television:
Campaign

ART DIRECTOR
Pete Favat

WRITER
Rich Herstek

AGENCY PRODUCER
Amy Feenan

PRODUCTION COMPANY
Picture Park

DIRECTOR
Pete Favat

CLIENT
Massachusetts Department
of Public Health

AGENCY
Arnold Communications/
Boston

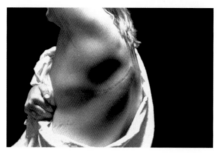

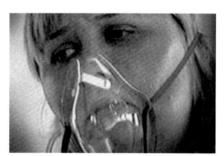

SUPER: *Transplants are not a cure.*

PAM: *My doctor called me at five in the morning. He said to come right away, they had a lung there waiting for me.*

DOCTOR: *This is an operation on a patient who has emphysema.*

PAM: *They wheeled me into a room and they put me on a metal table, and that's the last thing I remember...and when I woke up, what I had just done hit me like a ton of bricks. Unfortunately, my transplant failed and I have to go through this all over again.*

SUPER: *The pain never ends.*

SUPER: *1-800-TRY-TO-STOP.*

MERIT AWARD
Public Service/
Political Television:
Campaign

ART DIRECTOR
Pete Favat

WRITER
Rich Herstek

AGENCY PRODUCER
Amy Feenan

PRODUCTION COMPANY
Picture Park

DIRECTOR
Pete Favat

CLIENT
Massachusetts Department
of Public Health

AGENCY
Arnold Communications/
Boston

(We see a fifteen-year-old girl smoking a cigarette while a quote from an R.J. Reynolds Tobacco Co. memo fades up over her image one phrase at a time.)

SUPER: *"... the 14- to 18-year-old group is an increasing segment of the smoking population. RJR must soon establish a successful new brand in this market... 1976 R.J. Reynolds Tobacco Co.*

Document: Planning Assumptions and Forecast for the Period 1977–1986."

SUPER: *They knew. They always knew.*

SUPER: *It's time we made smoking history. Mass. Dept. of Public Health.*

For the full document visit www.quitnet.org. For information call 1-888-4-NO-TOBACCO.

SUPER: *125 th Annual Demon Awards.*

ANNOUNCER: *Welcome back to the 125th Demon Awards show, coming to you live from the banks of the beautiful River Styx in downtown Hades.*

PRESENTER: *In the category for the most deaths in a single year, the nominees are suicide...*

SFX: *Clapping and cheering throughout.*

SUPER: *Most deaths in a single year. Suicide.*

PRESENTER: *Illicit drugs...*

SUPER: *Most deaths in a single year. Illicit drugs.*

PRESENTER: *Tobacco...*

SUPER: *Most deaths in a single year. Tobacco.*

PRESENTER: *And murder.*

SUPER: *Most deaths in a single year. Murder.*

PRESENTER: *The envelope please. And the winner is...tobacco.*

ANNOUNCER: *This is tobacco's ninth consecutive win. Once again, tobacco killed more people than murder, suicide, and illicit drugs combined.*

TOBACCO: *I want to thank all you smokers out there; this one's for you.*

ANNOUNCER: *This broadcast has been brought to you by Truth. Quality providers of, well, the truth.*

SUPER: *Truth.*

MERIT AWARD
Public Service/
Political Television:
Campaign

ART DIRECTORS
Paul Keister
Dave Clemans

WRITERS
Tim Roper
Tom Adams

AGENCY PRODUCER
Terry Stavoe

**PRODUCTION
COMPANY**
JGF

DIRECTOR
Jeff Gorman

CLIENT
Florida Tobacco
Pilot Program

AGENCY
Crispin Porter &
Bogusky/Miami

MERIT AWARD
Consumer Radio: Single

WRITERS
Ron MacDonald
Lorraine Tao
Doug Robinson

AGENCY PRODUCER
Marion Bern

CLIENT
Labatt Breweries of Canada

AGENCY
Ammirati Puris Lintas/
Toronto

SFX: *Phone ringing.*

BOBBI: *Good morning. The Flower Emporium, Bobbi speaking.*

CAMERON: *Hi, Bobbi. How are you today? It's Cameron calling Out of The Blue. I was wondering if I could, umm, get some flowers, please, to be sent.*

BOBBI: *Sure.*

CAMERON: *What I'm trying to do here is this...really. There's this young lady I'm really trying to impress; we've gone on a few dates and things are going really well, and I really want to take it to the next level, and I thought that some flowers would be a great idea, don't you think that's neat?*

BOBBI: *Umm-hmm, sure is. Okay...*

CAMERON: *What kind of flowers do you recommend?*

BOBBI: *Roses.*

CAMERON: *How much per rose?*

BOBBI: *A dozen long stems is fifty dollars or five dollars per rose.*

CAMERON: *Okay. Now tell me, like, what would you want as a young lady. Like, what would you...*

BOBBI: *What would I want? Two dozen.*

CAMERON: *Two dozen? Let's do it.*

BOBBI: *Okay. And how are you...you're putting it on a credit card, right?*

CAMERON: *Can I do it COD?*

BOBBI: *Okay. You're ordering roses for her and you want it cash on delivery, so when we bring her the roses, from you, she's going to pay for them?*

CAMERON: *Perfect. Let's set it up.*

BOBBI: *Can you hold for a minute?*

ANNOUNCER: *Hey, I'm calling Out of The Blue, you could be next. Labatt Blue.*

MERIT AWARD
Consumer Radio: Single

WRITER
Matt Ashworth

AGENCY PRODUCER
Lisa Gatto

CLIENT
Millers Outpost

AGENCY
Butler Shine & Stern/
Sausalito

DON MORROW: *Meeting Women: A Simple Guide for Any Man, Even You. Lesson Two-If you're not talking, she can't figure out how dumb you really are.*

HEATHER: *Hi guys, it's me again. This week, we're going to cover actually talking to women. Let's say you see an attractive woman you'd like to meet. We'll start by reviewing what not to say.*

JOE: *You're really pretty, just like my old girlfriend.*

HEATHER: *Instead, try something like this:*

JOE: *You're really pretty, (different voice inserted) would you like to go shopping?*

HEATHER: *Here's another example:*

STEVE: *(in a "big and dumb" voice) You know what I really like? Professional wrestling.*

HEATHER: *A better choice would have been:*

STEVE: *You know what I really like? Professional (different voice inserted) ice dancing...and musicals.*

HEATHER: *Now before you actually approach a woman, you need the right clothes. Clothes that say you're not a dork before you open your mouth. Like Anchor Blue woven tops at Millers Outpost. They've got 'em right now at fifty percent off. That way, no matter how dumb you sound, at least she'll know you can dress yourself. All right? Let's try one more.*

MIKE: *Hi. You wanna make out?*

HEATHER: *Bad.*

MIKE: *Hi. You wanna (different voice inserted) read some poetry?*

HEATHER: *Good.*

DON MORROW: *Millers Outpost. It's a free country. Dress accordingly.*

MAN: *Capitol.*

CALLER: *Yeah, hi, I'm calling about the ad for the driver?*

MAN: *All right.*

CALLER: *Uh, I have a question for you. I don't have a car, but uh, I thought I could do some deliveries on my bicycle.*

MAN: *On your bicycle?*

CALLER: *Yeah, you know eat a couple PowerBars and ride around.*

MAN: *No, that's not gonna work. We don't make deliveries on bicycles.*

CALLER: *Even if I ate a couple PowerBars?*

MAN: *You're gonna look pretty funny going down the street on a bicycle with a portable toilet on it. Ain't ya?*

CALLER: *A portable toilet?*

MAN: *Uh-huh.*

CALLER: *Uh-huh, well I can attach it to my bike.*

MAN: *No, I don't think that's gonna work.*

CALLER: *You don't think?*

MAN: *No, I know it's not.*

CALLER: *Even if I could eat a PowerBar?*

MAN: *It's not, it's not gonna work, dude.*

CALLER: *I have some...a lot of energy.*

MAN: *It's not gonna work, dude. We've gotta a van for you to drive, man.*

CALLER: *You do?*

MAN: *Yeah, you got a driver's license?*

CALLER: *Yeah, but I don't like driving that much and thought I...*

MAN: *It's not gonna work, dude.*

CALLER: *Well, do you deliver any other smaller things that I could do on my bike?*

MAN: *No, we don't have nothing you can do on your bike.*

CALLER: *All right, I guess I will just have to look somewhere else. Thanks.*

ANNOUNCER: *PowerBar energy bars. Balanced nutrition and lasting energy for everyday life and then some. Power on.*

MERIT AWARD
Consumer Radio: Single

WRITER
Aaron Stern

AGENCY PRODUCER
Rob Sondik

CLIENT
PowerBar

AGENCY
Citron Haligman
Bedecarre/
San Francisco

GUY: *I ah theekee thoo you thoo ay thanthayer.*

TRANSLATOR: *I am speaking to you through a translator.*

GUY: *Thoo weegthogo I bunned my thung va-way ba-wee why eedeen a mow-ten ahva peee-tha.*

TRANSLATOR: *Two weeks ago, I burned my tongue very badly while eating a molten lava pizza.*

GUY: *I thoo wav ha thum cooo fuh nethee haddee.*

TRANSLATOR: *I should have had some Cool from Nestea handy.*

GUY: *Buh I dithunth.*

TRANSLATOR: *But I didn't.*

GUY: *Unfothunately, I hath notheen coo to dweenk.*

TRANSLATOR: *Unfortunately, I had nothing cool to drink.*

GUY: *After I bunned my thung.*

TRANSLATOR: *And, I am a geek.*

GUY: *Tha nowa I thad.*

TRANSLATOR: *I'm out of my head.*

GUY: *Dough! Withun thoo me!*

TRANSLATOR: *Don't listen to me!*

GUY: *Hey! Dough, thoopid!*

TRANSLATOR: *I am so stupid...*

GUY: *Lithun thoo wha I thayeen!!*

TRANSLATOR: *I ate molten lava pizza without having any Cool from Nestea in the house.*

ANNOUNCER: *Cool from Nestea. Cools you to the core.*

MERIT AWARD
Consumer Radio: Single

WRITER
Mike Lescarbeau

AGENCY PRODUCER
Kirsten Taklo

CLIENT
Nestea

AGENCY
Fallon McElligott/
Minneapolis

MERIT AWARD
Consumer Radio: Single

WRITER
Steve Dildarian

AGENCY PRODUCER
Cindy Epps

CLIENT
Anheuser-Busch

AGENCY
Goodby Silverstein &
Partners/San Francisco

SFX: "Bud" and "er" throughout, swamp sounds.

LOUIE: Hey, Frank?

FRANK: Yeah, Louie?

LOUIE: When I get down there with the frogs...

FRANK: Uh-huh?

LOUIE: I'm not gonna say, "weis."

FRANK: But that's your line.

LOUIE: I think the line is overused.

FRANK: Louie, it's called Bud-weis-er. There's no room for a rewrite.

LOUIE: Yeah, but anyway after their big guy says "Bud," I'm gonna deliver a twenty-five-second dissertation on "born on dating."

FRANK: You're gonna do what?

LOUIE: It's a nice departure from the campaign.

FRANK: No, it's not.

LOUIE: Budweiser will like it.

FRANK: No they won't. They want funny ads.

LOUIE: Funny?

FRANK: Just do the tongue thing, they'll go crazy.

LOUIE: Da! Craz- there's nothing funny about Budweiser, Frank.

FRANK: Excuse me?

LOUIE: I mean, there's nothing funny about providing your customers with the freshest beer in the business.

FRANK: Why are you talking like this? Who are you?

LOUIE: Just talkin' about Budweiser, king of beers since 1876.

FRANK: Oh, I don't believe it, Louie.

LOUIE: What?

FRANK: You've sold out.

LOUIE: I have not sold out!

FRANK: Yes you have. You're like a company mouthpiece all of a sudden.

LOUIE: Frank, Frankie, you have no idea what these people are payin' me.

FRANK: Payin' you? So that's what this is all about, huh?

LOUIE: No, it's not! It's about "born on dating."

FRANK: It's about the money.

LOUIE: What, what did I say? Born on dating?

FRANK: What are they paying you under the branch on this one?

LOUIE: Two guys walk into a bar, one guys says, "Born on dating..."

FRANK: Oh, this is a sad, sad day.

ANNOUNCER: Anheuser-Busch. St. Louis, Missouri.

MERIT AWARD
Consumer Radio: Single

WRITER
Steve Dildarian

AGENCY PRODUCER
Cindy Epps

CLIENT
Anheuser-Busch

AGENCY
Goodby Silverstein &
Partners/San Francisco

SFX: Swamp sounds.

LOUIE: Ah, Frank?

FRANK: Yeah, Louie?

LOUIE: This summer is gonna be fun.

FRANK: Oh yeah, why's that?

LOUIE: Now that I'm working for Budweiser-

FRANK: Uh-huh.

LOUIE: I've rented out a summer branch.

FRANK: Summer branch, really?

LOUIE: Yeah, it's a low slung branch right over the water.

FRANK: Those branches are expensive, you should save your money.

LOUIE: Ah, not this summer.

FRANK: No?

LOUIE: I'm gonna stock the fridge with Budweiser and buy a two-month supply of hot dogs.

FRANK: Yeah, that's a smart investment, hot dogs.

LOUIE: We'll invite the iguana girls over-

FRANK: Hmm.

LOUIE: And turn up the radio. (He does his version of a club tune with a driving bass line). Brrrrr chick chicka-

FRANK: What's that?

LOUIE: Boom boom boom-

FRANK: Is that you?

LOUIE: Club Louie... this is gonna be fun.

FRANK: Hey, hey, Club Louie, what about our fly fishing trip?

LOUIE: Frankie, I'm a celebrity now, I need to lead a more flamboyant lifestyle. Chickey chickey boom boom...

FRANK: A flamboyant lifestyle?

LOUIE: Yeah, nocturnal living... late nights and cold Bud. Boom boom...

FRANK: Hey, hey, chicky chicky boom boom. What's happened to you Louie? Would you listen to yourself? What are you doing?

LOUIE: Frankie, Frankie, I'm sorry I - I got carried away.

FRANK: All right, tell me about it.

LOUIE: I'm still the same old Louie.

FRANK: I hope so, I like that Louie.

LOUIE: However, I would like you to start calling me Louis.

FRANK: I'm not gonna call you Louis.

LOUIE: The reptile formerly known as Louis?

FRANK: No.

LOUIE: Chickey chickey boom boom...

FRANK: Ah man, here we go again.

ANNOUNCER: Anheuser-Busch. St. Louis, Missouri.

SFX: *Swamp sounds.*

LOUIE: *Hey, Frankie?*

FRANK: *Yeah.*

LOUIE: *I'm gonna settle this Texas thing once and for all.*

FRANK: *Ah, how's that Louie?*

LOUIE: *Well, since my apologies haven't worked, I'm gonna let the ferret do the talking.*

FRANK: *The ferret?*

LOUIE: *Oh yeah, the coyotes and the prairie dogs really respect him.*

FRANK: *Oh, that says a lot.*

LOUIE: *He's a pillar in their community.*

FRANK: *I'm sure.*

LOUIE: *Hey ferret, get over here!*

FERRET: *"Squeak."*

LOUIE: *Hey buddy, I want you to make an announcement for me.*

FERRET: *"Squeak."*

LOUIE: *I'll feed you the lines, you deliver the speech.*

FERRET: *Squeak.*

LOUIE: *Okay, here we go: "Fellow Texans..."*

FERRET: *"Squeak."*

LOUIE: *"I did not realize that the middle frog was from the Lone Star State."*

FERRET: *"Squeak squeak."*

LOUIE: *"His recent bump-off attempt, and subsequent nervous tic development, have caused me great sadness."*

FERRET: *"Squeak squeak squeak squeak."*

LOUIE: *Is he translating this correctly?*

FRANK: *I don't know, sounds like gibberish.*

LOUIE: *Ferret, is this a word-for-word translation?*

FERRET: *"Squeak."*

LOUIE: *I don't understand what that means.*

FRANK: *Nah, it's gettin' lost — I don't know...*

LOUIE: *What does that mean? I don't trust this guy. Just repeat the lines!*

FERRET: *"Squeak."*

LOUIE: *Let me hear it again! Tell the Texans I'm sorry.*

FERRET: *"Squeak."*

LOUIE: *I got a bad feeling about this.*

FRANK: *Yeah, you got to keep it simple.*

LOUIE: *Get out! You're fired again!*

FERRET: *"Squeak."*

ANNOUNCER: *Anheuser-Busch. Houston, Texas.*

MERIT AWARD
Consumer Radio: Single

WRITER
Steve Dildarian

AGENCY PRODUCER
Cindy Epps

CLIENT
Anheuser-Busch

AGENCY
Goodby Silverstein
& Partners/
San Francisco

SFX: *Swamp sounds.*

LOUIE: *Hey, Frank?*

FRANK: *Yeah?*

LOUIE: *The iguanas are having a party this weekend.*

FRANK: *I know, we should bring along some Budweiser.*

LOUIE: *I'm not worried about the Budweiser –*

FRANK: *Hmm.*

LOUIE: *I'm worried about our pick-up lines.*

FRANK: *What do you mean?*

LOUIE: *I mean I'm tired of sitting on the branch with you every Saturday night.*

FRANK: *Speak for yourself, I've had a few dates.*

LOUIE: *Hey, hey, that thing with the newt was not a date, Frank.*

FRANK: *Wh-what are you talking about?*

LOUIE: *You were helping her hunt for moths.*

FRANK: *So whatever. It was a date, okay?*

LOUIE: *Let's work on the lines –*

FRANK: *We were out together.*

LOUIE: *How about this –*

FRANK: *What?*

LOUIE: *What's a beautiful iguana like you doing in a rat-infested swamp like this?*

FRANK: *Louie, that's the oldest line in the book. All right, it's played.*

LOUIE: *Okay, okay, how about...your eyes are like huge bulging spheres which can rotate in any direction.*

FRANK: *Ah, you're nuts. You're getting nowhere with that. You need a more romantic approach, Louie.*

LOUIE: *Yeah, like what?*

FRANK: *Like you just send them a Budweiser from across the swamp.*

LOUIE: *Okay, I like that.*

FRANK: *Then you crawl up slowly –*

LOUIE: *I like that.*

FRANK: *And say, I couldn't help but notice how the moonlight reflects off of your sticky, gelatinous tongue.*

LOUIE: *Oh Frank, that's disgusting.*

FRANK: *It's not disgusting. It's certainly no worse than your lines.*

LOUIE: *What? Romeo you are not.*

FRANK: *Hey, I've had much success with that line.*

ANNOUNCER: *Anheuser-Busch. St. Louis, Missouri.*

MERIT AWARD
Consumer Radio: Single

WRITER
Steve Dildarian

AGENCY PRODUCER
Cindy Epps

CLIENT
Anheuser-Busch

AGENCY
Goodby Silverstein
& Partners/
San Francisco

MERIT AWARD
Consumer Radio: Single

WRITER
Peter Robertson
Susan Hosking

AGENCY PRODUCER
Esther Watkins

CLIENT
TVNZ

AGENCY
Saatchi & Saatchi/
Auckland

VOICE 1: *Hello.*

VOICE 2: *Hey, is it still cool for Sunday, come over, watch TV?*

VOICE 1: *Who's this?*

VOICE 2: *It's me.*

VOICE 1: *Me who?*

VOICE 2: *No, let's not play games here, I'll be over at 8:30 to watch Montana Sunday Theater on TV One, looks very good...*

VOICE 1: *You've got the wrong person here, I think.*

VOICE 2: *Sunday, 8:30, TV One.*

VOICE 1: *What about it?*

VOICE 2: *It's called "The Uninvited."*

SFX: *Laughter. Then phone ringing.*

VOICE 3: *Barry speaking.*

VOICE 2: *Hey, hey it's me. Hey umm, Sunday night, still cool?*

VOICE 3: *Hello, Barry speaking...*

VOICE 2: *Hello, is Sunday night still cool...Gary? Barry?*

VOICE 3: *Yeah.*

VOICE 2: *Gary?*

VOICE 3: *G'day, Gary, how are ya...*

SFX: *Phone ringing.*

VOICE 4: *Hello.*

VOICE 2: *Hey it's me, haven't heard from you for a while.*

VOICE 4: *Aaah...*

VOICE 2: *Aaah, yeah, hey is it still cool to come over on Sunday, watch TV?*

VOICE 4: *Sunday?*

VOICE 2: *Yeah, we, yeah we talked about it, remember, 8:30.*

VOICE 4: *Naaah...*

VOICE 2: *That thing on TV One, Montana Sunday Theater on TV One.*

VOICE 4: *Who, who are you talking to?*

VOICE 2: *I'm talking to you.*

VOICE 4: *Huh, you, 8:30, what, what's the program?*

VOICE 2: *Mmmm, it's called "The Uninvited."*

SFX: *Laughter.*

VOICE 2: *It's a sci-fi thriller about unwelcome visitors.*

MERIT AWARD
Consumer Radio: Single

WRITER
Allan Carver

AGENCY PRODUCER
Allan Carver

CLIENT
Cable Atlantic

AGENCY
Target Marketing &
Communications/
Newfoundland

BOY: *I will now recite the New York alphabet. "BEEP"ing A, "BEEP"ing B, "BEEP"ing C, "BEEP"ing D...*

ANNOUNCER: *Worried about what your child is picking up these days? Tune into The Family Channel on Channel 44. It's quality programming with the warmth and wonder of Disney. The whole family will enjoy it. And there's no commercials between 8:00 and 3:00 every day. The Family Channel. Just one of the great new channels in the "Show-Stoppers" package from Cable Atlantic.*

SFX: *Swamp sounds.*

LOUIE: *Hey, Frank?*

FRANK: *Yeah.*

LOUIE: *Did you know Budweiser's the official beer of Major League Baseball?*

FRANK: *Really? That's great.*

LOUIE: *Yeah, so I thought it'd be nice if we sang a little song.*

FRANK: *Yeah, good idea, I'm ready.*

LOUIE: *Okay, just follow my lead.*

FRANK: *I'm with ya.*

LOUIE: *Hey ferret, you ready over there?*

FERRET: *"Squeak."*

FRANK: *Yeah, okay.*

LOUIE: *(Clears throat.) Take me out to the ball game.*

FRANK: *Take me out to the crowd.*

FERRET: *Squeak squeak squeak squeak squeak squeak.*

FRANK: *Oh yeah.*

LOUIE: *I don't care if I never get back, so let's root, root, root for the home team.*

FRANK: *If they don't win it's a shame. 'Cause it's...*

FERRET: *Squeak-squeak-squeak, squeak, squeak, squeak...*

LOUIE, FRANK AND FERRET:... *at the old ball game!*

LOUIE: *Hey, I like that, I like that. That-that was okay.*

FRANK: *Yeah, I thought the ferret could sing.*

LOUIE: *Oh, he's got a lovely voice.*

FRANK: *Yeah, got flow in there.*

LOUIE: *Hey, one more time!*

FRANK: *Yeah!*

LOUIE: *Take me out to the ball game...*

FRANK: *Hmm-hmm-hmm.*

FERRET: *Squeak squeak squeak squeak squeak.*

FRANK: *Oh he's good, he's good.*

LOUIE: *I love this guy!*

LOUIE, FRANK AND FERRET: *Buy me some peanuts and cracker jacks...*

ANNOUNCER: *Anheuser-Busch. St. Louis, Missouri.*

MERIT AWARD
Consumer Radio:
Campaign

WRITER
Steve Dildarian

AGENCY PRODUCER
Cindy Epps

CLIENT
Anheuser-Busch

AGENCY
Goodby Silverstien
& Partners/
San Francisco

SFX: *Phone ringing*

VOICE 1: *Hello*

VOICE 2: *Oh hi, how are you?*

VOICE 1: *I'm alright, how are you?*

VOICE 2: *Good, hey it's me, is Sunday still cool ?*

VOICE 1: *I don't know who me is.*

VOICE 2: *Me, me, me, me, me,me.*

VOICE 1: *You don't know who you are talking to there.*

VOICE 2: *I do know who I'm talking to. Hey, is Sunday night still cool, I could come over at about 8:30 to watch TV at your place, Montana Sunday Theatre on TV One, 8:30.*

VOICE 1: *Yeah that's fine.*

VOICE 2: *Okay, well I'll see you on Sunday.*

VOICE 1: *Okay, see ya.*

VOICE 2: *Hey you wanna, know the programme...*

VOICE 1: *Bye.*

VOICE 2: *You want to know... where are you going ?*

SFX: *The phone goes dead.*

SFX: *Phone ringing.*

VOICE 3: *Hey*

VOICE 2: *Hey it's me. Hey is it still cool for Sunday night?*

VOICE 3: *What...?*

VOICE 2: *TV*

VOICE 3: *TV?*

VOICE 2: *Yeah TV One. 8:30, cool?*

VOICE 3: *What, what, what's, what are you talking about?*

VOICE 2: *8:30 Sunday night, Montana Sunday Theatre, me and you, we talked about it ages ago, remember...?*

VOICE 3: *No, who, who'd you want, who's this ?*

VOICE 2: *It's me, I've, hey okay so I'll see you about 8:30 Sunday, it's on TV One. Looks pretty good.*

VOICE 3: *Hah, hah, rightho !*

VOICE 2: *No, looks pretty good...*

VOICE 3: *Yeah cool.*

VOICE 2: *It's called – The Uninvited !*

SFX: *Laughter*

VOICE 2: *It's a sci-fi thriller about unwelcome visitors.*

MERIT AWARD
Consumer Radio:
Campaign

WRITERS
Peter Robertson
Susan Hosking

AGENCY PRODUCER
Esther Watkins

CLIENT
TVNZ

AGENCY
Saatchi & Saatchi/
Auckland

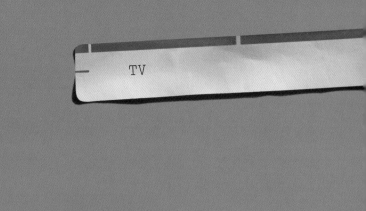

TV

MERIT AWARD
Consumer Television:
Over :30 Single

ART DIRECTOR
Walter Campbell

WRITER
Tom Carty

AGENCY PRODUCER
Yvonne Chalkley

PRODUCTION COMPANY
Academy Commercials

DIRECTOR
Jonathan Glazer

CLIENT
Guinness

AGENCY
Abbott Mead Vickers.
BBDO/London

FRANCO (ITALIAN WITH ENGLISH VOICEOVER):

My brother's a hero. A champion. He went to the games. He came fourth. But to the village he was first. Everybody loves him.

He's the reason I own a bar. After all this time they still want to see him swim. Every year we have a mad race. When he reaches the buoy, I start the clock. Marco against the pint. They expect.

"But I'm getting older," he says. "One day I'll lose," he says. "Don't worry," I say. "You'll never lose."

ANNOUNCER: *It takes 119.5 seconds to pour the perfect pint.*

SUPER: *Guinness. Good things come to those who wait.*

MERIT AWARD
Consumer Television:
Over :30 Single

ART DIRECTOR
Tim Vaccarino

WRITER
Shane Hutton

AGENCY PRODUCER
Bill Goodell

PRODUCTION COMPANY
HSI Productions

DIRECTOR
Gerard De Thame

CLIENT
Volkswagen

AGENCY
Arnold Communications/
Boston

MUSIC: *Techno.*

(A Jetta is driving in a light drizzle with a couple inside. The young woman pushes in a cassette and music starts. Then the couple notices that their windshield wipers, the men's feet on the sidewalk, the newspaper a man is opening to read, a man's yo-yo, a man's broom sweeping, the hand signal to cross the street, the basketball a young man is bouncing and the boxes being unloaded from a delivery truck are all moving in time with the music. As the couple's Jetta stops at the corner, a passing truck splashes water from a puddle.

DRIVER: *That was interesting.*

ANNOUNCER: *The all new Volkswagen Jetta. Sometimes everything just comes together.*

SUPER: *Drivers wanted. Volkswagen.*

ANNOUNCER: *On the road of life there are passengers, and there are drivers.*

GERM 1: *Attention!*

GEORGE C. SCOTT: *To the world at large... we are merely Germs... small, insignificant bacterial growth. But today we stand united knowing full well the glorious reward that awaits each and every one of us. Sure we are just germs... looking out I see more... I see... heroes. Are we ready?*

GERM 1: *Ready Sir!*

GEORGE C. SCOTT: *Do me proud!!*

GERM 3: *One, two, three...*

SFX: *Germs yelling and cheering.*

SUPER: *It's not TV. It's HBO.*

GEORGE C. SCOTT: *This moment will live forever!*

SFX: *Cleaning woman spraying disinfectant on remote control.*

MERIT AWARD
Consumer Television
Over :30 Single

ART DIRECTOR
Don Schneider

WRITER
Michael Patti

AGENCY PRODUCERS
Regina Ebel
Becky Friedman
Rani Vaz

PRODUCTION COMPANY
PYTKA

DIRECTOR
Joe Pytka

CLIENT
HBO

AGENCY
BBDO/New York

MUSIC: *"Someone to Watch over Me"*

A guardian angel guides a man through his day protecting him from a variety of calamities. When the angel becomes engrossed in "Men in Black" playing on HBO in a storefront window, his charge is crushed by a falling piano.

SUPER: *It's not TV. It's HBO.*

MERIT AWARD
Consumer Television
Over :30 Single

ART DIRECTOR
Don Schneider

WRITER
Michael Patti

AGENCY PRODUCERS
Regina Ebel
Becky Friedman
Rani Vaz

PRODUCTION COMPANY
PYTKA

DIRECTOR
Joe Pytka

CLIENT
HBO

AGENCY
BBDO/New York

MERIT AWARD
Consumer Television:
Over :30 Single

ART DIRECTOR
Richard Flintham

WRITER
Andy McCleod

AGENCY PRODUCER
Howard Spivey

PRODUCTION COMPANY
Academy Commercials

DIRECTOR
Peter Cattaneo

CLIENT
Volkswagen Group UK

AGENCY
BMP DDB/London

(Dialogue is in German with English subtitles.)

WOMAN: *Hello, come in.*
(She ushers a couple into the hallway.)

MALE GUEST: *So, this is your new "pad," eh?*

FEMALE GUEST: *We've been dying to see it.*

WOMAN: *Let me show you around.*
(The woman walks briskly along the hall, opening doors, allowing the couple only the briefest of glimpses.)

WOMAN: *Lounge. Kitchen. Bedroom, guest bedroom, and bathroom. (The woman stops and opens a door at the end of the hall with a flourish.)*

WOMAN: *And this... is the garage. It's a lovely garage with plenty of room for bits and pieces. It has good lighting powered by seven 120-watt fluorescent tubes. There's space for shelves, roof rack, stuff like that. It's seven meters long and five meters, eighty centimeters wide. Approximately. The garage door opens when you press this button... or by remote control from outside... the locks were made by Gruber Locks of Munich. South facing... (The scene fades to black and then a shot of the V6 Passat. We hear her voice continuing.)*

SUPER: *Passat V6. A car born out of obsession.*

SUPER: *Volkswagen.*

MERIT AWARD
Consumer Television:
Over :30 Single

ART DIRECTORS
Sarah Barclay
Tony Greenwood

WRITERS
Tony Greenwood
Sarah Barclay

AGENCY PRODUCER
Jenny Livingston

PRODUCTION COMPANY
Window Productions

DIRECTOR
Ray Lawrence

CLIENT
Conference of Australian
Milk Authorities

AGENCY
Clemenger BBDO/Melbourne

(A sprightly elderly man kisses an elderly woman goodbye. He then takes off down a path, jumps the front gate and keeps on walking. He turns into another house, where a different elderly woman opens the door.)

SUPER: *Robert Daly. Age sixty-seven. Retired milkman.*

(The man and woman share a warm embrace.)

SUPER: *Still doing the rounds.*

(He drinks a large glass of milk.)

SUPER: *Milk. Legendary stuff.*

(At a meeting of the World Telekinesis Confederation, three men demonstrate their powers of telekinesis. One bends a fork, another lifts a manhole cover. Both receive polite applause. But the final man who opens and pours a bottle of Budweiser receives a standing ovation only to be outdone by an audience member who drinks the beer telekinetically.)

SFX: Audience reactions; beer bottle opening, pouring and being drunk.

SUPER: Budweiser. www.budweiser.com. This Bud's for you.

MERIT AWARD
Consumer Television:
Over :30 Single

ART DIRECTOR
Andy Anema

WRITER
Don Pogany

AGENCY PRODUCER
Greg Popp

PRODUCTION COMPANY
A Band Apart Commercials

DIRECTOR
Charles Wittenmeier

CLIENT
Anheuser-Busch

AGENCY
DDB Needham/Chicago

SUPER: Attention: Not everyone in this ad will have a Miller Time. But you might. Miller strategic learning.

MUSIC: "Miller Time" theme.

(Inside an office, we see a scientist-type guy holding a dog bone. A dog is standing next to him. People at the window are watching what's going on.)

SCIENTIST: We all know how a dog reacts when he sees something he really likes.

(The scientist gives the bone to the dog, the dog's tail wags.)

SCIENTIST: Unexpectedly, I have noticed this same behavior in this young man.

(Scientist points to the young man with a pointer.)

MUSIC: Quirky rock music, "I can't control my arm..."

(After the man grabs the Miller Lite bottle, his arm starts wagging and he spills the beer. After that, we see a scientific blind test where a second scientist gets hit in the nose with the bottle when the young man wags his arm.)

SCIENTIST: Can you turn this into something good?

(We see the guy with the wagging arm behind a drum kit, holding Miller Light bottles with drumsticks stuck into them.)

SUPER: Miller Time.

SUPER: www.millerlite.com

MERIT AWARD
Consumer Television:
Over :30 Single

ART DIRECTOR
Paul Malmstrom

WRITER
Linus Karlsson

AGENCY PRODUCER
Kristoffer Knutson

PRODUCTION COMPANY
Partizan

DIRECTOR
Traktor

CLIENT
Miller Brewing Company

AGENCY
Fallon McElligott/Minneapolis

MERIT AWARD
Consumer Television:
Over :30 Single

ART DIRECTOR
Paul Malmstrom

WRITER
Linus Karlsson

AGENCY PRODUCER
Kristoffer Knutson

PRODUCTION COMPANY
Partizan

DIRECTOR
Traktor

CLIENT
Miller Brewing Company

AGENCY
Fallon McElligott/Minneapolis

SUPER: *Not everyone in this ad will have a Miller Time. But you might.*

MUSIC: *"Miller Time" theme.*

MUSIC: *Robust, Western-style music.*

(A family of settlers is on a horse-drawn wagon. A woman points to a spot near the woods.)

SUPER: *Hey, let's live in the woods.*

(We see shots of settlers chopping down trees, pulling them out of woods and building a house. Then family sits at a picnic table in front of their new cabin enjoying Miller Lite. We see a "beaver" watching the family "stealing" his trees.)

MUSIC: *The Western-style music suddenly stops.*

(A man dressed in a beaver suit jumps out of the woods on a 125cc motorcross bike.)

MUSIC: *A rock song with the lyrics "Evil Beaver."*

(The beaver drives like crazy, jumps off the bike and begins devouring the house. The family puts up a fight, but after the beaver gnaws the grandpa's wooden leg in half, they flee. The beaver sits by a pile of sawdust, pouring a Miller Lite into a glass. He toasts the camera.)

SUPER: *Miller Time.*

SUPER: *www.millerlight.com*

SUPER: *Dick. This commercial is made and approved by me (Dick's signature).*

MERIT AWARD
Consumer Television:
Over :30 Single

WRITERS
Filip Nilsson
Fredrik Jansson

AGENCY PRODUCER
Maria Bergkvist

PRODUCTION COMPANY
Atmosfar

DIRECTOR
Jorgen Loof

CLIENT
IKEA Sweden

AGENCY
Forsman & Bodenfors/
Gothenburg

MUSIC: *"Shorty" by The Wannadies.*

(A small boy in basketball clothes comes home, looking grumpy. He joins his family at the dinner table and serves himself an enormously heaped plate of mashed potatoes. The boy eats and eats, with incredible determination, while his parents watch in disbelief. The rest of the family leaves the table, but he keeps eating. Finally done, the boy leaves the table and walks upstairs. When he enters his room, he glances up at the life-size cardboard cut-out of his favorite basketball player standing in a corner. The boy pulls out his extendable bed, stretches out and lies very still.)

SUPER: *Stuff to grow up with. Children's IKEA.*

SUPER: *Sarajevo 1984*

ALMA: *It was like a fairy tale. I was one of 800 girls. (Pointing to picture) I'm really here.*

ADEMIR: *I was a kid from Sarajevo, just a little kid, but now, you know, I am capital of the world.*

EMINA: *We never thought, in fact, that that time was just calm before the storm.*

SFX: *Gunfire, screams, and sirens.*

ADEMIR: *First, I heard grenades. On my balcony, I could see Zetra burning.*

EMINA: *Zetra was really a place for young people. (Holding up photo of ice skating arena). That is inside of lZetra. We felt like sport has died in Sarajevo.*

ALMA: *I can't put together these two things – the flame of the Olympics and flame of destroying.*

ADEMIR: *People have to realize that it is time to change their gun for hammer, Sirens for songs.*

EMINA: *These who are up in the hills could never convince me that we cannot live together. We have 50 nations fighting for medals, not for territory.*

ADEMIR: *You can destroy things, you know, but what happened to us when the Olympics came to Sarajevo, this we have kept alive.*

SUPER: *In 102 years, the Olympic flame has been extinguished 41 times.*

It's spirit, not once.

SUPER: *John Hancock*

Worldwide sponsor

MERIT AWARD
Consumer Television:
Over :30 Single

WRITER
Jamie Mambro

ART DIRECTOR
Ernie Schenck

AGENCY PRODUCER
Scott Hainline

PRODUCTION COMPANY
@radical.media

DIRECTOR
Tarsem

CLIENT
John Hancock Insurance

AGENCY
Hill Holliday Connors
Cosmopulos/Boston

(Two drivers turn their heads to look at a beautiful woman, both crashing their cars. A third car comes along, a Toyota Corolla, and now the woman turns her head and she walks into a light pole.

SUPER: *Look out for the new Corolla. Toyota.*

MERIT AWARD
Consumer Television:
Over :30 Single

ART DIRECTOR
Geir Florhaug

WRITER
Paal Tarjei Aasheim

AGENCY PRODUCER
Peter Boe

PRODUCTION COMPANIES
Big Deal Film
Palma Picturer

DIRECTOR
Marius Holst

CLIENT
Toyota Norge

AGENCY
New Deal DDB/Oslo

MERIT AWARD
Consumer Television:
Over :30 Single

ART DIRECTOR
Greg Martin

WRITER
Mike McKenna

AGENCY PRODUCERS
David Eddon
Barbara Simon

PRODUCTION COMPANY
Blink

DIRECTOR
Ivan Zacharias

CLIENT
COI/Army

AGENCY
Saatchi & Saatchi/London

SUPERS: *You're behind enemy lines.*

You've located their fuel dump.

But have they located you?

Do you hide?

Or fight?

You do both.

Because you're qualified in telecommunications.

Your qualifications will be recognized even when you're not.

SFX: *Artillery strike on fuel dump.*

SUPER: *Army. 0345 300 111. Be the best.*

MERIT AWARD
Consumer Television:
Over :30 Single

ART DIRECTOR
Joaquin Lira

WRITER
Raffa Rodriguez

AGENCY PRODUCER
Lisa Dee Twinam

PRODUCTION COMPANY
The End

DIRECTOR
Jaume

CLIENT
Miller Brewing Company

AGENCY
Square One/Dallas

SUPER: *Miller Time*

MUSIC: *"Miller Time" theme*

(On a deserted stretch of highway a roadside stand sign reads "Tamales & Miller Lite." The proprietor, a mysterious red-haired Asian man awakens from a trance when a car approaches. The driver gets out, walks toward the stand. With lightning-fast quickness the proprietor sweeps a pile of dust from one of the chairs, sets down a fork and serves a tamale before his customer is even seated. The customer sits down and is served a Miller Lite with the same amazing quickness. The customer attempts to grab the Miller Lite but the proprietor gestures that he should try the tamale first. The customer shows disappointment before trying tamale, and then the heat of the tamale causes him to combust and turn into a pile of dust. Pleased, the proprietor returns the Miller Lite to its rightful place in the tiny refrigerator.)

SUPER: *Miller Time.*

(A diverse series of characters deliver separate lines of a monologue describing their "other life" playing Playstation.)

VARIOUS SPEAKERS:
For years I've lived a double life.
In the day I do my job,
I ride the bus,
Roll up my sleeves with the hoi polloi.
But at night I live a life of exhilaration,
Of missed heartbeats and adrenalin,
And, if the truth be known,
A life of dubious virtue.
I won't deny I've been engaged in violence,
Even indulged in it.
I have maimed and killed adversaries,
And not merely in self defense.
I have exhibited disregard for life,
Limb,
And property,
And savored every moment.
You may not think it to look at me,
But I have commanded armies,
And conquered worlds.
And though in achieving these things
I have set morality aside,
I have no regrets.
For though I've led a double life
At least I can say,
I have lived.

SUPER: *Do not underestimate the power of Playstation.*

MERIT AWARD
Consumer Television:
Over :30 Single

ART DIRECTOR
Ed Morris

WRITER
James Sinclair

AGENCY PRODUCER
Diane Croll

PRODUCTION COMPANY
Gorgeous

DIRECTOR
Frank Budgen

CLIENT
Sony Playstation

AGENCY
TBWA GGT Simons
Palmer/London

(A man, a woman, and a baby are in a living room.)

SUPER: *Greenside, 6:50 PM.*

SFX: *Clock ticking, noises from the TV.*

SFX: *Music and clapping from the television.*

GAME SHOW HOST: *Welcome back for the ultimate round of Master Genius. Our finalist... Brian Roberts. Your last question... a tough one... mathematics... If the radius of a circle is 2.228 meters, what is the circumference? Just to the nearest whole number... Fifteen seconds, Brian.*

ANNOUNCER: *An education plan from Standard Bank will help you provide for your children's future. So you can make sure they reach their full potential.*

(We see the baby has arranged his blocks so that the number I14 stands alone.)

BRIAN: *Fourteen meters.*

GAME SHOW HOST: *Correct!*

SFX: *Applause.*

(Baby gurgles delightedly and starts clapping. Mom looks over at the baby and nudges Dad.)

MOM: *Look, love! He's clapping!*

ANNOUNCER: *Standard Bank. With us, you can go so much further.*

MERIT AWARD
Consumer Television:
Over :30 Single

ART DIRECTOR
Andrew Lang

WRITER
Frances Luckin

AGENCY PRODUCER
Helena Woodfine

PRODUCTION COMPANY
Velocity Afrika

DIRECTOR
Keith Rose

CLIENT
Standard Bank

AGENCY
TBWA Hunt Lascaris/
Johannesburg

MERIT AWARD
Consumer Television:
Over :30 Single

ART DIRECTOR
Jonn Boiler

WRITER
Glenn Cole

AGENCY PRODUCER
Charles Wolford

PRODUCTION COMPANY
A Band Apart Commercials

DIRECTOR
John Woo

CLIENT
Nike International

AGENCY
Wieden & Kennedy/
Amsterdam

(While waiting for a delayed flight, a group of the world's greatest soccer players stage an impromptu game in the airport.)

SUPER: *Nike swoosh.*

MERIT AWARD
Consumer Television:
Over :30 Single

ART DIRECTOR
Armando Hernandez

WRITER
Enrique Soler

AGENCY PRODUCER
Roger Barrera

PRODUCTION COMPANY
2001

DIRECTOR
Pucho Mentasi

CLIENT
United Airlines

AGENCY
Young & Rubicam/Miami

SFX: *Jet engine winding down.*

(Passengers thank the crew as they exit.)

MAN 1: *What a wonderful flight!*

MAN 2: *Marvelous!*

OLD LADY: *Oh, Captain.*

MAN 2: *I want to stay.*

YOUNG WOMAN: *Call me.*

YOUNG MAN: *Great flight, dude!*

SUPER: *With an award for the best overall service.*

SFX: *Camera flash.*

SUPER: *You'll find it hard to leave our planes.*

MAN 2: *I'm not leaving. No way.*

FLIGHT ATTENDANT: *Sir, sir.*

SUPER: *United Airlines. Rising.*

MUSIC: *"It's Been a Long Time Coming" by Crosby, Stills and Nash.*

(A boat is floating down a river. We see son on boat looking out window.)

SON: *Dad was here. Didn't talk about it much. Said you had to be there. Well, here I am.*

(Son disembarks, walks through village on river bank.)

SON: *Never talked about it much. Said you had to be there. Well, here I am.*

SON *(ON PHONE): Hey old man. How you doing?*

FATHER: *Ty, you still in Singapore?*

SON: *No. I'm on leave. I'm in Vietnam.*

FATHER: *Vietnam?*

SON: *Yeah.*

FATHER: *Want to talk about it?*

SON: *Yeah. I do. I sure do.*

SUPER: *AT&T. It's all within your reach.*

MERIT AWARD
Consumer Television:
Over :30 Single

ART DIRECTORS
Eric Steinhauser
Peter Levathes

WRITERS
Peter Levathes
Eric Steinhauser

AGENCY PRODUCER
Ken Yagoda

PRODUCTION COMPANY
PYTKA

DIRECTOR
Joe Pytka

CLIENT
AT&T

AGENCY
Young & Rubicam/
New York

SUPER: *Not everyone in this ad will have a Miller Time. But you might.*

MUSIC: *"Miller Time" theme*

(A beautiful young woman is sitting on a blanket having a picnic with a robot. He plays some sad song on the guitar for her as she sings along.)

SFX: *Robot-type sounds.*

(The robot grabs the Miller Lite, pours it all over himself and blows up. The woman carries the robot to the local repair shop. The repair guy throws the robot into a crushing mill. Seconds later, the robot appears as a big chunk of metal going into a bin for recycling.)

SUPER: *Later that year.*

(The woman, still sad, is sitting by the side of a country lane. A young man appears, gives her a can of Miller Lite.)

SFX: *Robot-type sounds.*

(She sees a little diode on the side of the can, realizes it's him and presses can to her face.)

SUPER: *Miller Time.*

SUPER: *www.millerlite.com*

SUPER: *Dick. This commercial is made and approved by me (Dick's signature).*

MERIT AWARD
Consumer Television:
Over :30 Campaign

ART DIRECTOR
Paul Malmstrom

WRITER
Linus Karlsson

AGENCY PRODUCER
Kristoffer Knutson

PRODUCTION COMPANY
Partizan

DIRECTOR
Traktor

CLIENT
Miller Brewing Company

AGENCY
Fallon McElligott/
Minneapolis

MERIT AWARD
Consumer Television:
Over :30 Campaign

ART DIRECTOR
Alexandra Taylor

WRITER
Adam Kean

AGENCY PRODUCERS
Sally-Ann Dale
Barbara Simon

PRODUCTION COMPANY
Paul Weiland Film Company

DIRECTOR
Alexandra Taylor

CLIENT
COI/Army

AGENCY
Saatchi & Saatchi/London

SUPER: *The town has been attacked by enemy soldiers.*

SUPER: *They've killed her husband... and raped her.*

SUPER: *The last thing she wants to see are more soldiers.*

SUPER: *But not all soldiers are men.*

SFX: *Stamping feet.*

SUPER: *Army. Be the best.*

MERIT AWARD
Consumer Television
:30 Single

ART DIRECTOR
Kathy Larkin Redick

WRITERS
David Lipson
Vincent Walker

AGENCY PRODUCER
Tom Twomey

PRODUCTION COMPANY
Concrete Productions

DIRECTOR
John Adams

CLIENT
Cherokee Casino

AGENCY
Ackerman McQueen/
Irving

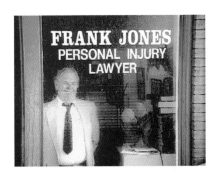

(A disheveled man sitting behind a desk is looking out his street level office window, having nothing better to do.)

SFX: *Squeaky desk fan, radio playing lightly in the background.*

(A runaway bus comes into view.)

SFX: *Tires screeching. Bus crash impact, glass shattering.*

(The man, witnessing the entire accident, grimaces and then smiles. We see the sign on his window: Frank Jones. Personal Injury Lawyer.)

SUPER: *Feeling Lucky?*

SUPER: *Cherokee Casino.*

(A fan is sitting on top of a table. A dog walks in, sits down in front of chair and stares up at fan. The dog jumps up on the chair and puts one paw on the table. We see the dog in front of the fan, panting while the wind blows on his face.)

ANNOUNCER: *Get ready. The new Volkswagens are coming.*

SUPER: *Drivers Wanted. Volkswagen.*

MERIT AWARD
Consumer Television
:30 Single

ART DIRECTOR
Don Shelford

WRITER
David Weist

AGENCY PRODUCER
Paul Shannon

PRODUCTION COMPANY
Satellite

DIRECTOR
Jhoan Camitz

CLIENT
Volkswagen

AGENCY
Arnold Communications/
Boston

SFX: *Radio makes light pop.*

(The mother offers the baby to her brother, and he is initially reluctant to take it. However, after some encouragement he takes the baby and holds it awkwardly in his arms. He clearly has never held a baby before.)

RADIO DJ: *We'll be right back after the break...*

RADIO: *...with twin air bags and ABS for...*

(The mother looks anxiously at the father and the father looks back at her. They both look at the baby.)

RADIO: *...an on the road price of...*

(Just in time the father leans over and switches the radio off.)

SUPER: *Volkswagen Golf. Surprisingly ordinary prices.*

MERIT AWARD
Consumer Television
:30 Single

ART DIRECTORS
Andrew Fraser
Ewan Paterson

WRITERS
Andrew Fraser
Ewan Paterson

AGENCY PRODUCER
Howard Spivey

PRODUCTION COMPANY
Stark Films

DIRECTOR
Steve Reeves

CLIENT
Volkswagen Group UK

AGENCY
BMP DDB/London

MERIT AWARD
Consumer Television
:30 Single

ART DIRECTOR
Wayne Best

WRITER
Adam Chasnow

AGENCY PRODUCER
Liz Graves

PRODUCTION COMPANY
JGF

DIRECTOR
Jeff Gorman

CLIENT
FOX Sports

AGENCY
Cliff Freeman and
Partners/New York

(A father is walking with his kids at night in a zoo. The dad shines a flashlight into a cage and searches around. The cage is empty.)

DAD: *Nothing. (Sighs.) Monkey cage.*

GIRL: *I don't see any monkeys.*

DAD: *Oh, there's an animal.*

(Shines his flashlight on a squirrel.)

DAD: *All right, let's go home.*

SUPER: *Get everything out of the way.*

SUPER: *There's a full day of Super Bowl pregame coverage.*

SUPER: *FOX Super Bowl XXXIII. Pregame 11 AM ET/8 AM PT.*

DAD: *Happy?*

MERIT AWARD
Consumer Television
:30 Single

ART DIRECTORS
Taras Wayner
Roger Camp

WRITER
Kevin Roddy

AGENCY PRODUCER
Liz Graves

PRODUCTION COMPANY
HKM

DIRECTOR
Noam Murro

CLIENT
FOX Sports

AGENCY
Cliff Freeman and
Partners/New York

(Two guys are standing near a tall ladder next to the side of a barn. One of the guys grabs a rope attached to a tree and climbs to the top of the ladder. Once at the top, he takes a big jump and swings down, crashing face first into the side of the barn and falling to the ground.)

SFX: *"Thud" of guy hitting ground.*

(The other guy looks at the guy lying there.)

OTHER GUY: *That sounded like Anderson.*

(In actual game footage Brady Anderson makes a catch by crashing into the outfield wall. We hear the thud via sounds of the game.)

GAME ANNOUNCER: *Brady Anderson at the wall... leaps and makes a spectacular catch. Wow, now you have to hope he's all right.*

SUPER: *FOX Sounds of the Game. Don't Try It At Home.*

SUPER: *Major League Baseball.*

SUPER: *FOX Saturday Game of the Week*

(A guy fills a shopping cart with concrete blocks, bags of cement; begins pushing cart fast across parking lot. Cart smashed into another guy crouching in parking lot wearing catcher's gear.)

GUY 1: *Did that look like Bernie Williams?* (Actual Catcher cam game footage of Bernie Williams charging home plate.)

Game Announcer: *Here comes Williams... he's out at the plate. A major collision but Wilson was able to hang on...*

SUPER: *FOX Catcher Cam. Don't Try it at Home.*

SUPER: *Major League Baseball. FOX Saturday Game of the Week.*

MERIT AWARD
Consumer Television
:30 Single

ART DIRECTORS
Taras Wayner
Roger Camp

WRITER
Kevin Roddy

AGENCY PRODUCER
Liz Graves

PRODUCTION COMPANY
HKM

DIRECTOR
Noam Murro

CLIENT
FOX Sports

AGENCY
Cliff Freeman and
Partners/New York

(A guy is standing next to a horse. Another guy, dressed in catcher's gear, comes and crouches down behind the horse.)

GUY 1: *Ready?*

GUY 2: *Yep.*

(First guy slaps horse on rear end. Horse reacts, kicking guy in catcher's mask.)

GUY 1: *That, uh, look like the foul tip into Rodriguez?*

(We see actual Catcher Cam footage of Rodriguez getting hit by foul tip.)

GAME ANNOUNCER: *Rodriguez really gets nailed on this one. Even off his mask that's gotta hurt. Makes you wonder why anyone wants to be a catcher. Tools of ignorance or not, that's gotta hurt.*

SUPER: *FOX Catcher Cam. Don't try it at home.*

SUPER: *Major League Baseball.*

SUPER: *FOX Saturday game of the week.*

MERIT AWARD
Consumer Television
:30 Single

ART DIRECTORS
Taras Wayner
Roger Camp

WRITER
Kevin Roddy

AGENCY PRODUCER
Liz Graves

PRODUCTION COMPANY
HKM

DIRECTOR
Noam Murro

CLIENT
FOX Sports

AGENCY
Cliff Freeman and
Partners/New York

MERIT AWARD
Consumer Television
:30 Single

ART DIRECTORS
Taras Wayner
Roger Camp

WRITER
Kevin Roddy

AGENCY PRODUCER
Liz Graves

PRODUCTION COMPANY
HKM

DIRECTOR
Noam Murro

CLIENT
FOX Sports

AGENCY
Cliff Freeman and
Partners/New York

SFX: *Speeding truck.*

MAN: *Yeah, that looked like a Johnson fastball.*

GAME ANNOUNCER: *Johnson is really bringing the heat today. All game long it's been grab a bat... have a look... and take a seat.*

SUPER: *FOX Catcher Cam. Don't try it at home.*

SUPER: *Major League Baseball.*

SUPER: *FOX Saturday game of the week.*

MERIT AWARD
Consumer Television
:30 Single

ART DIRECTOR
Kilpatrick Anderson

WRITER
Kevin Roddy

AGENCY PRODUCER
Nick Felder

PRODUCTION COMPANY
MJZ

DIRECTOR
Rocky Morton

CLIENT
FOX Sports

AGENCY
Cliff Freeman and
Partners/New York

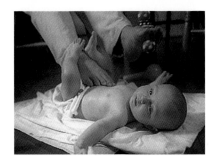

(A pair of men's feet, acting amazingly like hands, adeptly change an infant's diaper and fasten it with a diaper pin.)

ANNOUNCER: *These feet belong to Roger Camp, an extraordinary man who overcame a tremendous challenge. Roger is determined to lead an ordinary life, to perform the everyday tasks that you and I take for granted...so he won't miss a second of FOX Sports.com. Whether it's daily insights from John Madden or real-time scores and stats, it's like having the NFL on FOX, online.*

(Man shakes rattle with toes over baby on the floor on a blanket.)

SUPER: *foxsports.com. Making A Difference.*

ANNOUNCER: *Meet Wayne Best. He saw kids in his community without direction and did something about it. He got them off the street and put them to work, teaching important lessons in community service, responsibility and helping others. So he can spend all his time on foxsports.com. Where he enters his Zip Code to get the latest on his favorite home teams. It's like FOX Sports Net, online.*

SUPER: *foxsports.com. Making a difference.*

MERIT AWARD
Consumer Television
:30 Single

ART DIRECTOR
Kilpatrick Anderson

WRITER
Kevin Roddy

AGENCY PRODUCER
Nick Felder

PRODUCTION COMPANY
MJZ

DIRECTOR
Rocky Morton

CLIENT
FOX Sports

AGENCY
Cliff Freeman and
Partners/New York

WOMAN: *Action adventure?*

CLERK 1: *Sure. Follow me.*

(Clerk leads woman to action adventure section. There we see an older cowboy teaching two clerks how to throw a fake punch.)

COWBOY: *So the trick is to come as close as you can to the person and let the camera do the rest... Do it.*

(Clerk 2 rears back and hits Clerk 3 square in the face. Clerk 3 cries out in pain. Cowboy turns to Clerk 2.)

COWBOY: *That's a good start-except we don't want to actually hit the person... Do it again.*

(Clerk 2 rears back and again hits Clerk 3 square in the face. Clerk 3 again cries out in pain.)

COWBOY: *Okay. Let's try one more where you don't actually hit him... Do it.*

(Clerk 2 rears back and hits Clerk 3, who drops to his knees, grabbing the cowboy on the way down.)

COWBOY: *Ooooohhh. That was so close.*

SUPER: *Welcome to Hollywood.*

SUPER: *Hollywood Video.*

MERIT AWARD
Consumer Television
:30 Single

ART DIRECTOR
Matt Vescovo

WRITER
Eric Silver

AGENCY PRODUCER
Nick Felder

PRODUCTION COMPANY
Tate & Partners

DIRECTOR
Baker Smith

CLIENT
Hollywood Video

AGENCY
Cliff Freeman and
Partners/New York

MERIT AWARD
Consumer Television
:30 Single

ART DIRECTOR
Matt Vescovo

WRITER
Eric Silver

AGENCY PRODUCER
Nick Felder

PRODUCTION COMPANY
Tate & Partners

DIRECTOR
Baker Smith

CLIENT
Hollywood Video

AGENCY
Cliff Freeman and
Partners/New York

WOMAN: *Hi. Could you tell us a little about this movie?*

(The clerk gestures for couple to wait one second and then knocks on cabinet under desk.)

CLERK: *Don, we need you up here.*

(The cabinet door slides open and we see a man in a suit crammed inside. The man then pops up, looks at the movie box, and begins speaking in a movie trailer announcer's voice.)

DON: *From flesh to steel. From blood to blade. From man to mutant. Evil has a new enemy. Justice has a new weapon. And the world has a new hero.*

CLERK: *That was real nice, Don.*

DON: *Uh-huh.*

SUPER: *Hollywood Video.*

MERIT AWARD
Consumer Television
:30 Single

ART DIRECTOR
Roger Camp

WRITER
Eric Silver

AGENCY PRODUCER
Nick Felder

PRODUCTION COMPANY
Hungry Man

DIRECTOR
John O'Hagan

CLIENT
Outpost.com

AGENCY
Cliff Freeman and
Partners/New York

SPOKESMAN: *We want people to remember our name, Outpost.com. That's why we went to day care centers all across this great country of ours and met with the youngsters.*

(We see footage of six-year-old kids running around day care center laughing, etc.)

SPOKESMAN: *Then we permanently tattooed their foreheads with our name.*

(We see tattoo artist and kids with huge Outpost.com tattoos on their heads. The kids are now crying.)

SPOKESMAN: *Excessive? Maybe. But we're on a mission.*

SUPER: *Send complaints to Outpost.com.*

SUPER: *Outpost.com. The place to buy computer stuff online.*

SUPER: *Miller Time.*

MUSIC: *"Miller Time" theme.*

(We see a man through his apartment window, heading for the fridge. The man reaches in and pulls out a bottle of Miller Lite, reads the cap on the bottle. Reluctantly, he starts dancing. The man dances for a while, then looks at cap again. We can see that it says "Twist to open." He starts dancing again, this time a bit more determined.)

SUPER: *www.millerlite.com*

SUPER: *Dick. This commercial is made and approved by me (Dick's signature).*

MERIT AWARD
Consumer Television
:30 Single

ART DIRECTOR
Harvey Marco

WRITER
Dean Buckhorn

AGENCY PRODUCER
Jack Nelson

PRODUCTION COMPANY
HSI

DIRECTOR
Gerard de Thame

CLIENT
Miller Brewing Company

AGENCY
Fallon McElligott/
Minneapolis

SUPER: *Manson parole hearing.*

MANSON: *First of all, I give you respect and want peace. I do not enter into your circle. What you do in that circle is your business. You step in this circle and I'll deal with you. Do you understand me now?*

SUPER: *No chance.*

SUPER: *Ameristar.*

SFX: *Coins hitting metal tray.*

SUPER: *Chance.*

MERIT AWARD
Consumer Television
:30 Single

ART DIRECTOR
Matt Mowat

WRITER
Chuck Meehan

AGENCY PRODUCER
James Horner

PRODUCTION COMPANIES
Five Union Square Productions
Maiden Lane Productions

DIRECTOR
Tom Schiller

CLIENT
Ameristar Casinos

AGENCY
Goldberg Moser O'Neill/
San Francisco

MERIT AWARD
Consumer Television
:30 Single

ART DIRECTOR
Matt Mowat

WRITER
Chuck Meehan

AGENCY PRODUCER
James Horner

PRODUCTION COMPANY
Five Union Square Productions

DIRECTOR
Tom Schiller

CLIENT
Ameristar Casinos

AGENCY
Goldberg Moser O'Neill/
San Francisco

ANNOUNCER: *Stevie Moyer will be attempting a forward three-and-one-half somersault with two-and-one-half twists.*

SUPER: *No chance.*

SUPER: *Ameristar.*

SFX: *Coins hitting metal tray.*

SUPER: *Chance.*

MERIT AWARD
Consumer Television
:30 Single

ART DIRECTOR
Jim Carroll

WRITERS
John Brockenbrough
Chris Brignola

AGENCY PRODUCER
Liz Hodge

PRODUCTION COMPANY
Chelsea Pictures

DIRECTOR
Nicholas Barker

CLIENT
Excite

AGENCY
Lowe & Partners/SMS/
New York

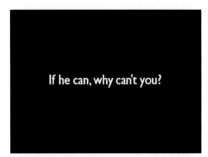

SUPER: *With Excite.com, he met his wife in an online chat room.*

SUPER: *If he can, why can't you?*

SUPER: *Excite.com*

SUPER: *With Excite.com, she instantly sends photos to friends around the world.*

SUPER: *If she can, why can't you?*

SUPER: *Excite.com*

MERIT AWARD
Consumer Television
:30 Single

ART DIRECTOR
Jim Carroll

WRITER
John Brockenbrough

AGENCY PRODUCER
Liz Hodge

PRODUCTION COMPANY
Chelsea Pictures

DIRECTOR
Nicholas Barker

CLIENT
Excite

AGENCY
Lowe & Partners/SMS/
New York

SUPER: *With Excite.com, he got a free e-mail account.*

SUPER: *If he can, why can't you?*

SUPER: *Excite.com*

MERIT AWARD
Consumer Television
:30 Single

ART DIRECTOR
Jim Carroll

WRITER
John Brockenbrough

AGENCY PRODUCER
Liz Hodge

PRODUCTION COMPANY
Chelsea Pictures

DIRECTOR
Nicholas Barker

CLIENT
Excite

AGENCY
Lowe & Partners/SMS/
New York

MERIT AWARD
Consumer Television
:30 Single

ART DIRECTORS
Rob Potts
Yan Elliott

WRITERS
Andy Jex
Jim Hosking

AGENCY PRODUCER
Zoe Bell

PRODUCTION COMPANY
Spectre

DIRECTOR
Daniel Kleinman

CLIENT
Van Den Bergh Foods

AGENCY
Mother/London

(Gavin is eating Super Noodles on the Sofa. Thomas, his toddler son, sits with him.)

JENNY (Off camera): *I'm really dreading tonight, do you know that. I could do with staying in and watching the telly. I don't know why Kate has to get me to vet every single bloke she goes out with. It's ridiculous. I don't know why she can't trust her own instincts. I go through this every time. I'm gonna be late – did I leave my shirt in there?... Gav... am I talking to myself?*

(Gavin eating Super Noodles, instinctively wipes mouth on fabric draped over sofa.)

JENNY: *Gav? Hello? Am I talking to myself...?*

(Gavin, realizing he has just wiped his mouth on Jenny's shirt, puts the shirt next to Thomas and flicks some noodles on the toddler. Jenny enters to discover shirt.)

JENNY: *Oh, Thomas!*

GAVIN: *All very well doing that, mate. Ruined the shirt-marvelous.*

ANNOUNCER: *Batchelors Super Noodles. We call them super, you buy them.*

MERIT AWARD
Consumer Television
:30 Single

ART DIRECTOR
Eric Aronin

WRITER
Eric Aronin

PRODUCTION COMPANY
Backyard Productions

DIRECTOR
Rob Pritts

CLIENT
Stand-Up NY

AGENCY
Ogilvy & Mather/New York

There's a time and a place for comedy.

DOCTOR: *All right, I want you to take a deep breath and hold it... Hold it.*

SFX: *Crinkly examination-table paper.*

DOCTOR: *Okay, let it out now. Once more. Okay, fine. Take my fingers and squeeze them as hard as you can. That's good. Now the other hand. Now pull.*

(As the patient pulls his fingers, the doctor cuts a big fart.)

DOCTOR: *Gotcha!*

SUPER: *There's a time and a place for comedy. Stand-up NY Comedy Club.*

(A visibly disgusted man watches as his neighbor attempts to back his boat into driveway.)

ANNOUNCER: *This is enough to put a High Life man off his lunch. Time was, a man knew how to command his own vehicle. Just how far are we willing to fall? Better reacquaint yourself with the High Life, soldier, before someone tries to take away your Miller Time.*

SUPER: *Miller High Life.*

MERIT AWARD
Consumer Television
:30 Single

ART DIRECTOR
Jeff Williams

WRITER
Jeff Kling

AGENCY PRODUCER
Jeff Selis

PRODUCTION COMPANY
@radical.media

DIRECTOR
Errol Morris

CLIENT
Miller Brewing Company

AGENCY
Wieden & Kennedy/Portland

SFX: *Duct tape tearing.*

ANNOUNCER: *Even when a man has his toolbox handy, isn't it nice to turn to this all-purpose helper? The High Life man knows that if the pharaohs had duct tape, the Sphinx would still have a nose. We salute you, duct tape. You help a man get to Miller Time.*

SUPER: *Miller High Life.*

MERIT AWARD
Consumer Television
:30 Single

ART DIRECTOR
Jeff Williams

WRITER
Jeff Kling

AGENCY PRODUCER
Jeff Selis

PRODUCTION COMPANY
@radical.media

DIRECTOR
Errol Morris

CLIENT
Miller Brewing Company

AGENCY
Wieden & Kennedy/Portland

MERIT AWARD
Consumer Television
:30 Single

ART DIRECTOR
Jeff Williams

WRITER
Jeff Kling

AGENCY PRODUCER
Jeff Selis

PRODUCTION COMPANY
@radical.media

DIRECTOR
Errol Morris

CLIENT
Miller Brewing Company

AGENCY
Wieden & Kennedy/Portland

SFX: *Burgers sizzling on grill.*

ANNOUNCER: *Something's not quite right. There. Now that's a sandwich. There's only one beer that can stand up to a man's meal. Right again. That's living the High Life. That's Miller Time.*

SUPER: *Miller High Life.*

MERIT AWARD
Consumer Television
:30 Single

ART DIRECTOR
Jeff Williams

WRITER
Jeff Kling

AGENCY PRODUCER
Jeff Selis

PRODUCTION COMPANY
@radical.media

DIRECTOR
Errol Morris

CLIENT
Miller Brewing Company

AGENCY
Wieden & Kennedy/Portland

ANNOUNCER: *Sometimes a man gets too hungry to clean his hands properly. The powdered sugar on this donut puts a semi-protective barrier between your fingerprint and your nutrition. But even if some grease does get on that donut, that's just flavor to a High Life man.*

SUPER: *Miller High Life.*

ANNOUNCER: *Look at that bounty. Everything on the plate within the same uniform color range. If that isn't food for a man who can say what is. Tuck into that golden plate special with the only beer that fits the life to which you're called. The High Life. This is your Miller Time.*

SUPER: *Miller High Life.*

MERIT AWARD
Consumer Television
:30 Single

ART DIRECTOR
Jeff Williams

WRITER
Jeff Kling

AGENCY PRODUCER
Jeff Selis

PRODUCTION COMPANY
@radical.media

DIRECTOR
Errol Morris

CLIENT
Miller Brewing Company

AGENCY
Wieden & Kennedy/Portland

ANNOUNCER: *That last egg's looking real good. You've had quite a few, though. Maybe you shouldn't. But... if you make a light choice here, maybe you will have room for just one more. See there? When you live the High Life, you can live it both ways.*

SUPER: *Miller High Life.*

MERIT AWARD
Consumer Television
:30 Single

ART DIRECTOR
Jeff Williams

WRITER
Jeff Kling

AGENCY PRODUCER
Jeff Selis

PRODUCTION COMPANY
@radical.media

DIRECTOR
Errol Morris

CLIENT
Miller Brewing Company

AGENCY
Wieden & Kennedy/Portland

MERIT AWARD
Consumer Television
:30 Single

ART DIRECTOR
Rob Palmer

WRITERS
Jamie Barrett
Jim LeMaitre

AGENCY PRODUCER
Jennifer Smieja

PRODUCTION COMPANY
@radical.media

DIRECTOR
Frank Todaro

CLIENT
Nike

AGENCY
Wieden & Kennedy/Portland

ANNOUNCER: *"Golf's Not Hard!"* with Tiger Woods and the Air Zoom TW.

TIGER WOODS: *A common problem in golf is the slice. One solution is to play with a gallery.*

(He prepares to hit.)

TIGER: *Having women and children to my left and right is a handy reminder that I need to keep my clubface square...*

(He rips a three wood through a one foot-wide space in a gallery full of people.)

TIGER: *Now, let's see how this tip works for Joe, a 27 handicapper from Logansport... Go get 'em Joe!*

(Joe gets ready to hit ball with fake cut-out people making up the gallery on each side of him. Joe strikes the ball, obliterating three of the cut-out people.)

TIGER: *Joe overcompensated for his slice and hooked it. Something we'll be sure to work on next time!*

SUPER: *Nike.*

MERIT AWARD
Consumer Television
:30 Single

ART DIRECTOR
Linda Knight

WRITER
Kash Sree

AGENCY PRODUCER
Colleen Wellman

PRODUCTION COMPANY
Propaganda

DIRECTORS
Lasse Halstrom
Alfonso Cuaron

CLIENT
Nike

AGENCY
Wieden & Kennedy/Portland

SFX: *Alarm clock.*

(Camera follows a boy who begins his day using his feet to do most everything: open and close doors, flush the toilet, turn on the TV and change channels.)

SFX: *Soccer game on TV.*

(He dribbles a box of cereal and kicks it onto the table. Final shot is of the boy trying to raise a spoonful of cereal to his mouth with his feet.)

SUPER: *(What are you getting ready for?)*

SUPER: *Nike.*

WOMAN: *Good morning.*

(As she pulls a letter out of her mailbox, Tim Duncan swats it down... He is whistling "While Strolling Through the Park One Day" throughout. Another woman is arguing with store owner over the price of a melon.)

WOMAN: *Half off.*

MAN: *Are you crazy or something?*

(Tim Duncan swats melon down.)

(Duncan continues, swatting down a water container, a hotdog someone is holding, etc. Duncan tries to swat down a girl's lollipop, but it sticks to his hand. He unsticks it, gives it back and, shrugging, walks off.)

SUPER: *(What are you getting ready for?)*

SUPER: *Nike.*

MUSIC: *Steel drum.*

MAN: *Your sister's not the problem. I just don't want to spend two weeks cooped up with the rest of your family...*

(He chokes on a bite of steak.)

WOMAN: *What? Are you all right? Somebody help us!*

(Gabby Reese leaps up and spikes him in the back. The meat goes flying across the restaurant.)

SUPER: *(What are you getting ready for?)*

GABBY: *Rotation.*

(She and her teammates rotate seats.)

SUPER: *(What are you getting ready for?)*

SUPER: *Nike.*

MERIT AWARD
Consumer Television
:30 Single

ART DIRECTOR
Hal Curtis

WRITER
Chuck McBride

AGENCY PRODUCER
Donna Portaro

PRODUCTION COMPANY
Satellite

DIRECTOR
Jhoan Camitz

CLIENT
Nike

AGENCY
Wieden & Kennedy/Portland

MERIT AWARD
Consumer Television
:30 Single

ART DIRECTOR
Leslie Ali

WRITER
Derek Barnes

AGENCY PRODUCER
Beth Barrett

PRODUCTION COMPANY
Oil Factory

DIRECTORS
Dom&Nic

CLIENT
Nike

AGENCY
Wieden & Kennedy/Portland

MERIT AWARD
Consumer Television
:30 Single

ART DIRECTOR
Hal Curtis

WRITER
Chuck McBride

AGENCY PRODUCER
Jennifer Smieja

PRODUCTION COMPANY
HKM

DIRECTOR
Mike Mills

CLIENT
Nike

AGENCY
Wieden & Kennedy/Portland

(Jerome Bettis runs to the edge of the mountain and leaps off, tumbling down the mountain. He slams into a tree stump and over some rocks. After finally stopping, he gets up, brushes off his face mask, and runs back up the mountain.)

SUPER: (What are you getting ready for?)

SUPER: Nike.

MERIT AWARD
Consumer Television
:30 Campaign

ART DIRECTOR
Alan Pafenbach

WRITERS
Lance Jensen
Stuart D'Rozario

AGENCY PRODUCER
Bill Goodell

PRODUCTION COMPANY
Manifesto

DIRECTOR
Nick Lewin

CLIENT
Volkswagen

AGENCY
Arnold Communications/
Boston

Reverse engineered from UFOs.

MUSIC: Fluke's "Absurd"

SUPER: Reverse engineered from UFOs.

SUPER: Drivers wanted. Volkswagen.

(The loud sound of hammering echoes throughout a suburban development in the middle of the night. The hammering is interrupted every so often by screams. Lights start to come on in the windows of houses. In the backyard of one of the houses, a man is hammering away, building an outdoor deck. Working in the dark, he is smashing his fingers with the hammer.)

SUPER: *Get everything out of the way.*

SUPER: *There's a full day of Super Bowl pregame coverage.*

SUPER: *FOX Super Bowl XXXIII. Pregame 11 AM ET / 8 AM PT.*

MERIT AWARD
Consumer Television
:30 Campaign

ART DIRECTOR
Wayne Best

WRITER
Adam Chasnow

AGENCY PRODUCER
Liz Graves

PRODUCTION COMPANY
JGF

DIRECTOR
Jeff Gorman

CLIENT
FOX Sports

AGENCY
Cliff Freeman and
Partners/New York

(A guy is standing next to a horse. Another guy, dressed in catcher's gear, comes and crouches down behind the horse.)

GUY 1: *Ready?*

GUY 2: *Yep.*

(First guy slaps horse on rear end. Horse reacts, kicking guy in catcher's mask.)

GUY 1: *That, uh, look like the foul tip into Rodriguez?*

(We see actual Catcher Cam footage of Rodriguez getting hit by foul tip.)

GAME ANNOUNCER: *Rodriguez really gets nailed on this one. Even off his mask that's gotta hurt. Makes you wonder why anyone wants to be a catcher. Tools of ignorance or not, that's gotta hurt.*

SUPER: *FOX Catcher Cam. Don't try it at home.*

SUPER: *Major League Baseball.*

SUPER: *FOX Saturday game of the week.*

MERIT AWARD
Consumer Television
:30 Campaign

ART DIRECTORS
Taras Wayner
Roger Camp

WRITER
Kevin Roddy

AGENCY PRODUCER
Liz Graves

PRODUCTION COMPANY
HKM

DIRECTOR
Noam Murro

CLIENT
FOX Sports

AGENCY
Cliff Freeman and
Partners/New York

MERIT AWARD
Consumer Television
:30 Campaign

ART DIRECTOR
Matt Vescovo

WRITER
Eric Silver

AGENCY PRODUCER
Nick Felder

PRODUCTION COMPANY
Tate & Partners

DIRECTOR
Baker Smith

CLIENT
Hollywood Video

AGENCY
Cliff Freeman and
Partners/New York

MAN: *So you're saying select new releases are guaranteed every single day of the week?*

CLERK: *That's right.*

(Fade to black. "Movie credits" start to roll, listing everyone responsible for previous five seconds of dialogue.)

SUPER: *Welcome to Hollywood.*

SUPER: *Hollywood Video.*

MERIT AWARD
Consumer Television
:30 Campaign

ART DIRECTOR
Matt Vescovo

WRITER
Eric Silver

AGENCY PRODUCER
Nick Felder

PRODUCTION COMPANIES
Tate & Partners
Moxie Pictures

DIRECTORS
Baker Smith
Todd Philips

CLIENT
Hollywood Video

AGENCY
Cliff Freeman and
Partners/New York

CLERK: *Okay, have these new releases back by Monday.*

WOMAN: *Isn't that five days?*

CLERK (*Begins singing; very campy*): *Five days to watch these movies.*

(Clerk 2 then slides across the floor, á la Fred Astaire.)

CLERK 2 (*SINGING*): *Five days including new releases.*

(Clerks start to sing and dance in unison.)

CLERKS: *Everything in the store is five days.*

(Clerks join hands and begin spinning each other.)

CLERK 1: *It can't be.*

CLERK 2: *It sure is.*

CLERK 1: *No way.*

CLERKS: *Five days.*

(Clerk 1 then accidentally throws Clerk 2 through plate glass window. Clerk 2 lies motionless. Clerk 1 goes on with the show.)

CLERK 1: *Each and every rental-five days.*

SUPER: *Welcome to Hollywood.*

SUPER: *Hollywood Video.*

SUPER: *Larry Shanet, President of Comedy Central.*

LARRY: *Hi, I'm Larry Shanet, President of Comedy Central. I'd like to remind you that Comedy Central has quality comedy program-ming while other networks don't. CNN, not funny. VH1, not funny. C-SPAN, not funny. The Discovery Channel, well, those baboons with the red asses, they're kind of funny. But how often do you see those things? Comedy Central, that's your best bet.*

SUPER: *Comedy Central.*

MERIT AWARD
Consumer Television
:30 Campaign

ART DIRECTORS
Lori Campbell
Stephen Pearson
Scott Vitrone

WRITERS
Lori Campbell
Stephen Pearson
Scott Vitrone

PRODUCTION COMPANY
Hungry Man

DIRECTORS
Hank Perlman
Mark Foster

CLIENT
Comedy Central

AGENCY
Dweck and Campbell/
New York

SUPER: *Miller Time.*

MUSIC: *"Miller Time" theme.*

(A great dane carries a Miller Lite in his mouth, then sets it down.)

GUY: *All right.*

SUPER: *"The things you do for beer!"*

SUPER: *Miller Time*

MERIT AWARD
Consumer Television
:30 Campaign

ART DIRECTOR
Harvey Marco

WRITER
Dean Buckhorn

AGENCY PRODUCERS
Jack Nelson
Julie Hampel

PRODUCTION COMPANIES
HSI

@radical media

DIRECTORS
Gerard de Thame
Tarsem

CLIENT
Miller Brewing Company

AGENCY
Fallon McElligott/Minneapolis

MERIT AWARD
Consumer Television
:30 Campaign

ART DIRECTOR
Matt Mowat

WRITER
Chuck Meehan

AGENCY PRODUCER
James Horner

PRODUCTION COMPANIES
Five Union Square Productions
Maiden Lane Productions

DIRECTOR
Tom Schiller

CLIENT
Ameristar Casinos

AGENCY
Goldberg Moser O'Neill/
San Francisco

SUPER: *Manson parole hearing.*

MANSON: *First of all, I give you respect and want peace. I do not enter into your circle. What you do in that circle is your business. You step in this circle and I'll deal with you. Do you understand me now?*

SUPER: *No chance.*

SUPER: *Ameristar.*

SFX: *Coins hitting metal tray.*

SUPER: *Chance.*

MERIT AWARD
Consumer Television
:30 Campaign

ART DIRECTOR
Jim Carroll

WRITER
John Brockenbrough

AGENCY PRODUCER
Liz Hodge

PRODUCTION COMPANY
Chelsea Pictures

DIRECTOR
Nicholas Barker

CLIENT
Excite

AGENCY
Lowe & Partners/SMS/
New York

SUPER: *With Excite.com, she instantly sends photos to friends around the world.*

SUPER: *If she can, why can't you?*

SUPER: *Excite.com*

SUPERS: *Manicure: $15.*
Lace skirt: $85.
Vintage evening bag: $60.
Look on old boyfriend's face at the reunion: priceless.

SUPERS: *There are some things money can't buy.*
For everything else there's MasterCard.

ANNOUNCER: *Accepted all over, even beauty salons.*

SUPERS: *MasterCard.*

MERIT AWARD
Consumer Television
:30 Campaign

ART DIRECTOR
Jeroen Bours

WRITER
Joyce King Thomas

AGENCY PRODUCER
Sally Hotchkiss

PRODUCTION COMPANY
Tony Kaye & Partners

DIRECTOR
Tony Kaye

CLIENT
MasterCard

AGENCY
McCann-Erickson/
New York

SUPER: *Processing Goalie.*

SUPER: *Still processing.*

SUPER: *Time for a Pentium II processor?*

SFX. *Intel bong.*

SUPER: *Intel.*

MERIT AWARD
Consumer Television :30
Campaign

ART DIRECTOR
Walt Connelly

WRITER
Larry Silberfein

AGENCY PRODUCERS
Noel Tirsch
Tom Meloth

PRODUCTION COMPANY
Propaganda

DIRECTOR
Gore Verbinky

CLIENT
Intel

AGENCY
Messner Vetere Berger
McNamee Schmetterer/
EuroRSCG/New York

MERIT AWARD
Consumer Television
:30 Campaign

ART DIRECTOR
Paul Foulkes

WRITERS
Tyler Hampton
Jeff Odiorne

AGENCY PRODUCERS
Tiffany Richter
Chris Weldon

PRODUCTION COMPANY
Complete Pandemonium

DIRECTOR
Steve Williams

CLIENT
Electronic Arts

AGENCY
Odiorne Wilde Narraway
& Partners/San Francisco

(A conversation in a hardware store. We see cuts of game screens throughout.)

BIKER: *I'm racing...*

CLERK: *Oh...*

BIKER: *I'm moving pretty quick...*

CLERK: *Mm-hmm... the high speed...*

BIKER: *High speed stuff.*

SFX: *Music and motorcycle racing sounds.*

BIKER: *Which one would be better to knock a guy off a motorcycle? This one or this one? Whaddya think?*

CLERK: *Yeah, I think the 2-by-4's better.*

SFX: *Music and motorcycle racing sounds.*

BIKER: *I'm very impressed with your knowledge of road combat.*

CLERK: *Oh.*

ANNOUNCER: *Road Rash 3D. Soundtrack on Atlantic Records.*

SUPER: *Electronic Arts.*

MERIT AWARD
Consumer Television
:30 Campaign

ART DIRECTORS
Susan Westre
Per Robert Jacobson
Genevra Capece
Chris Curry

WRITERS
Steve Hayden
Chris Wall
Dan Burrier
Kate Levin
Philip McEvoy
Brendan Gibbons

AGENCY PRODUCERS
Lee Weiss
Jen Morelli
Oritte Bendory
Jenny Russo

PRODUCTION COMPANY
PYTKA

DIRECTOR
Joe Pytka

CLIENT
IBM

AGENCY
Ogilvy & Mather/New York

SUPER: *boondoggle.*

COMPUTER GUY: *You've been to some nice places.*

EXECUTIVE: *Yes, I have. Singapore is terrific.*

EXECUTIVE: *That's the prime minister of some... something. (Picks up mask.) See this?*

COMPUTER GUY: *Scary.*

EXECUTIVE: *Fatima. Big star... Fifty-two countries, two years.*

COMPUTER GUY: *This new software I've installed, it's gonna save your life. It's called Lotus Notes. It lets you collaborate on projects all over the world. You never have to leave your office. It's gonna be great to have you around.*

SUPER: *Lotus Notes from IBM. Work Global. Stay Local.*

SUPER: *E-Business Solutions.*

SUPER: *BM. Solutions for a small planet.*

(As Tiger Woods begins his backswing on a fairway shot, a young man who has forced his way to the front of the gallery raises an "Applause" sign)

SFX: *Roar of crowd*

SPORTS COMMENTATOR: *Well I don't know what happened there, but I mean that's 30 yards too far to the right, and the lie didn't look too bad.*

SUPER: *It's a whole new game when you've got money on it.*

ANNOUNCER: *Superspreads. It's a whole new sports betting system.*

MERIT AWARD
Consumer Television
:30 Campaign

ART DIRECTORS
Paul Sanders
Rupert Allcock
Kristen Goudemond

WRITERS
Adam Wittert
Alexia Milner
Hugh Bush

AGENCY PRODUCER
Helen D'Hotman

PRODUCTION COMPANY
Glide Productions

DIRECTOR
Richard Williams

CLIENT
IGN Superspreads

AGENCY
Ogilvy & Mather Rightford
Searle-Tripp & Makin/
Johannesburg

RICH EISEN (On air): *Stuart and I get the playoff picture back from the darkroom when we come back.*

OFF CAMERA ASSISTANT: *We're clear!*

SUPER: *On set commercial break. 2:43 AM, August 18, 1998.*

EISEN: *Prompter's going too fast. I can't keep up!*

LOU DUVA (Sponging Eisen down): *It's not the teleprompter, it's you! Now stop the **##!!!$$##.*

EISEN: *My throat! I can hardly talk.*

DUVA: *Give'm some tea! Give'm some tea!*

EISEN: *I can't go back out there. I don't wanna go back out there. Cut me! Cut me, Lou!*

DUVA: *Come on, baby! Come on. Snap out of it! Don't be a lollipop. Get out there!*

EISEN (Back on air): *Well, without question these days, the word on everybody's lips...*

SUPER: *This is SportsCenter. ESPN.*

MERIT AWARD
Consumer Television
:30 Campaign

WRITER
Ernest Lupinacci

AGENCY PRODUCER
Peter Cline

PRODUCTION COMPANY
Hungry Man

DIRECTOR
Paul Norling

CLIENT
ESPN

AGENCY
Wieden & Kennedy/Portland

MERIT AWARD
Consumer Television
:30 Campaign

ART DIRECTORS
Hal Curtis
Linda Knight
Leslie Ali

WRITERS
Chuck McBride
Kash Sree
Derek Barnes

AGENCY PRODUCERS
Beth Barrett
Jennifer Smieja
Colleen Wellman

PRODUCTION COMPANIES
HKM
The Oil Factory
Propaganda

DIRECTORS
Mike Mills
Lasse Halstrom
Alfonso Cuaron
Dom&Nic

CLIENT
Nike

AGENCY
Wieden & Kennedy/
Portland

SFX: *Alarm clock.*

(Camera follows a boy who begins his day using his feet to do most everything: open and close doors, flush the toilet, turn on the TV and change channels.)

SFX: *Soccer game on TV.*

(He dribbles a box of cereal and kicks it onto the table. Final shot is of the boy trying to raise a spoonful of cereal to his mouth with his feet.)

SUPER: *(What are you getting ready for?)*

SUPER: *Nike.*

MERIT AWARD
Consumer Television
:30 Campaign

ART DIRECTORS
Arty Tan
Hal Curtis
Danielle Flagg

WRITERS
Jim LeMaitre
Chuck McBride
Jonathan Cude

AGENCY PRODUCERS
Kevin Diller
Jennifer Smieja
Donna Portaro

PRODUCTION COMPANIES
Propaganda
Satellite
Oil Factory

DIRECTOR
Vaughan Arnell
Jhoan Camitz
Dom&Nic

CLIENT
Nike

AGENCY
Wieden & Kennedy/
Portland

SFX: *Heart monitor, hospital ambience.*

(We follow Picabo Street in a wheelchair as she careens down a hospital corridor, down a stairwell, through a waiting room and out the door.)

SFX: *Ambulance, cars screeching.*

SUPER: *(What are you getting ready for?)*

SUPER: *Nike.*

SFX: *Ambient nighttime swamp sounds; birds calling, crickets chirping, etc.*

LOUIE: *Ferret, ferret, ferret. Do you even remember our original plan?*

SFX: *Ferret squeals affirmatively.*

LOUIE: *Oh, you do, huh? Well, you didn't stick to it, did you?*

SFX: *Ferret squeals "no."*

LOUIE: *What were you… nuts?*

SFX: *Thud as Louie's hand hits log.*

LOUIE: *Look at me…*

SFX: *Ferret squeals "what?"*

LOUIE: *…how can you even look at me? Turn away.*

SFX: *Ferret squeals in shame.*

SUPER: *Budweiser.*

MERIT AWARD
Consumer Television
:20 and Under: Single

ART DIRECTOR
Todd Grant

WRITER
Steve Dildarian

AGENCY PRODUCER
Cindy Epps

PRODUCTION COMPANY
Innervision Studios

DIRECTOR
Tom Rouston

CLIENT
Anheuser-Busch

AGENCY
Goodby Silverstein &
Partners/San Francisco

(Bride and groom are alone on the dance floor for their "first dance." Behind them we see two guys sneaking up on them with a punch bowl and then pour it on their heads.)

SUPER: *Must be football season.*

SFX: *Crowd cheering, airplane sounds.*

SUPER: *Southwest Airlines. Proud Sponsor of The NFL.*

MERIT AWARD
Consumer Television
:20 and Under: Single

ART DIRECTOR
Holland Henton

WRITER
Brian Brooker

AGENCY PRODUCER
Dottie Martin

PRODUCTION COMPANY
@radical.media

DIRECTOR
Frank Todaro

CLIENT
Southwest Airlines

AGENCY
GSD&M/Austin

MERIT AWARD
Consumer Television
:20 and Under: Single

ART DIRECTOR
Holland Henton

WRITER
Brian Brooker

AGENCY PRODUCER
Dottie Martin

PRODUCTION COMPANY
@radical.media

DIRECTOR
Frank Todaro

CLIENT
Southwest Airlines

AGENCY
GSD&M/Austin

GUY 1: *Great job on that paper jam.*

GUY 2: *I like how you handled that toner.*

SUPER: *Must be football season.*

SFX: *Crowd cheering, airplane sounds.*

SUPER: *Southwest Airlines. Proud Sponsor of The NFL.*

MERIT AWARD
Consumer Television
:20 and Under: Single

ART DIRECTOR
Holland Henton

WRITER
Brian Brooker

AGENCY PRODUCER
Dottie Martin

PRODUCTION COMPANY
@radical.media

DIRECTOR
Frank Todaro

CLIENT
Southwest Airlines

AGENCY
GSD&M/Austin

(A woman in a grocery store picks up a squash in the produce section. She accidentally drops it and a group of women suddenly dive on the squash as though it were a loose football.)

SUPER: *Must be football season.*

SFX: *Crowd cheering, airplane sounds.*

SUPER: *Southwest Airlines. Proud Sponsor of The NFL.*

{A statue of a naked discus thrower rotates slowly and dramatically and stops when the statue's rear end is center screen.)

SUPER: *Amsterdam 1998. The Gay Games. European Gay Ways. Official Tour Operator of the Gay Games. Packages Available.*

MERIT AWARD
Consumer Television
:20 and Under: Single

ART DIRECTOR
Ray Mendez

WRITER
Gregg Wasiak

AGENCY PRODUCER
Monique van Smaalen

PRODUCTION COMPANY
Slokkers Film Productions

DIRECTOR
Hein Groot

CLIENT
European Gay Ways

AGENCY
TBWA/Campaign Company/
Amsterdam

ANNOUNCER: *ABC's Cheap Cinema Theater presents...*

SUPER: *The English Patient.*

GUY: *AHHHHH!!! I'm hurt.*

WOMAN: *I'll take care of you.*

GUY: *I love you.*

ANNOUNCER: *Classic movies inexpensively re-created so you can skip the theater and spend more time watching TV.*

SUPER: *American Broadcasting Company.*

MERIT AWARD
Consumer Television
:20 and Under: Single

ART DIRECTORS
Cody Spinadel
John Shirley

WRITER
Michael Collado

AGENCY PRODUCER
Kara O'Neil

PRODUCTION COMPANY
Will Vinton Studios

DIRECTOR
Mike Wellins

CLIENT
ABC

AGENCY
TBWA/Chiat/Day/
Playa del Rey

MERIT AWARD
Consumer Television
:20 and Under: Campaign

ART DIRECTORS
Cody Spinadel
John Shirley

WRITER
Michael Collado

AGENCY PRODUCER
Kara O'Neil

PRODUCTION COMPANY
Will Vinton Studios

DIRECTOR
Mike Wellins

CLIENT
ABC

AGENCY
TBWA/Chiat/Day/
Playa del Rey

ANNOUNCER: *ABC's Cheap Cinema Theater presents...*

SUPER: *The Godfather.*

THUG: *They shot Sonny.*

SHOT GUY: *Ow. Ow. Ow.*

THUG: *They shot Frankie.*

SHOT GUY: *Ow. Ow. Ow.*

ANNOUNCER: *Classic movies inexpensively re-created so you can skip the theater and spend more time watching TV.*

SUPER: *American Broadcasting Company.*

MERIT AWARD
Consumer Television
:20 and Under: Campaign

ART DIRECTOR
Arty Tan

WRITER
Mike Folino

AGENCY PRODUCER
Jennifer Dennis

PRODUCTION COMPANY
Hungry Man

DIRECTOR
Hank Perlman

CLIENT
Nike

AGENCY
Wieden & Kennedy/
Portland

GUY 1: *No look, all net.*

SAMUEL JACKSON *(Off camera): Ohhhhhhhh!*

JACKSON: *Three guys playing Horse... it's FAN-tastic.*

SUPER: *Start the season. Hurry.*

SUPER: *Nike swoosh.*

SFX: *Crickets chirping, swamp sounds throughout.*

FROG 1: *Bud.*

LOUIE (Sing-songy, loud): *Weis.*

FROG 2: *Er.*

FRANK: *Oh, boy.*

LOUIE (Shouting): *Weis.*

FROG 2: *Er.*

LOUIE (Sing-songy): *Weis.*

FRANK: *Louie...*

LOUIE: *What?*

FRANK: *Just say the line.*

LOUIE: *That's what I'm doing.*

FRANK: *No, you're not. You're going (Sing-songy, loud) Weis.*

LOUIE: *These are my interpretations of the part.*

FRANK: *This isn't Shakespeare. You're replacing a stressed-out frog.*

LOUIE: *Hey, Frankie, you know what they say...*

FRANK: *What?*

LOUIE: *There are no small parts... only small lizards.*

FRANK: *Nobody says that.*

LOUIE: *I say it all the time.*

FROG 1: *Bud.*

LOUIE (Quickly): *Weis.*

FROG 2: *Er.*

SUPER: *www.budweiser.com*

FROG 1: *Bud.*

LOUIE (Quickly): *Weis.*

FROG 2: *Er.*

MERIT AWARD
Consumer Television:
Varying Lengths Campaign

ART DIRECTOR
Todd Grant

WRITER
Steve Dildarian

AGENCY PRODUCERS
Cindy Epps
Debbie King

PRODUCTION COMPANY
Innervision Studios

DIRECTOR
Tom Rouston

CLIENT
Anheuser-Busch

AGENCY
Goodby Silverstein &
Partners/San Francisco

ODD VOICE: *Sometimes I get distracted.*

Once I missed the beginning of "NFL 2night." I took my knowledge for granted. And it started to go away. Now my knowledge is back. That makes me happy.

SUPER: *NFL 2night. Tuesday-Friday at 7:30 PM on ESPN 2.*

MERIT AWARD
Consumer Television:
Varying Lengths Campaign

ART DIRECTOR
Guy Shelmerdine

WRITER
Grant Holland

AGENCY PRODUCER
Corey Bartha

PRODUCTION COMPANY
Propaganda

DIRECTOR
Dante Ariola

CLIENT
ESPN 2

AGENCY
Ground Zero/Marina del Rey

MERIT AWARD
Consumer Television:
Varying Lengths Campaign

ART DIRECTOR
Mike O'Sullivan

WRITER
Richard Maddocks

AGENCY PRODUCER
Liz Rosby

PRODUCTION COMPANY
Republic Films

DIRECTOR
Steve Saussey

CLIENT
Bluebirds Foods

AGENCY
MOJO Partners/Auckland

(A news anchorman from Indian television is interrupted by sudden hammering in the background.)

TWISTIE 1: *Sorry.*

TWISTIE 2: *I'm sorry too.*

SUPER: *It's a straight world without twisties.*

MERIT AWARD
Consumer Television:
Varying Lengths Campaign

ART DIRECTORS
Yan Elliott
Rob Potts
Paul Bruce
Franklin Tipton

WRITERS
Jim Hosking
Andy Jex
Ben Mooge
Scott Leonard

AGENCY PRODUCER
Zoe Bell

PRODUCTION COMPANY
Spectre

DIRECTOR
Daniel Kleinman

CLIENT
Van Den Bergh Foods

AGENCY
Mother/London

(Two men, late twenties, are in their kitchen with two bowls of steaming Super Noodles. Dan grabs the wok from the wall, strikes it hard with a large wooden garlic crusher. Dave fishes a noodle from his steaming bowl, flicks it at Dan with a martial arts movement.

DAVE: *You insult my honor!*

DAN: *Oooh, that's it, you in big trouble now.*

DAVE: *Oooh, you in so much trouble, I use the Monkey finger.*

(Dave flexes finger in Dan's direction.)

DAVE: *Aaaaghh! You idiot, you got me in the eye!*

DAN: *You fight, you fight you big coward...*

DAVE: *Stop it, stop it-enough! Stop it!*

ANNOUNCER: *Batchelors Super Noodles, is it me or are they just super!*

ANNOUNCER: *The word is triiodothyronine.*

SFX: *A few restless audience coughs, chair squeaks, a camera click.*

GIRL: *T...?*

SUPER: *No chance.*

SUPER: *Ameristar.*

SFX: *Coins hitting metal tray.*

SUPER: *Chance.*

MERIT AWARD
Consumer Television Under
$50,000 Budget: Single

ART DIRECTOR
Matt Mowat

WRITER
Chuck Meehan

AGENCY PRODUCER
James Horner

PRODUCTION COMPANY
Five Union Square Productions

DIRECTOR
Tom Schiller

CLIENT
Ameristar Casinos

AGENCY
Goldberg Moser O'Neill/
San Francisco

SUPER: *Manson parole hearing.*

MANSON: *First of all, I give you respect and want peace. I do not enter into your circle. What you do in that circle is your business. You step in this circle and I'll deal with you. Do you understand me now?*

SUPER: *No chance.*

SUPER: *Ameristar.*

SFX: *Coins hitting metal tray.*

SUPER: *Chance.*

MERIT AWARD
Consumer Television Under
$50,000 Budget: Single

ART DIRECTOR
Matt Mowat

WRITER
Chuck Meehan

AGENCY PRODUCER
James Horner

PRODUCTION COMPANY
Maiden Lane Productions

DIRECTOR
Tom Schiller

CLIENT
Ameristar Casinos

AGENCY
Goldberg Moser O'Neill/
San Francisco

MERIT AWARD
Consumer Television Under
$50,000 Budget: Single

ART DIRECTOR
Paul Foulkes

WRITERS
Tyler Hampton
Jeff Odiorne

AGENCY PRODUCERS
Tiffany Richter
Chris Weldon

PRODUCTION COMPANY
Complete Pandemonium

DIRECTOR
Steve Williams

CLIENT
Electronic Arts

AGENCY
Odiorne Wilde Narraway &
Partners/San Francisco

(A conversation in a hardware store. We see cuts of game screens throughout.)

BIKER: *See that long crowbar there?*

CLERK: *Long crowbar.*

BIKER: *Yeah.*

CLERK: *Where's that at?*

SFX: *Music and motorcycle racing sounds.*

BIKER: *I'm gonna hook a guy and pull him right off.*

CLERK: *Ah, that's a good one.*

BIKER: *Huh?*

CLERK: *That's a good one.*

BIKER: *You think I'm kidding, don't you?*

CLERK: *No.*

ANNOUNCER: *Road Rash 3D. Soundtrack on Atlantic Records.*

SUPER: *Electronic Arts.*

MERIT AWARD
Consumer Television Under
$50,000 Budget: Single

ART DIRECTOR
Paul Foulkes

WRITERS
Tyler Hampton
Jeff Odiorne

AGENCY PRODUCERS
Tiffany Richter
Chris Weldon

PRODUCTION COMPANY
Complete Pandemonium

DIRECTOR
Steve Williams

CLIENT
Electronic Arts

AGENCY
Odiorne Wilde Narraway &
Partners/San Francisco

(A conversation in a hardware store. We see cuts of game screens throughout.)

BIKER: *I race about 130 miles per hour... four or five guys in my gang. We go wheelin' up the highway. The whole object: a) to win; b) to make sure that people stay outta my way.*

SFX: *Music and motorcycle racing sounds.*

(Biker encourages clerk to hit him with axe handle.)

BIKER: *Come on. Okay, that's good.*

SFX: *Music and motorcycle racing sounds.*

(Biker makes guitar noise.)

ANNOUNCER: *Road Rash 3D. Soundtrack on Atlantic Records.*

SUPER: *Electronic Arts.*

(A father shows his son scenes around town: from a bad accident to the raping of a woman in a cellar. Things children would see, if you let them watch TV by themselves.)

SUPER: *What you'd never show your children in real life they shouldn't see on TV.*

MERIT AWARD
Consumer Television Under
$50,000 Budget: Single

ART DIRECTOR
Patrick They

WRITERS
Johannes Krempl
Patrick They

AGENCY PRODUCER
Julia Frohlich

PRODUCTION COMPANY
Neue Sentimental Film/Berlin

DIRECTOR
Nico Beyer

CLIENT
SWR Television Baden-Baden

AGENCY
Ogilvy & Mather/Frankfurt

(As Tiger Woods begins his backswing on a fairway shot, a young man who has forced his way to the front of the gallery raises an "Applause" sign)

SFX: *Roar of crowd*

SPORTS COMMENTATOR: *Well I don't know what happened there, but I mean that's 30 yards too far to the right, and the lie didn't look too bad.*

SUPER: *It's a whole new game when you've got money on it.*

ANNOUNCER: *Superspreads. It's a whole new sports betting system.*

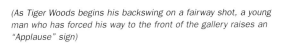

MERIT AWARD
Consumer Television Under
$50,000 Budget: Single

ART DIRECTORS
Paul Sanders
Rupert Allcock
Kristen Goudemond

WRITERS
Adam Wittert
Alexia Milner
Hugh Bush

AGENCY PRODUCER
Helen D'Hotman

PRODUCTION COMPANY
Glide Productions

DIRECTOR
Richard Williams

CLIENT
IGN Superspreads

AGENCY
Ogilvy & Mather Rightford
Searle-Tripp & Makin/
Johannesburg

MERIT AWARD
Non-Broadcast
Out-of-Home: Single

ART DIRECTOR
Peter Nicholson

WRITER
Scott Wild

AGENCY PRODUCER
Ben Latimer

PRODUCTION COMPANY
Headquarters

DIRECTOR
Joe Public

CLIENT
Adidas

AGENCY
Leagas Delaney/
San Francisco

MEL STOTTLEMEYER: *Coney, you got to rest that arm.*

MR. A: *Well, we got to help him.*

(The Yanks guys proceed to help Cone do everything from signing autographs to eating dinner to going to the bathroom.)

MR. A: *I'll take that, you got to rest your arm.*

MR. A: *Pitch a good one tonight.*

SUPER: *Only in New York.*

SUPER: *Adidas.*

MERIT AWARD
Foreign Language
Television: Single

ART DIRECTOR
Arnaud Roussel

WRITER
Arnaud Roussel

AGENCY PRODUCER
Corinne Persch

PRODUCTION COMPANY
Wanda/Paris

DIRECTOR
Arnaud Roussel

CLIENT
Volkswagen

AGENCY
DDB Advertising/Paris

(A snack bar near a highway. Sitting at the table are four bikers in leather motorcycle gear, crash helmets set beside them. They look glum; one of them even starts to cry.)

SUPER: *How would you feel being overtaken by a van.*

SUPER: *New Sharan Turbo 150 horsepower.*

(Spot opens with Santa grunting on the toilet. He lets out a sigh of relief and then sees there's no toiletpaper. He thinks for an instant then hops to the living room. There he finds a pile of letters, smiles and picks one.)

SUPER: *Are you planning to write to Santa Claus? Or, are you going to buy your gifts at C&A?*

MERIT AWARD
Foreign Language Television:
Single

ART DIRECTORS
Hernan Damilano
Javier Fabregas

WRITERS
Hernan Gonzalez
Damian Kepel

AGENCY PRODUCERS
Horacio Ciancia
Selva Dinelli

PRODUCTION COMPANY
2001

DIRECTOR
Pucho Mentasti

CLIENT
C&A

AGENCY
Vega Olmos Ponce/
Buenos Aires

(The TV screen is totally black. Then the remote control symbol for brightness appears.)

SUPER: *Bright.*

(The Daewoo Leganza appears from the blackness driving along a road. The images on screen are only in black and white.)

SUPER: *Color.*

(The color of the Leganza and the background is revealed as the dashed line stretches halfway across bottom of screen.)

SUPER: *Volume.*

(The volume line extends halfway across bottom of the screen, but there's no sound. It extends further; still no sound. Finally, volume reaches maximum capacity.)

SFX: *Very low engine hum. Loud frog croak.*

SUPER: *Daewoo Leganza.*

SUPER (In Korean): *Visible but not audible.*

MERIT AWARD
Foreign Language Television:
Single

ART DIRECTORS
Reed Collins
Richard Bullock

WRITERS
Richard Bullock
Reed Collins

AGENCY PRODUCERS
Jong Won Kim
Jo Ik Nyung

PRODUCTION COMPANY
Velocity Afrika

DIRECTOR
Tony Baggott

CLIENT
Daewoo

AGENCY
Welcomm Advertising/
New York

MERIT AWARD
Foreign Language Cinema:
Single

ART DIRECTOR
Sebastien Zanini

WRITER
Pierre Marie Faussurier

AGENCY PRODUCER
Jeremy Morichon

PRODUCTION COMPANY
Premiere Heure

DIRECTOR
Xavier Gianolli

CLIENT
Volkswagen

AGENCY
DDB Advertising/Paris

(A gallery guide leads a potential buyer through a painter's retrospective, describing the influences on each work. All of the paintings are very dark.)

GALLERY GUIDE: *First, his home village. The cradle, sort of... His mother. Interesting, no? Well, then came a series that was much more... His first love. And a self-portrait, obviously. He's honest, you see?*

(The paintings in the next room are bright and colorful.)

GALLERY GUIDE: *Here, all I know is that he had changed cars.*

SUPER: *Volkswagen Golf.*

MERIT AWARD
Multi-Media Campaign

ART DIRECTOR (PRINT)
Andy Azula

WRITER (PRINT)
Greg Hahn

ART DIRECTOR (TV)
Andy Azula

WRITER (TV)
Greg Hahn

AGENCY PRODUCER
Monika Prince

PRODUCTION COMPANY
Satellite

DIRECTOR
Spike Jonze

CLIENT
The Lee Apparel Company

AGENCY
Fallon McElligott/
Minneapolis

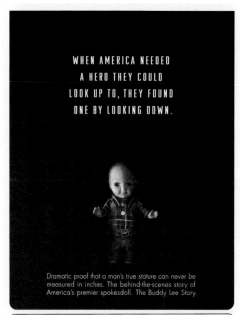

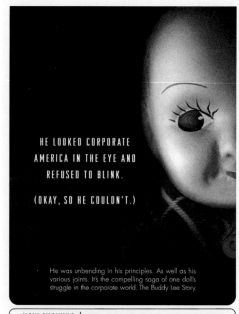

The career of Lee Jeans' "spokesdoll" Buddy Lee is documented with "archival" footage as we track his career from depression-era farmhand to "the toast of Madison Avenue" to "a fall to relative obscurity."

These "trailers" introduce "Buddy Lee as Buddy Lee in 'Buddy Lee, Man of Action.'"

In these two spots, Buddy Lee attempts to rescue a baby in a runaway car and save a kitten from a tornado. The car, with Buddy at the wheel, explodes into flames and the twister drives Buddy into a tree. As it turns out, the baby wasn't in the car and the kitten was safe all along but "man those are some jeans."

MERIT AWARD
Multi-Media Campaign

ART DIRECTOR
John Jay

WRITER
Jimmy Smith

ILLUSTRATOR
Katsura Moshino

PRODUCER
Cameron Shaw

CLIENT
Nike

AGENCY
Wieden & Kennedy/
Portland

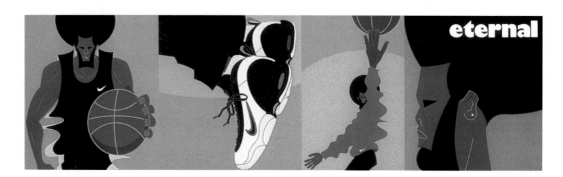

Peas Porridge Hop

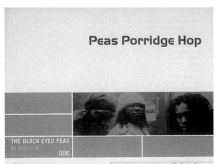

THE BLACK EYED PEAS
BY MESHACK
006

L.A.-based trio Black Eyed Peas are changing the face of hip-hop with their version of existence "Behind The Front" of the urban landscape.

Without the corn and cheese, Black Eyed Peas are gonna blow up without going Pop. They aren't exactly crossing over as much as building bridges for all to meet at the center.

One by one, Taboo, Apl*de*ap, and Will.I.Am serve up a tasty buffet of Hot Buttered Soul.

Time to motivate: TABOOH -- "Fallin' Up"

MESHACK Which one of the three are you? The Black, the Eye or the Pea?

TABOOH I think I would be the Pea for the positive and Pea for the phenomenal and Pea for the Phastest.

M Describe what the Black Eyed Peas are all about.

T We're about positive vibes and bringing back the music because trying to ride off gimmicks and trying to ride off other MCs' backs is stale and crusty. We're trying to bring back the live shows because there's a lotta groups out there that just go onstage with twenty homies and grab their nuts, yell in the mic, and that's all they do. We're trying to bring back the essence of doin' a show.

M What's your ethnic background and does that play a creative role in your work of art?

T Yeah because my background stems from Native American roots as well as Hispanic roots, meaning Mexican roots. And I feel that we get a lot of influence from Latin rhythms in our music and it plays a

big part in who we are as a group. We all stem from Latin backgrounds. For example, Will is from East Los Angeles. He grew up in a predominantly Mexican area. Then Apl is from the Philippines and that's a lot of what they listen to out there because they have Latin music out there. And with me it all coincides at the root.

M Comment on the current state of hip-hop and your role as a group in reincorporating live musicians and a live band into the mix.

T Right now hip-hop is asking for help and we're like in those cartoons when there's a big gray cloud overhead and it's dark. Then all of a sudden there's a ray of sunlight and the sound of angels: that's us! I feel like we're hip-hop's saviers in the sense that we're not doin' all that old typical stuff. We're comin' with different colors; everyone has a color but a lot of people choose to have the same color. It just so happens that we're on a different shade of color and we wanna make sure that people understand that they don't have to follow a "West Coast Gangsta" stereotype. You can be on some abstract stuff and still form your own path and be your own pioneer and innovator as Black Eyed Peas are.

M What is your role in the movement, energy, and traditional dance that you express live onstage?

T My job is to mainly hypnotize and make people feel what I feel onstage. And make sure that everybody in whatever place we perform receives high energy and

TIRED OF BEING TIRED
BY FURYIS STYLZE

Man I'm tired of being tired,
Tired of these cops harassing my people for no reason;
I see arrests & shoot-outs they happen all season;
Tired of watching my back for stick-up kidz who come quite often;
Tired of bad newz and funerals, familiar faces in a coffin;
Man I'm tired of being tired,
Tired of these young thugz looking at me like they want drama
Runnin the streets day & night disrespecting their mama;
I'm tired of seeing ya pantz hangin off your ass,
Sick a seeing you on the corner, when your ass should be in class;
Get your education baby. Education is the key;
But with ya eyez bloodshot it's kinda hard for you to see;
Man I'm tired of being tired,
So tired of the negative thoughts that throw ya mind off track;
I know we hustle to survive, but look at the effects of crack;
Ain't you tired of being a slave, can't you see how you behave;
It leads to incarceration, it leads to an early grave;
Man I'm tired of being tired,
I'm tired of wondering if we'll ever come together,
Sometimez I see it happening, sometimez I say never;
I'm so tired of being tired, but glad to see another day
So tired of strugglin just to earn an honest pay,
Mad at the world cause today wasn't my day;
I'm tired of the pain that guez away when I pray;
I'm tired of wishing for my dreamz to come true,
Man I'm just tired of being tired, so what about you?

TOP NIKE KICKS OF ALL TIME

Understand that these are my personal selections and have no bearing on sales figures or Nike preferences, etc.

019

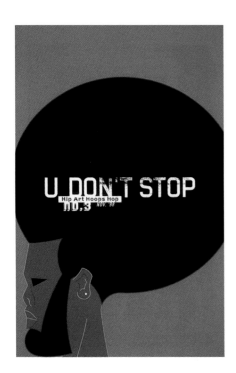

U DON'T STOP
Hip Art Hoops Hop
no.3 NOV. '98

U DON'T STOP
Hip Art Hoops Hop
no.1 JULY '98

MERIT AWARD
College Competition

ART DIRECTOR
Roman Tsukerman

WRITER
Roman Tsukerman

SCHOOL
Adhouse/New York

"Tracy Wong. I bet she's hot."

"I wanna work at Grey."

"Who's that old guy in the
Think Different Ad?"

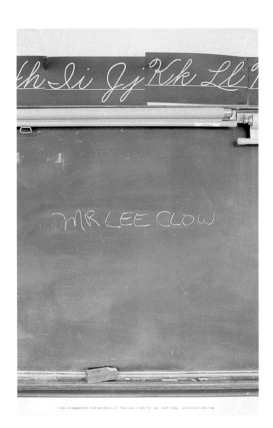

MERIT AWARD
College Competition

ART DIRECTOR
Brett Ingber

WRITER
Brett Ingber

SCHOOL
Art Center College of
Design/Pasadena

MERIT AWARD
College Competition

ART DIRECTORS
Dave Matli
Valeska Bachauer

WRITERS
Dave Matli
Valeska Bachauer

SCHOOL
Art Center College of
Design/Pasadena

With dual air bags, it's got all the flower power™
you need for a real 'sit in' with safety.

Drivers wanted.

lame copy. One good reason to read p16. inside Arnold Communications. One. a magazine

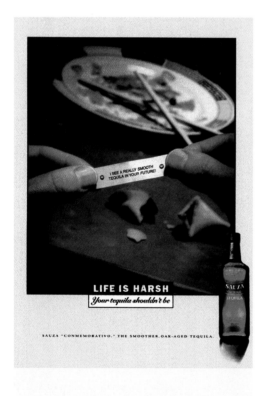

I SEE A REALLY SMOOTH
TEQUILA IN YOUR FUTURE!

LIFE IS HARSH
Your tequila shouldn't be

SAUZA "CONMEMORATIVO." THE SMOOTHER, OAK-AGED TEQUILA.

bad advertising. One good reason to read p8. techniques with Cliff Freeman. One. a magazine

TIME

The world's most interesting magazine.

retarded artdirection. One good reason to read p8. techniques with Bill Westbrook. One. a magazine

MERIT AWARD
College Competition

ART DIRECTOR
Dana Markee

WRITER
David Smith

SCHOOL
Brainco MSA/
Minneapolis

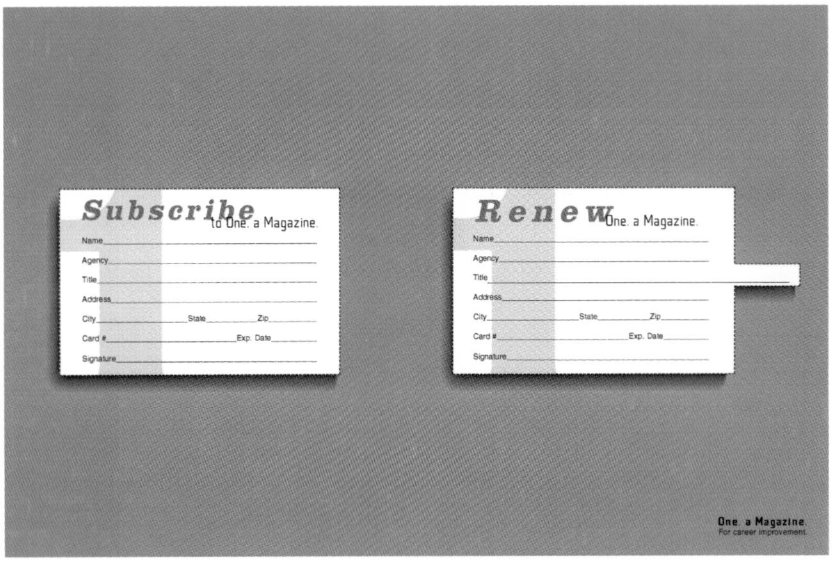

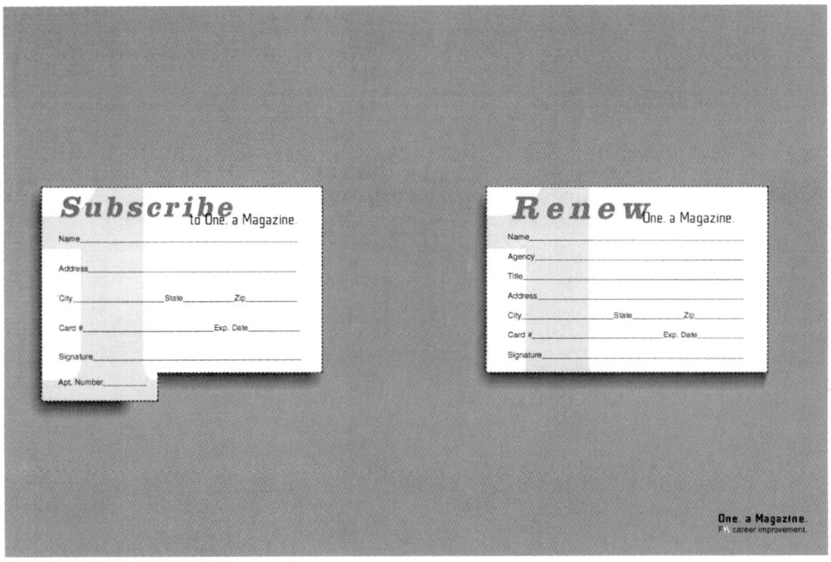

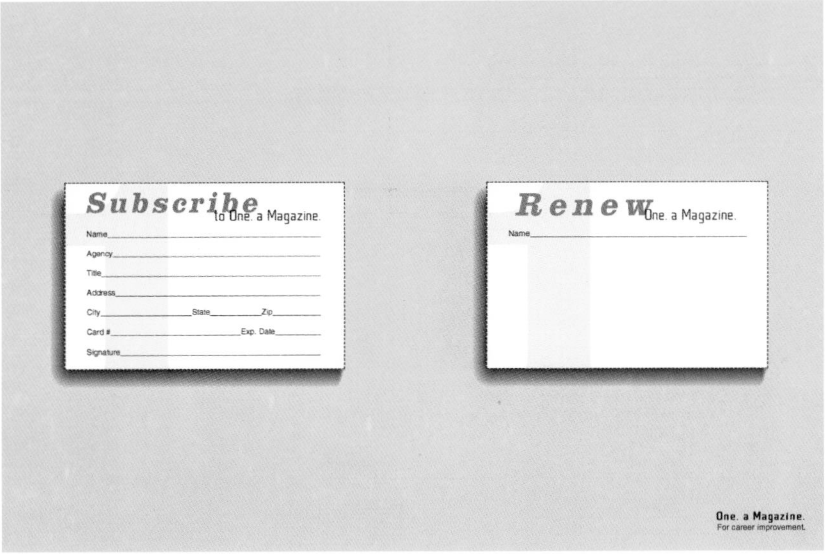

MERIT AWARD
College Competition

ART DIRECTOR
Rebecca Peterson

WRITER
Peter Shamon

SCHOOL
Creative Circus/Atlanta

Kind of a see-say
don't you think?

one. a magazine written by creatives
Thank God they only comment on advertising
www.oneclub.com

Oh come on,
is that all you could
come up with?

one. a magazine written by creatives
Thank God they only comment on advertising
www.oneclub.com

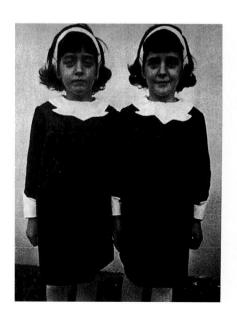

What, no third?

one. a magazine written by creatives
Thank God they only comment on advertising
www.oneclub.com

MERIT AWARD
College Competition

ART DIRECTOR
Donna Foster

WRITER
Matt Ledoux

SCHOOL
Creative Circus/
Atlanta

MERIT AWARD
College Competition

ART DIRECTOR
Mark Lawson

WRITER
Scott Newcombe

SCHOOL
Creative Circus/Atlanta

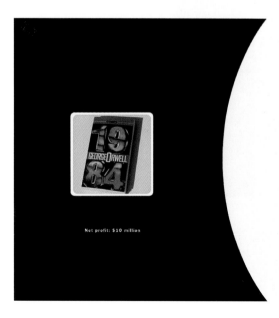

MERIT AWARD
College Competition

ART DIRECTOR
Jamie Day

WRITER
Jeremy Chin

SCHOOL
Creative Circus/Atlanta

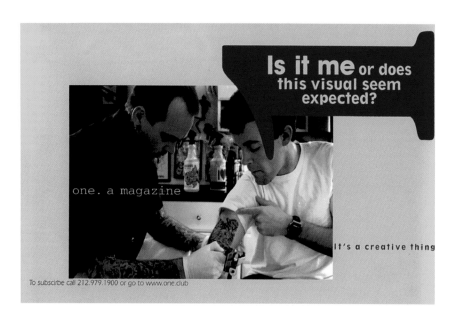

MERIT AWARD
College Competition

ART DIRECTORS
Esen Baykal
Andy Pearlman

SCHOOL
School of Visual Arts/
New York

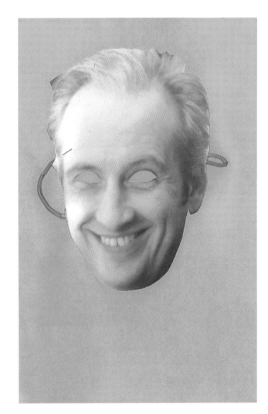

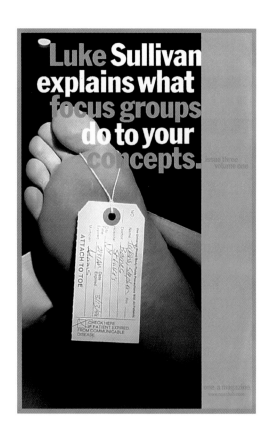

MERIT AWARD
College Competition

ART DIRECTOR
Cory Smith

WRITER
Joe Rose

SCHOOL
VCU Adcenter/Richmond

MERIT AWARD
College Competition

ART DIRECTOR
Eric Cosper

WRITER
Mike Sweeney

SCHOOL
VCU Adcenter/Richmond

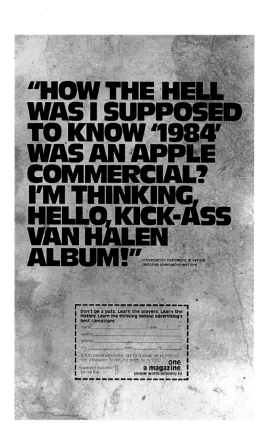

"HOW THE HELL WAS I SUPPOSED TO KNOW '1984' WAS AN APPLE COMMERCIAL? I'M THINKING, HELLO, KICK-ASS VAN HALEN ALBUM!"
—conversation overheard in Venice, California unemployment line

Don't be a putz. Learn the players. Learn the history. Learn the thinking behind advertising's best campaigns.

name _____ e-mail _____
agency _____
address _____
city _____ state _____ zip _____
$28.00 annual subscription rate for 4 issues. return form to: one. a magazine. 32 east 21st street. ny. ny 10010
payment enclosed ☐
bill me later ☐
one.
a magazine.
people worth listening to

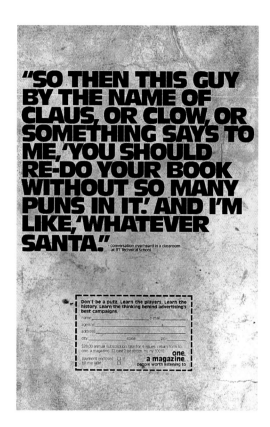

"SO THEN THIS GUY BY THE NAME OF CLAUS, OR CLOW, OR SOMETHING SAYS TO ME, 'YOU SHOULD RE-DO YOUR BOOK WITHOUT SO MANY PUNS IN IT.' AND I'M LIKE, 'WHATEVER SANTA."
—conversation overheard in a classroom at ITT Technical School

Don't be a putz. Learn the players. Learn the history. Learn the thinking behind advertising's best campaigns.

name _____ e-mail _____
agency _____
address _____
city _____ state _____ zip _____
$28.00 annual subscription rate for 4 issues. return form to: one. a magazine. 32 east 21st street. ny. ny 10010
payment enclosed ☐
bill me later ☐
one.
a magazine.
people worth listening to

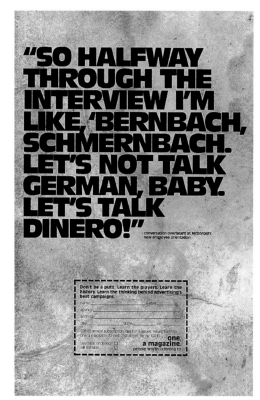

"SO HALFWAY THROUGH THE INTERVIEW I'M LIKE, 'BERNBACH, SCHMERNBACH. LET'S NOT TALK GERMAN, BABY. LET'S TALK DINERO!"
—conversation overheard at McDonald's new employee orientation

Don't be a putz. Learn the players. Learn the history. Learn the thinking behind advertising's best campaigns.

name _____ e-mail _____
agency _____
address _____
city _____ state _____ zip _____
$28.00 annual subscription rate for 4 issues. return form to: one. a magazine. 32 east 21st street. ny. ny 10010
payment enclosed ☐
bill me later ☐
one.
a magazine.
people worth listening to

WE KNOW BUDDY LEE LIKE NO ONE ELSE DOES.

one. a magazine.

THERE'S MORE TO SELLING BEER THAN YOU THINK.

one. a magazine.

MERIT AWARD
College Competition

ART DIRECTOR
Steven G. Yee

WRITER
Marcel Jennings

SCHOOL
VCU Adcenter/Richmond

WOULDN'T YOU UNDERSTAND THE WORK BETTER
IF YOU SAW WHAT'S UNDERNEATH IT?

one. a magazine.

MERIT AWARD
College Competition

ART DIRECTOR
Imdan Achda

WRITERS
Tom Randall
Greg Lane

SCHOOL
VCU Adcenter/Richmond

MERIT AWARD
College Competition

ART DIRECTOR
Amanda Berger

WRITER
Steve McElligott

SCHOOL
VCU Adcenter/Richmond

Where would
we be without One?

Where would
we be without One?

MERIT AWARD
College Competition

ART DIRECTOR
Eric Cosper

WRITER
Mike Sweeney

SCHOOL
VCU Adcenter/Richmond

MERIT AWARD
College Competition

ART DIRECTOR
Greg Thomas

WRITER
Jon Burkhart

SCHOOL
VCU Adcenter/Richmond

We'll make it thicker when we find more good work.

one. a magazine. Written by creatives. for creatives. It's published quarterly and comes free with a One Club membership.
Annual rates are $28 USA, $36 Canada, and $38 International. Make checks payable to the One Club, or call to change your card.

name _____ agency _____

address _____ city/state/zip _____ email _____ **1**

Mail to:The One Club for Art & Copy, Inc. 32 East 21st Street New York,NY 10010 phone (212) 979-1900 fax (212) 979-5006 email oneclub@ inch.com

It folds like a junior account exec in a client meeting.

one. a magazine. Written by creatives. for creatives. It's published quarterly and comes free with a One Club membership.
Annual rates are $28 USA, $36 Canada, and $38 International. Make checks payable to the One Club, or call to change your card.

name _____ agency _____

address _____ city/state/zip _____ email _____ **1**

Mail to:The One Club for Art & Copy, Inc. 32 East 21st Street New York,NY 10010 phone (212) 979-1900 fax (212) 979-5006 email oneclub@ inch.com

It's spineless so marketing managers can relate to it.

one. a magazine. Written by creatives. for creatives. It's published quarterly and comes free with a One Club membership.
Annual rates are $28 USA, $36 Canada, and $38 International. Make checks payable to the One Club, or call to change your card.

name _____ agency _____

address _____ city/state/zip _____ email _____ **1**

Mail to:The One Club for Art & Copy, Inc. 32 East 21st Street New York,NY 10010 phone (212) 979-1900 fax (212) 979-5006 email oneclub@ inch.com

MERIT AWARD
Cellege Competition

ART DIRECTOR
Ronny Northrop

WRITER
Laura Barnes

SCHOOL
VCU Adcenter/Richmond

MERIT AWARD
College Competition

ART DIRECTOR
Jon Rosen

WRITER
Crockett Jeffers

SCHOOL
VCU Adcenter/Richmond